THE ART OF BIBLICAL HISTORY

Foundations of Contemporary Interpretation
Moisés Silva, Series Editor
Volume 5

THE ART OF BIBLICAL HISTORY

V. Philips Long

ZondervanPublishingHouse
Grand Rapids, Michigan

A Division of HarperCollins*Publishers*

THE ART OF BIBLICAL HISTORY
Copyright © 1994 by V. Philips Long

Requests for information should be addressed to:
Zondervan Publishing House
Grand Rapids, Michigan 49530

Library of Congress Cataloging-in-Publication Data

Long, V. Philips.
  The art of biblical history / V. Philips Long.
      p.   cm. – (Foundations of contemporary interpretation : v. 5)
  Includes bibliographical references and indexes.
  ISBN 0-310-43180-8 (soft cover)
1. Bible–Hermeneutics.   2. Bible–Historiography.   3. History (Theology).   4.
Christianity–Essence, genius, nature.   I. Title.   II. Series.
BS476.L64   1994   93-45030
220.6'7'01–dc20   CIP

Edited by Matthew J. Maloley
Interior designed by Louise Bauer

Printed in the United States of America

98 99 00 01 02 03 / DH / 10 9 8 7 6 5 4 3

Better the end of a matter than its beginning,
Better a patient spirit than a prideful one.
—Ecclesiastes 7:8

This work is dedicated with love and gratitude
to my wife, Polly,
and our children,
Philip, Taylor, Andrea, and Duncan.

They undoubtedly share Qoheleth's sentiment about
beginnings and endings, and have admirably exhibited
the patience of which he speaks.

"History is the only science enjoying the ambiguous fortune of being required to be at the same time an art."

—Johann Gustav Droysen

"History is the most difficult of the belles lettres, for it must be true."

—Garrett Mattingly

". . . the appeal of history to us all is in the last analysis poetic. But the poetry of history does not consist of imagination roaming large, but of imagination pursuing the fact and fastening upon it."

—G. M. Trevelyan*

*All quoted in J. Axtell, "History as Imagination," *The Historian: A Journal of History* 49 (1987): 453.

CONTENTS

EDITOR'S PREFACE

This work completes the seven-volume series Foundations of Contemporary Interpretation. It seems rather appropriate that the last volume to appear should be the one on history. Few distinctives of Christian theology are as foundational in character and pervasive in their consequences as the conviction that the Bible is historically trustworthy. Attempts to salvage Christianity while abandoning that conviction invariably result in a message so crippled at its very roots that one has to wonder whether it is worth preserving at all.

Understandably, much of conservative biblical scholarship has been devoted to the defense of that conviction. And so it should be. What is not so clear is whether this great effort has always contributed positively to the interpretation of Scripture. The issue is not precisely that conservatives may have expended a disproportionate amount of time on historical apologetics to the detriment of other important fields of investigation (though perhaps a strong argument could be made in support of that judgment). Rather, the question needs to be asked whether the typical focus and approach run the risk of not doing justice to the character of Scripture itself. That there are some hermeneutical weaknesses in the traditional method is hardly to be disputed, and those weaknesses, no doubt, have contributed to the tendency of mainstream scholarship to downplay the historicity of biblical narrative.

There has long been a need for capable evangelical scholars to address this issue head-on. Those who have tried their hand at it have usually hesitated to go much below the surface (so that the product is little more than a reaffirmation of the traditional viewpoint) or they have adopted mainstream positions without

9

integrating them into basic tenets of the Christian faith (so that the term *evangelicalism* becomes progressively more diffused in application).

Each reader, of course, must decide whether Dr. Long has been successful in avoiding the Scylla of historical skepticism as well as the Charybdis of literary insensitivity. Given the controversial and emotional character of the subject, one can safely predict that at least some readers on both sides of the issue will find something to which they will object. Dr. Long's clear commitment to biblical historicity will, almost by definition, offend those who believe no one can be considered a scholar who does not find error, myth, or contradiction in the narratives of Scripture. By contrast, his very willingness to ask the hard questions—and thus inevitably to recognize the literary artistry of the narratives—may well put off readers who think there is only one kind of history-writing.

As the editor of the series, I may be suspected of prejudice in stating that Dr. Long has indeed been successful in meeting the goals set for this volume. Actually, he has far exceeded my expectations. There is not one significant issue that he has failed to take seriously. He has neither tried to camouflage his theological commitments nor sought to minimize the difficulties raised by the evidence. Within relatively short compass he has managed to cover complex subjects with both breadth and depth. And, to boot, he has accomplished it all with great clarity of writing and literary flair.

Dr. Long would be the first to recognize that many important questions are yet to be answered with definitiveness. Nonetheless, this volume is, in my opinion, the first to provide theological students with a truly solid foundation for the hermeneutics of biblical history. And they will ignore it to their peril.

MOISÉS SILVA

AUTHOR'S PREFACE

In a brief review of the first three volumes to appear in the Foundations of Contemporary Interpretation series, Robert Morgan comments that "judgment on the series as a whole must await the volume on history, the traditional rock of offence."[1] A comment such as this is an indication of the importance and magnitude of the questions to be addressed in the present study. What is the relationship between historical inquiry and biblical interpretation? Just how important are historical questions to biblical faith?

Colin Brown describes his own study of the relationship of history and faith as a personal exploration.[2] And, indeed, any who set out to probe this topic soon find themselves explorers in a vast terrain, oft-traveled but far from tamed, studded with bibliographic mountains the tops of which few have ever seen and philosophical seas the depths of which few, if any, have plumbed.[3] In this landscape I feel myself very much a traveler, and not a very seasoned one at that. I cannot claim to have conquered all the bibliographic mountains, though I have begun the ascent on not a few. Nor can I claim to have touched bottom in the philosophical seas, though I have navigated the shallows of some of them and at least peered into their mysterious depths, which I find both

[1] *Expository Times* 101 (1990): 210.

[2] *History and Faith: A Personal Exploration* (Grand Rapids: Zondervan, 1987).

[3] In fact, comprehensive exploration may no longer even be possible; cf. F. R. Ankersmit's comments on the "present-day overproduction in our [the historical] discipline. We are all familiar with the fact that in any imaginable area of historiography, within any specialty, an overwhelming number of books and articles is produced annually, making a comprehensive view of them all impossible" ("Historiography and Postmodernism," *HTh* 28 [1989]: 137).

alluring and foreboding—one cannot dismiss the possibility of drowning in them!

It is often said of journeys that "getting there is half the fun." This is true; and it would be a pity, as we traverse the topography of our topic, not to take time to consider significant landmarks along the way. But since most readers of this volume will be not simply sightseers but travelers desiring to discover what lies at journey's end, and since the time allotted for our journey is limited, it will be necessary to place reasonable limits on side-trips as we seek to discover a route that will lead across the terrain and to our destination. The route I have chosen is but one of several routes by which we might set out to explore the historical character of the Bible. I do not even claim that it is the best route, but I do think that it deserves more frequent travel than it has received thus far.

The title of this book was chosen for several reasons. First, echoing as it does the titles of two recent works by Robert Alter, *The Art of Biblical Narrative* and *The Art of Biblical Poetry*,[4] it expresses my conviction that advances in the literary study of the Bible, typified by such works as Alter's or by the more monumental work of Meir Sternberg, *The Poetics of Biblical Narrative*,[5] have much to contribute to our understanding of the Bible not only as literature but as a source of historical information as well. As Burke Long has succinctly remarked, "Given our lack of varied sources, if one is to understand Israel's history, one must first investigate with more literary sensitivity its styles of telling history."[6] Second, the title reflects my feeling that we may learn much about *verbal representation*—which I would adopt as a provisional, working definition of history-writing—by exploring points of analogy with modes of *visual representation* such as representational painting or portraiture. Third, if we understand *art* in our title as connoting not simply craft or artistry, but also slant and perspective, then the title may serve to suggest the

[4]New York: Basic Books, 1982 and 1985, respectively.

[5]Subtitled *Ideological Literature and the Drama of Reading* (Bloomington: Indiana University Press, 1985).

[6]"Historical narrative and the fictionalizing imagination," *VT* 35 (1985): 416.

Bible's widely recognized trio of interests in matters theological, historical, and literary. How these three interests are coordinated in the biblical texts is, as Sternberg remarks, "a tricky question,"[7] and one that we shall want to explore.

I have structured the discussion around fundamental questions regarding the historical character of the Bible and of the Christian faith: (1) Is the Bible a history book? If it is not, as is consistently pointed out by biblical scholars and theologians of virtually all stripes, what is it? What is its essential character, its *macro-genre*, as it were? (2) What do we mean by *history* anyway? What is *history?* (3) Does the Bible need to be historical to be true? If truth can be imparted in fictional stories, such as parables, is the question of historicity at all important? (4) If biblical scholarship strives for objectivity (while recognizing that subjectivity in interpretation can never be entirely eliminated), why do biblical scholars differ so widely in their historical conclusions? (5) When we read the Bible, how do we know whether what we are reading is to be understood as history, as parable, or as fable? How can we determine which parts of the Bible convey historical information?

Since the purpose of the present volume is to offer principles of interpretation as regards both the historical character of the Bible and the character of biblical historiography (history-writing), and since the size of the volume is limited, I shall not attempt anything like a comprehensive survey of "historiographical" passages in the Bible. I shall focus, rather, on the principal questions. Most of my examples will be drawn from the narrative portions of the Bible, since among those who believe that the Bible exhibits a historiographical impulse (that is, an intent to represent and reflect on past events) it is generally agreed that this impulse is most clearly evidenced in the Bible's narratives. This is not to deny, of course, that a historical impulse is apparent also in many poetical passages, such as the Song of the Sea (Exod. 15), the Song of Deborah (Judg. 5), the "historical psalms," the prophetic writings, and so forth.

Before launching into our subject, I would like to pause to thank the many who in one way or another have helped me with

---

[7] *Poetics of Biblical Narrative,* p. 41.

this project. A number of friends, some of whom are also colleagues, have read portions of the manuscript in progress and offered helpful advice. Improvements have often resulted from their counsel, while responsibility for flaws that remain is mine alone. Thanks are due to the late Dr. Raymond L. Dillard for reading and commenting on my section on Chronicles, to Dr. Richard S. Hess for similarly treating my section dealing with archaeology, and to Dr. Tremper Longman III for initially getting me interested in the project and for encouraging me along the way as regards both content and completion.

Thanks are also due to Dr. David M. Howard for his careful reading and evaluation of the work at an intermediate stage and to the students of two sessions of Trinity Evangelical Divinity School's Ph.D. seminar on biblical historiography, who graciously read and reviewed the work as it then was. I would also like to express appreciation to students at Covenant Theological Seminary, who read and commented on the work in several different drafts. Among these, special thanks go to David Wilcher for his assistance in the preparation of indices. Among my colleagues, I owe a debt of gratitude to Drs. C. John Collins, Esther L. Meek, and Robert W. Yarbrough for taking time from busy schedules to help me with the project. And I am particularly grateful to James L. Meek, who read the work in its fuller form and suggested many helpful modifications. I also want to thank the administration and the board of trustees of Covenant Theological Seminary for granting sabbatical leaves that enabled me to engage in intensive research and writing at Tyndale House in Cambridge. Tyndale House generously made its facilities available to me and my family during two short sabbatical stints and during my years of Ph.D. research; the benefits of library access and of personal contact with those working at Tyndale have been inestimable.

During my latest sabbatical leave, three individuals gave of their time not only to read the manuscript in its final draft but also to spend hours in conversation with me; thus, special thanks go to Dr. Iain W. Provan, to Dr. Phillip E. Satterthwaite, and to my former Ph.D. adviser, Dr. Robert P. Gordon. Special thanks go also to Dr. Moisés Silva, who, as general editor of the FCI series, has guided the work throughout, has read the manuscript at various stages, and has offered much good counsel and encouragement. Finally I thank my life-partner, Polly, for reading (and rereading) the work, for occasionally penning "so what?" in the margin, and for aiding me in the elimination of "zingers." We together thank our God and Father for the wonderful privilege of being about his business.

V. PHILIPS LONG

ABBREVIATIONS

Only titles that are cited more than once are included in this list.

AB	Anchor Bible
BTB	*Biblical Theology Bulletin*
CBQ	*Catholica Biblical Quarterly*
FCI	Foundations of Contemporary Interpretation
HTh	*History and Theory*
JETS	*Journal of the Evangelical Theological Society*
JSOT	*Journal for the Study of the Old Testament*
JSOTS	Journal for the Study of the Old Testament Supplement Series
Proof	*Prooftexts: A Journal of Jewish Literary History*
SBLDS	Society of Biblical Literature Dissertation Series
ScotBEv	*Scottish Bulletin of Evangelical Theology*
SJOT	*Scandinavian Journal of the Old Testament*
Them	*Themelios*
TrinJ	*Trinity Journal*
TynB	*Tyndale Bulletin*
VT	*Vetus Testamentum*
VTSup	Supplements to *Vetus Testamentum*
WBC	Word Biblical Commentaries
WTJ	*Westminster Theological Journal*

INTRODUCTION

Consider the following narrative:

> The two brothers had been in the attic for nearly two hours when they came upon something that intrigued them more than all their previous discoveries. Much of what they had already found was what they had expected: old letters and photographs at once inviting and discreetly forbidding perusal; items of clothing too frayed or unfashionable to be worn but too fraught with memories to be discarded; boxes of old books decrepit with age and, in the case of the favored, with much use; odd bits of furniture with careers cut short by injury or rivalry but resting serenely in the dimly lit confidence of eventual rediscovery and rehabilitation by a future generation; stacks of sheet music that chronicled the first fifty years of the twentieth century and whose melodies were as much a part of the boys' concept of "grandmother" as was the scent of the roses that she had so lovingly cultivated; sun hats and fishing poles that brought back memories of Granddad and of the "good old days" when speckled trout and spanish mackerel were plentiful on the grass flats of the Gulf of Mexico.

> These and many other discoveries were made as the boys explored the attic, but it was a small painting, carefully wrapped in brown paper, that most intrigued them. In the painting was a young girl sitting before a piano, atop which was an embroidered cloth. On the cloth lay cut roses, garden gloves, and shears. Leaning against the piano stool was a field hockey stick and at its base a basketball. The style and condition of the painting indicated considerable age. Particularly striking was the face of the girl, which, though rendered with an economy of brush strokes, suggested experience of life and wisdom unusual in a child so young. Most peculiar was the depiction of the girl's right hand, which displayed what appeared to be a second thumb!

17

Upon uncovering this curious painting, the boys immediately set about to discover its nature. The medium appeared to be oil paint. No signature was apparent—though, as best the boys could judge such things, the artist seemed to have been quite accomplished. The question that most interested them was whether the painting was a portrait, perhaps of a member of the family, or some other type of painting—a kind of visual parable perhaps, or just an interesting example of "art for art's sake." Their first impression was that the scene seemed somewhat artificial—pianos are hardly normal resting places for gardening tools or sports equipment. Nevertheless, the girl's appearance was more suggestive of personality and individuality than would be expected in a "young maiden" painting of the generic variety.

The tentative theory that soon emerged was that the painting must indeed be a portrait, the oddly arranged assortment of props serving to indicate not idiosyncratic house-keeping but the young girl's budding interests. Should this theory be correct, then the painting might even be of the boys' grandmother in her youth. Her interests in music and gardening were well-known and could still be corroborated by material evidence from the attic itself. Of her athletic prowess the boys knew little, though the thought that further searching in the attic might turn up a hockey stick excited them. Troubling for their theory, however, was the matter of the extra thumb, for in their experience their grandmother had never sported more than the usual complement of digits. Perhaps the extra thumb could be explained simply as a symbol of unusual precocity on the keyboard; the matter, however, bore further investigation.

Before ending their exploration of the attic, the boys turned up some evidence that tended to corroborate the portrait theory. Several other paintings were discovered in a corner, among them three more paintings of people and two landscapes. Three of the paintings were signed by the same artist, and given the similarities in style and the fact that the paintings were all found in the same attic, the boys felt it likely that all the paintings were by the one artist. Both landscapes were quite freely rendered, the artist apparently taking as much delight in the potentialities of the medium as in the subject itself.

The boys scrutinized the paintings of the people particularly closely and concluded that the positioning of the subject and the presence of a limited number of props in each painting tended to confirm their portrait theory. The artist's apparently strict adherence to the normal organization of physical features, however, left them even more undecided as to the significance of the extra thumb in the first painting. The additional paintings confirmed their common-sense judgment that in the artist's world, as in theirs, people have but one thumb per hand. Nevertheless, if the artist had felt free to include a symbolic thumb in one painting, why had no symbols been included in the others?

Determining that their investigation had been advanced as far as possible on the basis of the evidence before them, the boys exited the attic to take their inquiry farther afield. Searching out their mother at her desk, they presented her with the six paintings and mooted their theory that four of them must be portraits. This theory she was able to confirm, even to the point of giving names to the faces. The boys had been right in their assumption that the props in each of the portraits were included to give a fuller picture of the subject's character and interests and not to give information about where the items were normally kept.

On the matter of the extra thumb, while the mother granted the logic of the boys' empirical argument that its significance must be only symbolic (in all their experience with hands, they had never encountered one with six digits), she told them that in this case they must allow an exception. It seemed that their grandmother had been born with a thumblike appendage on her right hand. The slight embarrassment that this had caused her as a child had been somewhat compensated by her ability to play chords on the piano forbidden to most other mortals. As she approached age twelve, however, her parents began to reason that a suitor someday might be more attracted by physical normalcy than musical virtuosity, and they wisely decided to have the surplus appendage surgically removed.

On the matter of whether the portrait in question offered a good likeness of the boys' grandmother as a young girl, the mother was not in a position to render an opinion, except to observe that it seemed to have been the artist's intention to give a fair representation and, if the artist whose signature appeared on one of the landscapes was responsible also for the portrait in question, she had it on good authority that he had enjoyed an outstanding reputation for doing justice to his subjects. As for the two landscapes, the mother was unable to decide whether they were intended to record the artist's impression of specific vistas, were meant simply to present scenes typical of the gulf coast, or were created solely for their aesthetic appeal.

What can we learn from this strange tale? In what possible sense does it relate to the issue of biblical historiography, which is our present concern? While analogies are never perfect and should not be over-pressed, there are a number of parallels between the boys' attempts to explore the nature and significance of the artwork they discovered and the challenges that face those who would understand the Bible.

The boys' first challenge was to determine the genre (type or kind) of the painting of the young girl. They quickly recognized that the object before them was a painting and not, for example, a photograph. This perception was arrived at automatically and intuitively—though, had argument become necessary, the boys might have observed that the texture of the work's surface revealed brush strokes and not the fine-grained detail typical of photographs and that, at any rate, the apparent age of the work would place its creation in a period prior to the development of the techniques of color photography.

Having arrived at a very general genre description (i.e., *painting*), the boys sought to become more specific. The question that particularly intrigued them was whether and in what sense the painting might be referential, that is, depictive of a reality outside itself. If so, and not just art for art's sake, was it a representation of a particular person in a particular setting, perhaps even one of their ancestors, or simply a picture of what a typical young girl of the period might have looked like? Although the composition of the painting (e.g., the particular placement of some of the objects) suggested a certain intentional artificiality of arrangement, the painting overall gave a realistic impression. The rendering of the young girl's face in particular showed careful selection of detail, suggestive of a desire to capture a true likeness, and was accomplished with an economy of strokes that attested to the genius of the artist. Tentatively, the boys decided that the artwork before them was essentially representational, though the referential aspect was considerably more pronounced in some passages (e.g., the girl's face and figure) and less so in others (e.g., the props were rather loosely rendered and background objects only indicated by blocks of color).

Those who would read the Bible with understanding are similarly faced with the challenge of genre recognition. At a very general level, the Bible is literature, or, more specifically, a unified collection of literary works. Going beyond this very basic recognition, one may distinguish broadly between passages that tend to be more poetic in character and those that are in prose.[1] Further still, these basic divisions may be subdivided into subordinate categories and so on to the point of diminishing returns. Thus, genre description may take place on various levels of generality. I shall have more to say about genre criticism in chapter 1. The point that needs to be made at this juncture is simply this: The Bible is literature, but to recognize it as such does not settle the question of reference (whether it refers to realities beyond itself, real people and real events) any more than the boys' recognition of the work before them as a painting foreclosed the question of whether the painting was representational or nonrepresentational. Much of the Bible gives the impression of, and some of it explicitly presents itself as, *representational* literature—history-writing. It will be important for our consideration of biblical historiography to consider the relationship between subject matter and artistic medium. This will be the focus of chapter 2.

Now back to the boys in the attic. We may recall that their tentative decision that the painting before them must be representational was arrived at initially through close inspection of the painting itself, that is, on the basis of *internal evidence*. Certain features were somewhat perplexing, such as the unusual arrangement of props and especially the surplus thumb. But the boys were able to overcome this difficulty by nuancing their understanding of the painting's genre. In a portrait, for example, some artificiality in the arrangement of props would be quite acceptable. Further, a portrait might well tolerate some deviation from strict literality in the interest of capturing some aspect of the subject's essence. This

---

[1]See, e.g., D. J. A. Clines, "Story and Poem: The Old Testament as Literature and Scripture," *Interpretation* 34 (1980): 115–27.

made room for the boys' hypothesis that the entirely unnatural thumb must be a symbol of something else.

To this stage in the investigation the boys had proceeded largely on the basis of internal evidence, though some external considerations had already begun to creep in. Without their experience of life and the world, for example, the boys would never have been able to distinguish between the normal and the abnormal. Moreover, without some understanding of the conventions of portraiture the boys would have had no basis for classifying their painting as a portrait; they might have decided that the painting was a more or less realistic depiction of a particular person, but they would not have known to call it a portrait. Discovery of comparative material (more paintings) tended to confirm their tentative genre decision. None of the figures in the three additional portraits displayed any unusual features, however. This led the boys to conclude, falsely as it turned out, that the extra thumb in the first painting must indeed be a mere symbol and not a feature to be taken literally. It was in conversation with their mother that the boys learned that their concept of the "possible" needed expanding. The "possible," they discovered, should not in every instance be limited to the "normal," for their grandmother had in fact been born with an abnormality.

Again, there seem to be parallels between the way the boys assessed the visual art before them and the way biblical interpreters should assess the literature of the Bible. In either endeavor, the proper place to begin is with a close inspection of the work itself. The focus should be on both form and content. Careful reading of biblical texts will inevitably turn up perplexing features from time to time, features that call for explanatory theories. Tentative ideas regarding the text's specific genre will begin to emerge as reading proceeds, and these will require testing and perhaps modification as the investigation continues. The wider context and comparative literature (whether biblical or extrabiblical, ancient or modern) will often shed light on the biblical text, but again the interpreter must resist the urge to allow the "normal" to delimit the field of the "possible."

When once the boys' deduction that the first painting must

be a portrait of their grandmother had been confirmed by their mother, their attention turned to the question of whether or not the portrait captured a good likeness. In rendering an opinion on this matter, the mother did two things. First, she moved beyond the basic genre descriptor *portrait* to inquire after the artist's specific intentions. What style of portrait did he intend? In fact, of course, as the artist was unavailable for interview or investigation, her aim was to discern the intentionality apparent in the execution of the work itself—what might be called *embodied intention*. It was her judgment that the artist's style and detail suggested an intention to capture, to the extent allowed by the chosen medium, the essence of the visual appearance and character of the subject.

Now, the mere intention to achieve a good likeness does not in itself guarantee a good likeness, as many a mediocre portrait artist (and even a good artist on a bad day) can readily attest. Thus, before rendering an opinion on the painting in question, it was necessary for the mother to move on to a second consideration. Was the artist skilled in his craft? Strictly speaking, of course, some might wish to debate the identity of the artist—after all, the painting in question was unsigned, and even were it signed, the signature could be a forgery. The mother felt convinced, however, on what appeared to her to be reasonable grounds, that the artist was to be identified with the one whose signature appeared on several of the other paintings. Having made this identification, the mother felt herself in a position to attest to the artist's high level of competence. Her final deduction, based on these several considerations, was that the portrait was quite likely a fine representation of the boys' grandmother at a young age.

Biblical interpretation also tends to move beyond the basic question of genre to ask more specific questions. Having once identified a given text as, for example, historiography (a form of representational literature), interpreters will want to ask, What kind of historiography? If the author (or authors; the singular is used merely as a term of convenience) offers no statement of intention or, as is often the case in biblical literature, is not even identified, interpreters will focus on embodied intention, insofar as this may be inferred from the work itself on the basis of its literary strategies, compositional structure, selection of detail, and manner of expression.

At this stage the interpreter is sharpening the question of the text's *truth claim*. The genre descriptor, historiography, already implies a basic claim to referentiality; the added nuance is to ask after the level of detail and precision intended. What kind of likeness of reality is the narrator attempting to create? When once a decision on this matter is reached, the interpreter is faced with a second question, How capable is the narrator of achieving his intention? How competent is he in his craft? Here questions of biblical introduction (isogogics)—authorship, date, provenance— may become important. Here, too, the fundamental issue of the Bible's ultimate author(ity) must be considered. It is one thing to discern what a work intends (truth claim), it is quite another to decide whether it succeeds (truth value). Interpreters' opinions on the latter question are inevitably affected, at least in part, by their view of the identity and competence of the work's creator.

Shifting gears, now, we may use the story of the boys in the attic to introduce a further issue that must be considered in any discussion of biblical historiography. Our focus in this instance will not be on the genre of the painting in the story, but on the genre of the story itself. While in most contexts genre decisions are made intuitively and almost unconsciously, the reader may have experienced some difficulty in deciding just what the story of the boys in the attic is meant to be, particularly since the text's form and content are not exactly what one would expect in a book on biblical interpretation.

The reader has perhaps thought to ask whether the story is true or not. As it happens, a straightforward answer to this question cannot be offered, at least not until more thought is given to the genre of the story. The descriptors applied to the text— narrative, story, tale—are too general to get the reader very far in discovering the text's intended purpose. Even the authorship of the text may be in some doubt. The apparent significance of the fact that the story is found between the covers of a book upon which the present author's name appears, is somewhat offset by the fact that the text is formally distinguished, by its differing layout, from the main text.

Readers familiar with the convention in academic writing of citing sources for all excerpted materials might deduce from the lack of any such ascription that the little story must be the work of the author of the larger work; but, of course, literary conventions (even academic ones) may at times be modified or even disregarded by a given author. I may, for example, simply have forgotten to cite my source, or I may have chosen not to do so to make a point. Much of the biblical literature, as far as human authorship is concerned, is officially anonymous, and in many, even most, such instances, the human author may be beyond discovering.

To continue our discussion of the little story, then, let me confess to having composed it. And let us assume, very hypothetically, for the sake of discussion, that I have composed it perfectly to accomplish my intended purpose—that is to say, the truth value of each and every truth claim made by the text is assured. Even so, before I can answer the question regarding the story's truth, I must ask what you understand to be the purpose (and consequent truth claims) of the story.

We are back to the issue of genre. If you are asking, as you probably are, whether the sequence of events actually happened, the answer is no. If you are asking whether particular details in the story correspond to reality, the answers will vary. Did the painting of the young girl actually exist? No. Was someone's grandmother actually born with a surplus thumb? Yes, my own in fact. Was my grandmother a noted gardener and musician? Yes. Did my grandfather enjoy fishing and sometimes take me with him? Yes. Did my grandmother actually use her third thumb to play the piano before losing it to the surgeon's scalpel? Yes! Many of the details of the story are true, others are not, but the episode itself never took place. Does this make me a liar? I would argue that it does not, though were you to misconstrue the truth claim of the story to include factuality of the event and then learn that the event never took place, you might think me so.

To be fair, however, the truth question must be properly cast. Is the story true in terms of its intended purpose? Since the story is included in a book on biblical interpretation, the reader may well have surmised that its purpose is to illustrate some of the issues faced by those interpreting the Bible. For this purpose it is

not important whether the events described actually took place or
not. They may have, or they may not have; it does not matter.
Even to ask if the story is "true," without qualifying the question,
may seem a little out of place, since the story's purpose is to
illustrate a point and not to *affirm* or *establish* it.

It would be more appropriate to ask if the story succeeds in
accomplishing its purpose. That the story is a fiction is acceptable,
since its purpose is essentially illustrative and didactic (even though
this or that item of detail may refer to some aspect of reality).
Were the story meant to establish a truth on the basis of the
sequence of events recorded, however, then the factuality of the
sequence would be a much more pressing question. We shall look
more closely at these issues in chapter 3.

As we move now to take up in turn certain basic questions
relating to the historical character of the Bible, we do well to
recognize that the Bible contains various kinds of stories, some
meant to illustrate truth and others meant to establish it. The
fictional scenario above is intended to introduce some of the kinds
of issues that biblical interpreters encounter when they seek to
come to terms with the Bible in all its historical, theological, and
literary complexity. These issues will be given closer attention in
the chapters that follow.

1

HISTORY AND THE GENRE(S) OF THE BIBLE

Is the Bible a History Book?

The simple answer to the question posed in the title to this chapter is *no, the Bible is not a history book*.[1] But this is just the kind of question to which a simple (simplistic?) answer should not be given, at least not without going on to say what else the Bible is not. It is also not a science book, a law book, an ethics book, a theology book, or even a book of literature or politics (the list could go on). The Bible may be of vital interest in each of these areas, but its essence cannot be reduced to any one of them. If the question means to get at the essential nature of the Bible, then *history book* is not an adequate answer. It is important to recognize the all-encompassing character of the question, however, lest one fall prey to the kinds of false dichotomies often encountered in discussions of the historical character of the Bible—namely, the Bible is not history but literature, or the Bible is not history but theology.[2] The Bible, in terms of its essence, cannot be fully and adequately described by any of the above labels.

---

[1]At least not in the sense of being a history *textbook*. This point is widely acknowledged across the theological spectrum; see Moisés Silva, "The Place of Historical Reconstruction in New Testament Criticism," in *Hermeneutics, Authority, and Canon,* ed. D. A. Carson and J. D. Woodbridge (Grand Rapids: Zondervan, 1986), p. 109.

[2]Cf., e.g., G. Garbini: The Bible is "no longer politics or religion or history— but only ideology" (*History and Ideology in Ancient Israel* [London: SCM, 1988], p. xvi; cf. pp. xiv–xv, 14, 176); cf. also T. L. Thompson, following N. P. Lemche: "In terms of genre, the biblical traditions are rather origin traditions than

What then is the Bible? Much of the modern problem of
biblical interpretation is linked to what Robert Morgan describes
as "concealed disagreements" about how the subject matter of the
Bible is to be defined: "Some call the Bible superstition, others the
word of God."[3] The definition likely to enjoy widest acceptance is
that the Bible is a *religious book*. As the canonical Scriptures of two
of the world's major religions, Judaism (Hebrew Bible = Old
Testament) and Christianity (Old and New Testaments),[4] the
Bible certainly qualifies as a religious book.

But is *religious book* an adequate definition? To some it will
seem so. To secular interpreters, for example, the Bible may
appear to be just one religious book among many. For confessing
Christians, however, the Bible is not simply *a* religious book but
the religious book of their community of faith (though some in this
group may assume that the Bible's authority is not intrinsic but is
simply accorded to it by the community of faith itself).[5] For those
Christians who would take their cue from the Bible's own self-
understanding, the Bible is not simply *a* religious book or even *the*
religious book of a given community but, rather, *the* religious
book that is above all others and quite distinct from all others—its
very words being "God-breathed" (2 Tim. 3:16).[6]

historiography" (*Early History of Israel: From the Written and Archaeological Sources,*
Studies in the History of the Ancient Near East 4, ed. M. H. E. Weippert [Leiden:
E. J. Brill, 1992], p. 168).

[3]R. Morgan, with J. Barton, *Biblical Interpretation* (Oxford: Oxford University
Press, 1988), p. 19.

[4]M. Weinfeld ("Old Testament—The Discipline and Its Goals," in *Congress
Volume Vienna 1980,* ed. J. A. Emerton, VTSup 32 [Leiden: E. J. Brill, 1981],
p. 423) mentions also Islam, referring to the Old Testament as "the basis of the
three great world religions and of Western culture in general."

[5]Cf. Morgan (*Biblical Interpretation,* p. 7): "Where texts are accepted as authoritative within a community it is the community's authority that is invested in them."
For a critical review of Morgan's book, see A. C. Thiselton, "On Models and
Methods: A Conversation with Robert Morgan," in *The Bible in Three Dimensions,*
ed. D. J. A. Clines et al., JSOTS 87 (Sheffield: JSOT, 1990), pp. 337–56 (esp. pp.
353–55).

[6]See, e.g., D. A. Carson and J. D. Woodbridge, eds., *Scripture and Truth* (Grand
Rapids: Zondervan, 1983); *idem, Hermeneutics, Authority, and Canon;* G. Fackre,
"Evangelical Hermeneutics: Commonality and Diversity," *Interpretation* 43 (1989):
117–29.

THE BIBLE'S MACRO-GENRE
AND THE ISSUE OF TRUTH

What view one takes on the question of the Bible's essential nature, what we might call its *macro-genre,* will have far-reaching implications for how one assesses the truth value of the text. Secular readers, the first group described above, will find it easy to assume that the Bible, as just one religious book among many, may often be lacking in truth value. Confessing Christians, the second group, will at least want to regard the Bible as true in some sense—for example, "true for me." They will ascribe to the Bible at least a relative or subjective truth value. Christians of the third group, among whom I wish to be included, will hold that the Bible is true in a much more sweeping sense and will assume, consciously or unconsciously, that the Bible's truth claims (i.e., what the Bible teaches, commands, promises, and threatens) and its truth value (i.e., the veracity and/or authority of these speech acts) coincide.[7] Having said this, I must emphasize that one's commitment to the truth value of the Bible does not automatically settle the question of the truth claim(s) of any given text. It is one thing to believe the Bible to be true; it is another to understand what it says.[8]

This point may be illustrated by imagining a situation in which you tell me that you have written something that you would like me to read. Let us assume that I believe you to be both trustworthy and competent and thus have confidence in the truth value of what you write. Despite this confidence, if you offer no further comment, and if the circumstances surrounding our conversation offer no hint, I shall have very little idea of what it is you have written (i.e., what its genre, and thus its truth claim, is). Is it a telephone message, a list of things you would like me to do,

---

[7]On the diversity of the Bible's truth claims, see K. J. Vanhoozer, "The Semantics of Biblical Literature: Truth and Scripture's Diverse Literary Forms," in *Hermeneutics, Authority, and Canon,* ed. Carson and Woodbridge, pp. 49–104.

[8]That this important distinction sometimes becomes blurred is illustrated by the fact that "for many believers, unfortunately, assurance that the Bible is true appears to be inseparable from assurance about traditional interpretive positions, so that if we question the latter we seem to be doubting the former" (M. Silva, "Old Princeton, Westminster, and Inerrancy," *WTJ* 50 [1988]: 78).

a complaint, a poem, a joke, a riddle, a grocery list, a letter of recommendation, a contract, an essay, or what? The fact that I have confidence in your veracity and competence will, of course, influence the attitude with which I approach what you have written and the manner in which I respond, once I understand it. But my confidence in you does not guarantee that I will have an easy time comprehending what you have written.

All this is to make the point that questions of truth value and truth claim are essentially distinct. On the one hand, one's assumption regarding the likely truth value of the Bible is fundamentally affected by one's assessment of the macro-genre (or, more properly, the essential character or ontological status) of the Bible. If the Bible is a merely human document, then it may well be untrustworthy; if it is the very word of God, then the assumption will be the opposite.[9] On the other hand, one's discernment of the particular truth claims of the Bible requires that more specific genre decisions be made. Since the Bible comprises a collection of works of diverse literary genres, the truth claim(s) of this or that biblical text (what this or that text intends to convey, command, etc.) can be discovered only as each text is read on its own terms, with due recognition of its genre and due attention to its content and wider and narrower contexts.

THE BIBLE AS A FOREIGN BOOK

Something like genre recognition plays an important role in all forms of communication. People who have never experienced a foreign culture may not be very aware of this fact, since within

---

[9]To Morgan's assertion (*Biblical Interpretation*, pp. 278–79) that "a secular and pluralist culture no longer thinks of the Bible as the Word of God, and to start out with that claim would be to break off communication with the world outside," I would respond (1) that despite his reference to *pluralism*, Morgan may be assuming too monolithic an understanding of the modern world, and (2) that this may be, in any case, just the kind of question that "the world outside" should not be trusted to answer. On the matter of the Bible's trustworthiness, Vanhoozer ("Semantics of Biblical Literature") draws a helpful distinction between biblical *infallibility* (a term applicable to the full variety of Scripture's utterances) and biblical *inerrancy* (a subcategory of *infallibility* pertaining specifically to propositional statements).

their own culture they tend to make correct "genre decisions" automatically and even subconsciously, so that a break-down in communication seldom occurs.[10] But as soon as one enters a foreign culture the rules change. Not only is the language itself different, but even gestures may take on different significances, social expectations and rules of etiquette change, codes of friendship and hospitality may differ, and so on. "Culture shock," to a greater or lesser degree, is often the result. The following provides an extreme example of the potential for miscommunication and misunderstanding in cross-cultural situations.[11]

> They were new missionaries . . . alone in a remote tribal village. These two single women had the highest of goals . . . the best of intentions . . . the purest of motives: they were to translate the Bible into this, as yet, unwritten tribal language. But after a year's worth of labor, they had no results. Oh, they had been well received . . . at first! The tribe had even built them a small house, complete with screened-in porch. It was a hot muggy climate; with only a hint of a breeze right at daybreak. So, every morning they used to sit on that porch to read their Bibles and sip lime juice, the only refreshment they could find. But it seemed that rather quickly they became outcasts, with tribal members avoiding them, and they were unable to find someone to become their language helper. Just over a year later they and the mission decided something had to be done. A veteran missionary couple was sent to replace them. It seemed that in no time flat this couple had won the confidence of the tribe and began to make progress toward a translation. As they began to probe to find out why the two women had encountered such resistance, they were astonished to learn that the women had a reputation for exhibiting blatant immorality. The wives of the tribesmen even forbade their husbands and sons to go anywhere near the women. Inquiring further, the couple listened in utter shock to the tribesmen's description of the activity that had "confirmed" the two women's guilt: "Because *they drank lime juice*

---

[10]Cf. D. Patte's comments on the fairly reliable process by which the subconscious application of rules of intentionality within one's native culture allows the intentionality, and hence the communicative import, of a speech act to be discerned ("Speech Act Theory and Biblical Exegesis," *Semeia* 41 [1988]: 98).

[11]This is a slightly modified version of an account by missiologist M. Wilson (from a letter dated February 1986).

every morning!" You see, limes were the only citrus that grew near the village. For centuries the women of the tribe had drunk its juice in the belief that it was a "morning-after" contraceptive. The two single women, having been observed drinking it *every morning,* were thus a scandal in the village. The tribal people assumed that they had had gentlemen visitors each night. Of course, the truth is that there were no nightly visitors. The two women had no idea of what drinking a glass of lime juice meant in that culture. They had no idea of what that simple act was communicating.

If such misunderstandings can arise in cross-cultural situations today, is it any wonder that the Bible too can in places be misunderstood even by the most well-meaning of interpreters? The Bible is, after all, a *foreign* book, and though the existence of modern translations and a general, if diminishing, cultural familiarity with at least some of the Bible's contents can tend to dull our sensitivity to the Bible's foreignness, we overlook it at our own exegetical peril. After all, as Philip Hughes has observed, "the Bible is a collection of documents belonging to a period of history now long past. The most recent of its writings, those that comprise the books of the New Testament, are nineteen hundred years removed from the age in which we live."[12] If "every culture has its own sense of values," as Tomoo Ishida remarks, then the challenge of rightly interpreting literature from such distant and different cultures as the ancient Near Eastern world of the Old Testament or the first century world of the New Testament must not be underestimated. He writes:

> I am very doubtful of the ability of western society to understand the sense of values of Oriental countries, and vice versa. If we feel difficulties in understanding foreign cultures in our modern world, how can we correctly interpret the compositions from the ancient Near East which come to us not only from different cultures but from different and distant times?[13]

---

[12]"The Truth of Scripture and the Problem of Historical Relativity," in *Scripture and Truth,* ed. Carson and Woodbridge, p. 173.

[13]"Adonijah the Son of Haggith and His Supporters: An Inquiry into Problems About History and Historiography," in *The Future of Biblical Studies,* ed. R. E. Friedman and H. G. M. Williamson (Atlanta: Scholars Press, 1987), pp. 166–67.

One may not wish to adopt quite such a pessimistic view as this,[14] but the basic point is unassailable: "a naive application of modern western logic and judgement to the interpretation of ancient Near Eastern sources, including biblical literature, has [often] led us into error."[15] John Barton makes a similar comment with regard to criticisms sometimes leveled against various biblical passages: "An exclusive acquaintance with the literary genres available within our own culture can all too easily lead us to regard as impossible or composite works which are in fact entirely unproblematic within a different literary system."[16] Unless students of the Bible are willing to sacrifice, as it were, their monolingual and monocultural integrity—that is, unless they are willing, by an effort of imagination, to enter a cultural and literary world different in many respects from their own—even a high view of the Bible's veracity is no guarantee of a right view of its interpretation.

What is called for then, if mistakes are to be avoided, is the attainment of what has been called an *ancient literary competence*. The need to expend considerable effort to attain such competence is widely recognized among secular historians. S. W. Baron, writing on historical method, contends that the would-be interpreter must seek to discover the "intrinsic meaning of the source, not from some of his own scale of values, but that of the original writer or speaker."[17] C. Behan McCullagh illustrates how this works in practice:

[14]And, indeed, Ishida himself takes steps toward establishing, through the judicious use of the comparative method, "a set of criteria for interpretation that is free from the prejudices of our modern society" (ibid., p. 167).

[15]Ibid. (my insertion).

[16]*Reading the Old Testament: Method in Biblical Study* (London: Darton, Longman and Todd, 1984), p. 27. Barton cites the amusing example of French literary critics of the seventeenth and eighteenth centuries who, familiar only with the conventions of classical French tragedy, ridiculed Shakespeare's tragedies as "crude and barbaric in conception" or sometimes even refused to believe that they were "properly finished works at all."

[17]*The Contemporary Relevance of History: A Study of Approaches and Methods* (New York: Columbia University Press, 1986), p. 93.

There certainly is a danger that an historian who intuitively interprets the behaviour and products of people in other societies will use general knowledge appropriate to his own. This danger can be averted, however, if the historian immerses himself in the conventions of the society he is studying, learning the significance of its words and actions by studying them in different contexts. This is precisely what professional historians do, as J. H. Hexter has fully explained in his essay "The Historian and His Day" (Hexter, 1961). Hexter regularly spent nine or ten hours a day reading "things written between 1450 and 1650 or books written by historians on the basis of things written between 1450 and 1650" (p. 6). As a result he found that "instead of the passions, prejudices, assumptions and pre-possessions, the events, crises and tensions of the present dominating my view of the past, *it is the other way about*" (p. 9). . . . . Professional historians avoid the danger of interpreting the past by the conventions of the present: by building up a comprehensive knowledge of the conventions and preoccupations of the past.[18]

If, as G. B. Caird observes, the past "is not accessible to us by direct scrutiny, but only through the interrogation of witnesses," then perception of the past will depend in no small measure on "the historian's ability to 'speak the same language' as his source."[19] Unfortunately, not a few contemporary interpreters dismiss the notion of ancient literary competence as unattainable, and instead advocate ahistorical or even antihistorical approaches to biblical interpretation.[20] Meir Sternberg's criticism of such approaches, once heard, is as obvious as it is insightful:

> From the premise that we cannot become people of the past, it does not follow that we cannot approximate to this state by imagination and training—just as we learn the rules of any other cultural game—still less that we must not or do not make the effort. Indeed the antihistorical argument never goes all the way, usually balking as early as the hurdle of language. Nobody, to the best of my knowledge, has proposed that we each invent our own biblical

---

[18]*Justifying Historical Descriptions* (Cambridge: Cambridge University Press, 1984), p. 72.
[19]*The Language and Imagery of the Bible* (London: Duckworth, 1980), p. 202.
[20]I shall have more to say on this in chap. 4.

Hebrew. But is the language any more or less of a historical datum to be reconstructed than the artistic conventions, the reality-model, the value system?[21]

Sternberg emphasizes that if the task of becoming competent in the original languages of the Bible is as indispensable as it is demanding, then so too is the task of becoming competent in the literary conventions of the Bible and its neighboring cultures. "As with linguistic code, so with artistic code."[22] (I recognize, of course, that many readers of this book will have had no opportunity to learn either Greek, Hebrew, or Aramaic and therefore must rely on the judgments of experts as to how the various portions of the Bible are best translated. Similarly, there may be some need to rely on the aid of experts in seeking to develop an ancient literary competence.)[23]

The emphasis in the above discussion on the "foreignness" of the Bible may seem to suggest that the Bible is a closed book to all but specialists in the fields of ancient Near Eastern or Hellenistic languages and literatures. But this is not the case. Despite the many distinctives of the Bible's literary genres—its narratives, its poems, its epistles, and so forth—there is also considerable commonality between those genres and their modern-day counterparts, with which we are familiar. Were this not the case, comprehending them would be as inconceivable as comprehending a foreign language that shared no conceptual categories with our own (e.g., nouns, verbs, prepositions).[24] As Barton explains,

---

[21]*Poetics of Biblical Narrative*, p. 10.

[22]Ibid., p. 12.

[23]Recent books on the literature of the Bible that may prove useful to students include, in addition to the works of Alter and Sternberg already mentioned, J. Licht, *Storytelling in the Bible* (Jerusalem: Magnes, 1978); G. D. Fee and D. Stuart, *How to Read the Bible For All Its Worth*, 2d ed. (Grand Rapids: Zondervan, 1993); A. Berlin, *Poetics and Interpretation of Biblical Narrative* (Sheffield: Almond, 1983); T. Longman III, *Literary Approaches to Biblical Interpretation*, FCI 3 (Grand Rapids: Zondervan, 1987); M. A. Powell, *What Is Narrative Criticism?* (Minneapolis: Fortress, 1990); R. Alter, *The World of Biblical Literature* (New York: Basic Books, 1992); L. Ryken and T. Longman, *A Complete Literary Guide to the Bible* (Grand Rapids: Zondervan, 1993).

[24]Cf. R. Trigg, "Tales Artfully Spun," in *The Bible as Rhetoric: Studies in Biblical Persuasion*, ed. Martin Warner (New York: Routledge, 1990), p. 125: "The practice

"all literary study must assume that even quite remote cultures have *some* affinities with our own," so that, while we must "be on our guard, as biblical critics have sometimes failed to be, against thinking we know more than we do about the literary conventions of ancient Israel," we must not allow this realization to "drive us into a kind of critical nihilism according to which texts from the past are simply inscrutable."[25]

Robert Alter makes much the same point, contending that responsible biblical interpretation requires the adoption of a "self-conscious sense of historical perspective" that is alert to the "stubborn and interesting differences" between the world of the Bible and the modern world, but that at the same time recognizes that there are also "elements of continuity or at least close analogy in the literary modes of disparate ages," since "the repertory of narrative devices used by different cultures and eras is hardly infinite."[26]

In addition to drawing some reassurance from the significant degree of commonality between the literary forms of the biblical world and those of our own day, students of the Bible may be encouraged by what traditional Protestant thought has called the "perspicuity" (or clarity) of Scripture.[27] In a carefully nuanced discussion of the clarity or obscurity of the Bible, Moisés Silva notes that the doctrine of perspicuity, while not exempt from challenge or misunderstanding, is nevertheless a necessary corrective to the dispiriting misconception that the Bible is a book inaccessible to all but an elite few.[28] As formulated in the Westminster Confession of Faith, for example, the doctrine of the

of history and even the possibility of the translation of ancient languages depend on the assumption that there are major points of contact between what may seem alien worlds."

[25] *Reading the Old Testament*, pp. 28–29.

[26] "How Convention Helps Us Read: The Case of the Bible's Annunciation Type-Scene," *Proof* 3 (1983): 117–18.

[27] The perspicuity of Scripture is included along with the concepts of *sola scriptura* and the analogy of faith in Fackre's list of "standard features of traditional Protestant hermeneutics" ("Evangelical Hermeneutics," p. 123).

[28] *Has the Church Misread the Bible? The History of Interpretation in the Light of Current Issues*, FCI 1 (Grand Rapids: Zondervan, 1987), pp. 77–97.

perspicuity of Scripture offers encouragement to all students of the Bible, the "unlearned" as well as the "learned."[29] But, as Silva explains, it does not deny the value of diligent personal study, the importance of "specialists who seek to bridge the gap that separates us from the languages and cultures of the biblical writers," or the need for the illumination of the Spirit of God for the attainment of "saving understanding."[30] Nor does it deny that some readers of the Bible may become, as Paul puts it, "darkened in their understanding and separated from the life of God because of the ignorance that is in them due to the hardening of their hearts" (Eph. 4:18; cf. Rom. 1:21).[31]

In view of the degree of commonality between the literatures of various ages and cultures and in view of the Bible's clarity (perspicuity), every Bible reader (while recognizing that saving knowledge, like faith, is a gift of God) should be encouraged and challenged to know that with a good will and by the use of "ordinary means" a sufficient, if not comprehensive, understanding of biblical truth is attainable. Does this mean that the work of biblical scholars and specialists need be of little interest to ordinary readers? On the contrary, "leaning on the expertise of scholars who have specialized interest should be regarded as one more instance of using 'ordinary means' in the study of Scripture." To dismiss the work of scholars as irrelevant is to forget that the vast majority of people "cannot even read the Bible without depending on the scholarly work that has made Bible translations possible."[32]

These observations are true, but it should also be stressed

---

[29]See ibid., p. 85.

[30]Ibid., pp. 84, 89.

[31]The doctrine of the perspicuity of Scripture is similar in some respects to Sternberg's concept of the Bible's "foolproof composition," by which he means the ability of the biblical discourse to "bring home its essentials to all readers." The Bible may be "difficult to read, easy to underread and overread and even misread, but virtually impossible to, so to speak, counterread." Sternberg is alert to the fact that "ignorance, preconception, tendentiousness—all amply manifested throughout history, in the religious and other approaches—may perform wonders of distortion," but, nevertheless, "short of such extremes, the essentials of the biblical narrative are made transparent to all comers: the story line, the world order, the value system" (*Poetics of Biblical Narrative*, pp. 50–51).

[32]Silva, *Has the Church Misread the Bible?* p. 89.

that scholars can and do make mistakes and sometimes argue with great conviction and erudition for erroneous theories. It is therefore incumbent on ordinary readers, wherever possible, not simply to accept on faith this or that scholarly pronouncement, nor to be cowed by scholarly erudition or reputation, but to approach the contributions of scholars critically, testing them in the light of logic and common sense, and, preeminently, in the light of Scripture. Such was the treatment accorded no less a notable than the apostle Paul himself (Acts 17:11).

GENRE CRITICISM AND BIBLICAL INTERPRETATION

We turn now to look more closely at the work being done in the genre criticism of the Bible. The first thing that a newcomer to the discipline of genre criticism is likely to notice is the complexity of the field. Even the matter of how the term *genre* should be defined has not yet been finally settled. Among the better attempts at definition would be Barton's description of genre as "any recognizable and distinguishable type of writing or speech— whether 'literary' in the complimentary sense of that word or merely utilitarian, like a business letter—which operates within certain conventions that are in principle (not necessarily in practice) stateable."[33] Briefer is Collins's definition: "By 'literary genre' we mean a group of written texts marked by distinctive recurring characteristics which constitute a recognizable and coherent type of writing."[34]

While they are helpful as far as they go, such definitions as these remain quite general, and it seems fair to say with Grant Osborne that "the concept of genre, so central to hermeneutical theory in recent years, is an elusive one."[35] Among the possible reasons for this, the two following seem particularly noteworthy.

[33]*Reading the Old Testament*, p. 16.
[34]J. J. Collins, "Introduction: Towards the Morphology of a Genre," *Semeia* 14 (1979): 1; cf. also Longman, *Literary Approaches*, pp. 76-83.
[35]So begins Osborne's essay entitled "Genre Criticism—Sensus Literalis" (*TrinJ* 4 ns/2 [1983]: 1). Similarly, C. Blomberg (*The Historical Reliability of the Gospels* [Leicester: IVP, 1987], p. 235 n. 1) observes that while "genre has traditionally

First, the question of genre can legitimately be addressed to a particular writing on various levels of discourse. Earlier in this chapter, I rather loosely used the term *macro-genre* to refer to the essential character of the Bible as a whole, and I also used the term *genres* to refer to subunits or parts within the whole. It could be argued, of course, that a concept like genre, based as it is on the principle of a wide-ranging comparison of similar texts, is hardly applicable to the Bible.[36] There is a sense in which "the Bible by its very nature as divine revelation transcends 'all actual genres, since divine revelation could not be generic in a logical sense of the word.' "[37]

But even were we to avoid the term *genre* when speaking of the Bible as a whole, the problem of multi-level genre descriptions would still persist. For example, we can describe the book of Psalms at one level as a poetical book, at another level as a hymn book or a prayer book, and at another level still as a collection containing lament psalms, songs of thanksgiving, hymns, royal psalms, wisdom psalms, and the like. The books of 1 and 2 Samuel can be described at one level as (predominantly) narrative discourse, at another perhaps as royal apology (i.e., historiographic narratives defending theologically the legitimacy of the Davidic royal house), and at still another as a composition containing stories, sayings, proverbs, poems, songs, battle reports, genealogies, prayers, and prophecies.

One way scholars have sought to minimize the confusion is by limiting the use of the term *genre* to a particular level of discourse. Longman, for example, prefers to use "*genre* . . . to refer to a work as a whole and *form* to refer to a unit within a

been defined as a category of literary composition characterized by a particular style, form, or content, . . . the whole question of whether or not literature can be so categorized is one of increasing debate."

[36]As E. D. Hirsch has observed: "Anything that is unique cannot, with respect to those aspects which are unique, be a type" (*Validity in Interpretation* [New Haven: Yale University Press, 1967], p. 64).

[37]Osborne, "Genre Criticism," p. 3; quoting M. Beaujour. Osborne's criticism of Beaujour's position as ignoring "the analogical nature of God-talk as well as its human accommodation" (pp. 3–4) seems more appropriate in terms of the specific genres and subgenres within the Bible than of the Bible as a whole.

whole text.''[38] Similarly, Osborne, following J. A. Baird, distinguishes "genre, form and mode."

> Baird says that "form" is a literary device, based on the nature of the material, which is used to analyze small units of literature; "genre" takes several of these units and collects them into a single whole for the purpose of classification; and "mode" is even more diffuse, noting characteristics which (sometimes artificially) unite various forms or genres under a single rubric.[39]

Sidney Greidanus takes a similar three-tiered approach. He labels the Bible as a whole "proclamation"—this would be its *mode*. Under this general rubric he lists the following canonical *genres:* narrative, prophecy, wisdom, psalm, gospel, epistle, apocalypse. Narrowing the focus yet further, he mentions various specific *forms* that may occur in one or another of the above genres: law, dream, lament, parable, miracle, exhortation, autobiography, funeral dirge, lawsuit, pronouncement, report, royal accession, and passion.[40] Such terminological distinctions are useful but, unfortunately, have yet to become standardized.

A second feature of contemporary genre criticism that sometimes leads to confusion is the frequent application of genre labels derived from extrabiblical (and sometimes modern) literary and cultural contexts to biblical texts. While the use of extrabiblical literary terminology is to an extent unavoidable and indeed can be helpful in describing certain features in the biblical texts, it is important to bear in mind that genre categories that have been developed through the study of literatures outside the Bible may not be fully applicable to the biblical texts.[41]

Despite the above concerns regarding genre criticisms, it nevertheless remains the case that genre recognition, whether on a conscious or subconscious level, plays a vital role in all forms of

---

[38]*Literary Approaches,* p. 76, n. 3.

[39]"Genre Criticism," p. 4.

[40]*The Modern Preacher and the Ancient Text: Interpreting and Preaching Biblical Literature* (Grand Rapids: Eerdmans, 1988), pp. 20–23.

[41]Cf. W. G. Lambert, "Old Testament Mythology in Its Ancient Near Eastern Context," in *Congress Volume Jerusalem 1986,* ed. J. A. Emerton, VTSup 40 (Leiden: E. J. Brill, 1988), p. 127.

successful communication. At its best, genre criticism is not a *name game*[42] but an indispensable prerequisite for comprehending the *sensus literalis* of a text.[43] Blomberg writes: "To recognize what for a longer work of literature would be called its 'genre' is necessary for valid interpretation. Parables, for example, must not be interpreted like straightforward history; although they are very lifelike in many ways, Jesus may have included some details in them simply to make the stories lively and interesting."[44]

To illustrate this last point Blomberg cites the occasional misreading of "the story of the rich man and Lazarus (Luke 16:19–31)" as if it were concerned to present "a realistic depiction of life after death." In Blomberg's view, such an approach fails to recognize the true genre of the story, which he classifies as parable. To the objection that the passage is not labeled parable by the gospel writer, Blomberg points out that "approximately half the stories in the gospels which are commonly called parables are not specifically labelled as such, but they are recognized by the common form and structure which they share with passages specifically termed parables." In other words, they are recognized on the basis of *generic signals*.

Chief among the generic signals that Blomberg detects is the phrase with which the story opens, "A certain man was. . . ." He notes that the same phrase introduces "the two preceding parables of the prodigal son (15:11–32) and the unjust steward (16:1–13) and seems to correspond to the modern 'Once upon a time. . . .' Just as people today recognize such a phrase as the opening of a fairy-tale, so Jesus' audience would have been prepared by the start of a parable to recognize it as a fictitious narrative."[45]

A survey of other occurrences of the phrase "certain man" in Luke confirms Blomberg's point. It is a frequent formula in Jesus' parables, both in those that are explicitly labeled parables and in those that are not.[46] Given this *generic* (or more properly *formal*)

---

[42]Cf. G. W. Coats, ed., *Saga, Legend, Tale, Novella, Fable: Narrative Forms in Old Testament Literature*, JSOTS 35 (Sheffield: JSOT, 1985), p. 8.

[43]Cf. Osborne, "Genre Criticism," p. 5.

[44]*Historical Reliability*, p. 22.

[45]Ibid., p. 23.

[46]The former include Luke 12:16 (rich fool); 13:6 (fig tree); 15:3–4 (lost sheep); 19:12 (ten minas); 20:9 (tenants); and the latter include 10:30 (good Samaritan);

signal, we must ask why all commentators are not agreed that the story of the rich man and Lazarus is a parable. For one thing, modern interpreters may not be as quick to recognize the signal as Jesus' first-century audience would have been; this will depend on each interpreter's level of ancient literary and cultural competence. For another, a single indicator is not usually sufficient to determine genre. We may note, for example, that the phrase "certain man" occurs also at 14:2 in a nonparabolic context.[47] Finally, and perhaps most importantly, the fact that one of the characters in the story is given a name, Lazarus, may seem to suggest an element of historical specificity normally lacking in parables. The force of this last observation is much diminished, however, when one realizes that the name Lazarus means "God helps."[48] Hence it may have been used for its semantic or symbolic effect and not because a particular, historical person is in view. As J. A. Fitzmyer observes, "it is a fitting name for the beggar in this parable, who was not helped by a fellow human being, but in his afterlife is consoled by God."[49]

The above example illustrates how important the reader's linguistic and literary competence is for proper interpretation of textual discourse. This is as true for historical texts as for any other. As Michael Stanford puts it in *The Nature of Historical Knowledge*,[50] "the more we understand how a historian has done the work the better we can penetrate to what that work is about—the world of the past 'as it really was.'" That is to say, the better we pay "some attention to the glass through which we look, the better we shall understand what we are looking at." Alter makes the same point with respect to biblical interpretation when he

---

14:16 (great banquet); plus the three noted by Blomberg, 15:11 (prodigal son); 16:1 (unjust steward); 16:19 (rich man and Lazarus).

[47]According to most Greek witnesses.

[48]So J. Jeremias, *The Parables of Jesus*, rev. ed. (London: SCM, 1963), pp. 183, 185. The name, as J. A. Fitzmyer notes, is "a grecized, shortened form" of the Old Testament name Eleazar (*The Gospel According to Luke X–XXIV*, AB 28a [Garden City, N.Y.: Doubleday, 1985], p. 1131).

[49]Ibid.; see also p. 1130 for an explanation of how the rich man mistakenly came to be called "Dives" in postbiblical tradition.

[50]Oxford: Basil Blackwell, 1986, p. 137.

speaks of "a complete interfusion of literary art with theological, moral, or historiographical vision, the fullest perception of the latter dependent on the fullest grasp of the former."[51] In short, as I have written elsewhere, "an increased appreciation of the literary mechanisms of a text—*how* a story is told—often becomes the avenue of greater insight into the theological, religious and even historical significance of the text—*what* the story means."[52]

As important as linguistic and literary competence is, true communication between text and reader requires also a further point of shared understanding. Wittgenstein has stated: "If language is to be a means of communication there must be agreement not only in definitions but also (queer as this may sound) in judgments."[53] Putting it another way, Stanford contends that "if people are to talk to one another they must agree not only about words but about how they see the world."[54] The compatibility (or, as the case may be, incompatibility) of the view of the world held by the interpreter and the worldview evinced by the text is a significant conditioning factor in the interpretive process. I shall have more to say on this important issue in chapters 4 and 5.

Having stressed the importance of genre criticism in broad terms, we need now to consider several important qualifications, or cautions, lest genre criticism become an interpretive straitjacket.

First, we must recognize that genre criticism is primarily a *descriptive* and not a *prescriptive* enterprise. The genre classifications proposed by scholars are not to be regarded as inviolable rules of literature any more than the generalized descriptions of language found in grammar books are to be regarded as inviolable rules of speech.[55] Native writers or speakers are free to press the limits of genre, of which they may have little *conscious* awareness in any case. Still, just as it is useful for an outsider seeking to learn a foreign language to become acquainted with as much as possible of

---

[51]*Art of Biblical Narrative*, p. 19; cf. p. 179.

[52]V. Philips Long, *The Reign and Rejection of King Saul: A Case for Literary and Theological Coherence*, SBLDS 118 (Atlanta: Scholars Press, 1989), p. 14.

[53]*Philosophical Investigations*, part no. I, 242 (London: Basil Blackwell, 1968), p. 88; quoted by Stanford (*Nature*, p. 117).

[54]Ibid.

[55]Cf. Longman, *Literary Approaches*, pp. 77–78.

the grammar and syntax of that language, so it is very useful for the modern reader of the Bible to learn as much as possible of the Bible's literary grammar and syntax.

Second, we must resist the nineteenth-century notion that shorter, "purer" forms are early and "mixed" or "elaborated" forms are late. Under pressure from archaeological discovery and the logic of everyday experience, this old notion has been generally abandoned and a more fluid concept of genre has now emerged.[56] The result of this more fluid concept is the recognition "that no genre-class can have unrestricted access to any single generic trait."[57] This observation is significant when we come to ask about the historicity or historical intent of a given passage of Scripture. It is not sufficient simply to point to this or that individual trait, such as high literary style or a strong didactic intent, as signaling a nonhistoriographical genre or, conversely, to point to narrative form or elements of factual content as indicating a historiographical genre. As we shall see, such questions can only be decided on the basis of the broader context and the apparent overall purpose of the text under consideration.

Third, while genre criticism is fundamentally based on commonality and comparisons, it is reductionistic to assume that unique texts cannot exist. Allowance must be made for the possibility (and, considering the nature of the source, even probability) that biblical texts may explode the generic categories derived from comparisons with other literature. As Coats has observed, "Some species of literature—or of any kind of object—

---

[56]The "simplicity criterion" does continue to find expression occasionally. K. Koch, for example, in his study of the form-critical method, agrees with H. Gunkel that a "concise style" indicates greater antiquity and an "elaborated style" betrays a later period (*The Growth of the Biblical Tradition: The Form-Critical Method*, trans. S. M. Cupitt [London: Adam & Charles Black, 1969], p. 126). Nevertheless, Koch elsewhere allows that earlier, elaborated forms may have been condensed at a later period (see p. 201; cf. pp. 189, 211). C. Westermann also assumes the "simplicity criterion" in his influential *Basic Forms of Prophetic Speech*, trans. H. C. White (London: Lutterworth, 1967), pp. 24, 130–31, 148. For a recent critique of form criticism, including the "simplicity criterion," see J. Muddiman, "Form Criticism," in *A Dictionary of Biblical Interpretation*, ed. R. J. Coggins and J. L. Houlden (Philadelphia: Trinity Press International, 1990), pp. 240–43.

[57]Osborne, "Genre Criticism," p. 8.

may be genuinely unique, not readily subject to classification in a group."[58] The difficulty of finding extrabiblical literature comparable to the Gospels, for example, has led many scholars to the conclusion that "the Gospels are *sui generis* in the sense that they are 'a recombination of earlier forms and genres into novel configurations.' "[59]

One of the limitations of genre and form criticism is the fact that terms such as *saga, legend,* and even *historiography*—in fact, most of our genre labels—"have been drawn by and large from fields of literature outside the OT, indeed, from outside the period of time that produced the principal narratives." Thus, as Coats reminds us, the labels apply to the biblical literature "only with a limited degree of accuracy. . . . Giving a name to the genre is necessary but only as a convenience for the discipline."[60] Genre labels may even prove to be a liability if they prevent us from seeing that the Bible, if it is indeed the word of God, can be expected to surpass (as a whole and, we may assume, in some of its parts) the human productions of its day.[61] In this regard it may be appropriate to draw a comparison between Scripture (the written word) and Jesus (the living Word), "who as to his human nature was a descendant of David" (Rom. 1:3), but whose birth nevertheless could not be fully explained in human terms.

Fourth, since genre criticism by its very nature makes use of the comparative method, care must be taken that the comparative method does not become imperative. That is, the temptation must be avoided either to insist that only those biblical genres are possible that find analogies outside the Bible (see the preceding

---

[58]G. W. Coats, *Genesis: With an Introduction to Narrative Literature* (Grand Rapids: Eerdmans, 1983), p. 10.

[59]Osborne, "Genre Criticism," pp. 25–26; citing D. E. Aune.

[60]*Genesis*, p. 4. In other words, genre labels represent *etic* (non-native) as opposed to *emic* (native) categories. On the terminology *emic* versus *etic*, see M. G. Brett, "Four or Five Things to do With Texts: A Taxonomy of Interpretive Interests," in *Bible in Three Dimensions*, ed. Clines et al., esp. p. 363. On both the necessity and the danger of employing etic as well as emic categories, see Longman, *Literary Approaches*, pp. 52–53.

[61]See, e.g., E. L. Greenstein, "On the Genesis of Biblical Narrative," *Proof* 8 (1988): 347; Osborne, "Genre Criticism," p. 26.

paragraph) or to assume that whatever genres are attested outside the Bible may without qualification find a place in the Bible. If certain speech acts, such as lying or blasphemy, would be deemed unacceptable in the mouths of God's inspired messengers, then it stands to reason that certain genres might be deemed unacceptable in the biblical corpus.[62] In his study of Sumerian literature as a background to the Bible, W. W. Hallo comes to the following conclusion:

> The parallels I have drawn may in many cases owe more to a common Ancient Near Eastern heritage—shared by Israel—than to any direct dependence of one body of literature on the other. . . . Sometimes, as in the case of casuistic law, the biblical authors adopted these genres with little change; at other times, as in the case of individual prayer and congregational laments, they adapted them to Israelite needs; occasionally, as with divination and incantation, they rejected them altogether in favor of new genres of their own devising (in this case, prophecy).[63]

Finally, genre criticism must resist the temptation to focus exclusively on smaller units of discourse and instead must be alert to the way in which the genre of a larger discourse unit affects every smaller discourse unit within it. One of the drawbacks of form criticism and historical criticism as traditionally practiced is that these approaches have tended to focus primarily, if not

---

[62]I am aware of course of such passages as 1 Samuel 16 and 1 Kings 22, but these do not disprove the point being made. In 1 Samuel 16 the Lord provides Samuel with a "half-truth" to tell Saul—"I have come to sacrifice to the Lord" (v. 2)—which clearly echoes Saul's own attempted deception in the preceding chapter (cf. 15:15, 21) and suggests that Saul is getting his just desserts (cf. R. P. Gordon, "Simplicity of the Highest Cunning: Narrative Art in the Old Testament," *ScotBEv* 6 [1988]: 80; for a defense of the viewpoint that Saul's "sacrificial excuse" in 1 Samuel 15 is a prevarication, see my *Reign and Rejection*, pp. 145–46, 152). In 1 Kings 22:22, the Lord in his sovereignty releases a "lying spirit" (*rûaḥ šeqer*) to enter the mouths of Ahab's prophets, but even in this instance the true prophet of the Lord, Micaiah, ultimately speaks the truth.

[63]"Sumerian Literature: Background to the Bible," *Bible Review* 4/3 (1988): 38. One would perhaps want to qualify Hallo's last statement with some mention of prophecy as attested at Mari.

exclusively, on the smaller units, with far too little attention being given to the larger.[64]

David Clines points out that instead of treating the books of the Bible as "literary works that generate meaning through their overall shape, their structure, and their dominant tendencies, that is, through their identity as wholes," it has been customary for biblical scholarship to value them "piecemeal for their diverse contents."[65] This is an unfortunate tendency and one that runs directly counter to the fundamental principles of discourse. First among these principles, as articulated by Robert Bergen, is the fact that "language texts are composed of successively smaller organizational units of language." In other words, "language is multi-tiered."

> Letters and vowel points function as the lowest echelon in the Biblical language texts. These in turn form syllables, which may be used to create words. Words may be integrated into phrase patterns, which can be arranged into clauses, which in turn may be woven together into sentences. Sentences in turn may be ordered in such a way as to create paragraphs, which may be structured so as to create episodes (narrative discourse). Higher structures of language include (among others) episode clusters, stories, story cycles, subgenre, and genres. The number of organizational levels present within a text depends upon the complexity and type of the communication task.[66]

The second of Bergen's discourse principles is that "each successively higher level of textual organization influences all of the lower levels of which it is composed. Language is organized from the top down. . . . Upper levels of text organization, such as genre, place broad constraints on all lower levels. . . ."[67] This

---

[64]This complaint is at the heart of the synchronic versus diachronic debate in literary criticism; see Long, *Reign and Rejection*, pp. 7–20.

[65]*What Does Eve Do to Help? and Other Readerly Questions to the Old Testament*, JSOTS 94 (Sheffield: JSOT, 1990), p. 101.

[66]"Text as a Guide to Authorial Intention: An Introduction to Discourse Criticism," *JETS* 30 (1987): 327–36.

[67]Ibid., p. 330. Cf. Vanhoozer, "Semantics of Biblical Literature," p. 80: "Recent literary studies show that literary forms serve more than classificatory purposes. The genre provides the literary context for a given sentence and, therefore, partly determines what the sentence means and how it should be taken."

principle is of particular relevance when we begin to explore the
issue of the historicity or historical truth claims of a text. One
must consider the character and truth claims (the apparent
[embodied] intent) of the larger discourse unit before passing
judgment on the historical value of the smaller. In this task the
interpreter will find little help in the comparative method, for the
simple reason that, as Porter points out,

> in the cultures surrounding Israel, . . . literary forms are found
> almost entirely as separate units. In this sense it would be true to say
> that they are the raw materials of history, rather than history
> proper, although many of them are genuine historiography, in so
> far as they present interpretations and understanding of history and
> an awareness of direction within it. By contrast, in the Old
> Testament, all these elements, as far as the Pentateuch and the
> Former Prophets are concerned, are embedded in a chronologically
> added narrative. Nowhere else in the ancient Near East is there to be
> found anything strictly comparable to this collecting and arranging
> of traditions and documents as successive elements in larger corpora
> and, ultimately, into a single corpus.[68]

The ancient Near East, then, offers little that can compare to the
larger discourse units of the Old Testament—to say nothing of the
whole Old Testament, or the whole Bible! This fact, however,
does not justify a piecemeal approach to the biblical texts, as
tempting as it may be to focus exclusively on smaller units where
at least rough analogies in extrabiblical literature can be found. It is
not wrong, of course, to study the smaller units; it is indeed useful
and necessary. But final judgment on a smaller unit's import,
historical or whatever, must not be passed without first considering the larger discourse of which the smaller is a part.[69]

---

[68]J. R. Porter, "Old Testament Historiography," in *Tradition and Interpretation:
Essays by Members of the Society for Old Testament Study*, ed. G. W. Anderson
(Oxford: Clarendon Press, 1979), pp. 130–31.

[69]This is as true for the New Testament as it is for the Old—e.g., M. Davies
("Genre," in *Dictionary of Biblical Interpretation*, ed. Coggins and Houlden, p. 258)
has recently observed with respect to the New Testament epistles that "the
collection into a corpus of letters, originally occasioned by individual circumstances, modifies the genre, giving to all of them a representative character."

The following may serve as a brief example of the importance of considering the larger discourse unit before rendering
generic or form-critical verdicts. George Ramsey, in *The Quest for
the Historical Israel,* issues the following "common sense" judgment based on the "laws of nature": "We recognize that the story
told by Jotham (Judg. 9:7–15) is a fable, since trees do not talk. A
similar judgment is made about the story of Balaam's ass speaking
(Num. 22:28–30)" (p. 15).[70] But is this reasoning sound? Is the
fact that trees do not talk sufficient reason to label Jotham's speech
a fable? After all, according to the "laws of nature," bushes do not
burn without being consumed, and dead people do not rise from
the grave.

In the case of Jotham's speech, it is not the fabulous storyline
but, rather, the larger context that makes it unmistakable that
Jotham's speech is a fable. The verses that precede it introduce the
historical personages and the point of tension reflected in the fable,
and Jotham concludes his speech with direct references to the
same: "Now if you have acted honorably and in good faith when
you made Abimelech king, and if you have been fair to Jerub-
Baal. . . . But if you have not, let fire come out from Abimelech
and consume you, citizens of Shechem and Beth Millo, and let fire
come out from you, citizens of Shechem and Beth Millo, and
consume Abimelech!" (Judg 9:16, 20). The phrase "let fire come
out" is a repetition of the phrase found at the end of the fable:
"then let fire come out of the thornbush and consume the cedars of
Lebanon" (v. 15). This is clear evidence that Jotham's final words
in his speech (vv. 16–20) are an interpretation of his fable.

But what of the story of Balaam (Num. 22–24)? It too has its
"fabulous" elements (e.g., the appearance of the angel and the
speech of the donkey in chapter 23), but do these elements alone
make it a fable? The broader context apparently offers nothing that
would mark it out as such; no *interpretation,* for example, is given.
What one has, rather, is a story involving certain wondrous
occurrences within the larger account of the book of Numbers,

---

[70]London: SCM, 1982. On the problematic status of the concept of "autonomous
laws of nature," see J. C. Sharp, "Miracles and the 'Laws of Nature,' " *ScotBEv* 6
(1988): 1–19.

with no indication that a new formal literary type has been introduced. Thus, unless one is willing to argue that the book of Numbers as a whole must be characterized as fable, there appears to be no valid literary reason to label the Balaam stories as such.

GENRE CRITICISM AND THE RISE OF BIBLICAL POETICS

Form criticism may be described as a sort of lower-level genre criticism. It focuses on the smaller textual units that, in the case of biblical literature at least, are combined so as to form larger textual entities. As noted above, one of the deficiencies of the form-critical approach is that it can tend to overlook the significance of the larger discourse unit. Nevertheless, there are hopeful signs that increasing attention is being given to the larger units.

A convenient survey of higher-level genre criticism in New Testament studies is provided by Craig Blomberg.[71] He divides his discussion under the headings *Gospels, Acts, Epistles,* and *Revelation.* Of greatest interest for our present concern with biblical historiography are the first two categories. While recognizing that debate continues, Blomberg comes to rather positive conclusions on questions of historicity. After summarizing recent debates over the genre of the Gospels, Blomberg ultimately concludes that they may be identified as "theological histories of selected events surrounding the life and death of Jesus of Nazareth" (p. 42). Moreover, "Once allowance is made for paraphrase, abbreviation, explanation, omission, rearrangement and a variety of similar editorial techniques, one may remain confident that the gospels give trustworthy accounts of who Jesus was and what he did" (p. 41).[72]

Blomberg comes to similarly positive conclusions with

---

[71]"New Testament Genre Criticism for the 1990s," *Them* 15/2 (1990): 40–49.

[72]For a book-length defense of this position, see Blomberg's *Historical Reliability;* cf. also R. T. France, *The Evidence for Jesus* (Downers Grove, Ill.: InterVarsity, 1986); G. N. Stanton, *The Gospels and Jesus* (Oxford: Oxford University Press, 1989).

respect to the book of Acts: "As with the gospels, the Acts may be compared with a known genre of Hellenistic literature while at the same time retaining features which made it *sui generis*. Theological history may be the best label for the combination" (p. 42).[73]

In Old Testament studies, some of the more useful attempts at *higher-level* genre criticism might be broadly grouped under the rubric of biblical *poetics*. As described by Adele Berlin, poetics is "an inductive science that seeks to abstract the general principles of literature from many different manifestations of those principles as they occur in actual literary texts." Poetics serves interpretation, but is distinct from it. While interpretation focuses on an individual text, poetics canvases many texts in an attempt "to find the building blocks of literature and the rules by which they are assembled. . . . Poetics is to literature as linguistics is to language. . . . Poetics strives to write a grammar, as it were, of literature." Changing the analogy, Berlin explains that "if literature is likened to a cake, then poetics gives us the recipe and interpretation tells us how it tastes."[74]

So far, poetic criticism in Old Testament studies has focused largely on the higher-level genres of poetry and narrative. With respect to the former, influential works include James Kugel's *Idea of Biblical Poetry: Parallelism and Its History*,[75] Alter's *Art of Biblical Poetry*, and Adele Berlin's *Dynamics of Biblical Parallelism*,[76] to name but a few. The dust has not yet settled, but it is already apparent that significant new gains have been achieved, particularly in the corrective that has been issued to the older view, first espoused by Robert Lowth,[77] that Hebrew poetry is characterized by three types, and only three types, of parallelism: synthetic, antithetic, and synonymous. The recent studies have highlighted the ten-

---

[73]For a thorough and learned treatment of the question, see C. J. Hemer's *Book of Acts in the Setting of Hellenistic History*, Wissenschaftliche Untersuchungen zum Neuen Testament 49 (Tübingen: J. C. B. Mohr, 1989).

[74]*Poetics and Interpretation*, p. 15.

[75]New Haven: Yale University Press, 1981.

[76]Bloomington: Indiana University Press, 1985.

[77]*Lectures on the Sacred Poetry of the Hebrews*, trans. G. Gregory, new ed. with notes by C. E. Stowe (Andover: Codman Press, 1829).

dency of the second of the parallel (half-)lines to sharpen, intensify, and advance the thought of the first.[78]

Of greater pertinence to our concern with biblical historiography is the work being done in the area of biblical narrative discourse. The appearance of Alter's *Art of Biblical Narrative* in 1981 awakened new interest in the literary qualities of the Hebrew Bible, and a lively debate has followed. More substantial, and certainly no less controversial, is Sternberg's *Poetics of Biblical Narrative*, which first appeared in 1985.[79] These works and others like them have been less concerned with *classifying* the biblical texts than with exploring the specific *workings* of biblical narrative. This is a salutary emphasis, inasmuch as it aims to equip the interpreter with preunderstandings and reading strategies that are appropriate to the texts being studied. As for the impact that poetics may have on the historical study of the Bible, it is already apparent that phenomena in the biblical texts often cited by historical critics as tensions, contradictions, and the like are increasingly coming to be recognized as *narrative devices* employed by the biblical writers for communicative effect. It can only be hoped that the future will see increasing dialogue between the proponents of traditional historical criticism and those more versed in the poetics of biblical narrative. For if some of the insights of the latter are valid, then some of the historical conclusions of the former can no longer stand.[80]

Since poetics focuses on the internal workings of texts, it is an avowedly literary pursuit. This can and has seemed threatening

[78]For a convenient presentation of recent thinking on biblical poetry, see Longman, *Literary Approaches*, chap. 6.

[79]For a selective, comparative review of these works by Alter and Sternberg, see Long, "Toward a Better Theory and Understanding of Old Testament Narrative," *Presbyterion* 13 (1987): 102–9.

[80]I shall have more to say on these matters in the pages that follow; cf. also chap. 1 of Long, *Reign and Rejection*. A disappointing feature of D. Damrosch's otherwise stimulating book, *The Narrative Covenant: Transformation of Genre in the Growth of Biblical Literature* (San Francisco: Harper & Row, 1987), is his ready acceptance of the results of conventional source and redaction criticism, with little apparent consideration of how these results are often undermined by recent studies in biblical poetics; see, e.g., R. Polzin's critique in his review article "1 Samuel: Biblical Studies and the Humanities," *Religious Studies Review* 15/4 (1989): esp. 304–5.

to those more concerned with the historical and theological significance of the Bible. But as Sternberg has cogently argued, these three interests should not be set in opposition. He insists that "Biblical narrative emerges as a complex, because multifunctional, discourse. Functionally speaking, it is regulated by a set of three principles: ideological, historiographic, and aesthetic. How they cooperate is a tricky question."[81] It is the nature of this cooperation, especially between the historical and the aesthetic (literary) aspects, that we shall consider in the next chapter. But first, let us consider an example of how consciousness of genre is basic to proper interpretation.

AN EXAMPLE: JUDGES 4 AND 5

In broad generic terms, Judges 4 is prose and Judges 5 is poetry. Since both chapters treat the same basic episode (the defeat of Sisera and his Canaanite forces by Deborah, Barak, and especially Jael), these two chapters offer a nice example of the importance of interpreting biblical passages in the light of the genres in which they are cast. Not surprisingly, differences between the two renditions of the defeat of Sisera have elicited lively discussion and an extensive literature. For our own purposes, two recent treatments will be highlighted.

The first is Halpern's study, most recently published as chapter 4, "Sisera and Old Lace: The Case of Deborah and Yael," in his book *The First Historians: The Hebrew Bible and History*.[82] In this book Halpern defends the thesis that some biblical authors "who wrote works recognizably historical" had "authentic antiquarian intentions" in the sense that "they meant to furnish fair and accurate representations of Israelite antiquity" (p. 3). As sensible as this basic thesis is, some of the ways Halpern attempts to demonstrate its validity are open to question. With respect to Judges 4 and 5, for example, Halpern's aim is to show that the prose account of Judges 4 is a well-intended, if somewhat flawed,

---

[81]*Poetics of Biblical Narrative*, p. 41.
[82]San Francisco: Harper & Row, 1988.

attempt to distill *history* from the poetry of Judges 5. To do this, Halpern proposes the following criterion for detecting dependence of one text on another:

> Short of secure dating, only one circumstance permits confidence as to the relationship between parallel texts: there must be substantive points of difference, preferably several, such that one text only could be derived from the other. In practice, this means that the author of the derivative version must have interpreted the source in a manner with which the modern analyst takes issue: if the two agree, no basis for arbitrating priority remains. (p. 77)

One cannot help wondering how fairly a modern interpreter who adopts this criterion will be able to approach the texts in question. Looking for grounds to take issue with the writer of Judges 4, Halpern does not take long to find them. Preeminently, he cites "two disparities between the accounts [which] have, since the nineteenth century, provoked comment" (p. 78). The first is that while the poetical account, the Song of Deborah, mentions at least six tribes as participating in the defeat of Sisera, the prose account mentions only Zebulun and Naphtali. The second "concerns the manner of Sisera's demise." In chapter 4 Jael drives a tent peg through the skull of the sleeping Sisera, while in chapter 5, on Halpern's reading, Jael "sneaks up behind him and bludgeons him, so that he collapses at her feet (5:24–27)" (p. 78).

Regarding the first difficulty, Halpern notes that Malamat and Weiser have suggested readings that, if correct, would harmonize the apparent discrepancies between the tribal references in Judges 4 and 5. He also admits that "the historian of Judges 4" may have read the pertinent verses along the same lines that Weiser suggests. Nevertheless, he continues to maintain that the differences are such as to prove the dependence of Judges 4 on Judges 5.

My intention here is not to debate the merits of either Malamat's or Weiser's harmonizations (or of others that have been suggested) but to assess briefly the merits of Halpern's own method. Space limitations do not permit a full evaluation, but it seems fair to say, as a first general observation, that Halpern approaches the song of chapter 5 with expectations respecting sequencing and chronology that are too rigid for dealing with poetry.[83]

Second, he does not appear to make adequate allowance for the imagistic character of poetry. He is of course correct that in the prose account there is "no question of [Sisera's] falling after the blow (4:17–22)," at least not in the literal sense of *falling down*— Sisera is already sleeping. It is noteworthy, however, that when the prose narrative itself recounts Jael's presentation of the slain Sisera to Barak, it describes Sisera as *nōpēl mēt*, "fallen dead" (4:22). English translations tend to render this phrase "lying dead" (e.g., NRSV) or to leave the participle *nōpēl* untranslated—"dead" (so NIV), but it remains the case that the prose account uses the same verb that is used to describe Sisera's "falling" in the poetical account (5:27). This suggests that the imagery in the poem should not be pressed in too literalistic a direction.

This observation is in general agreement with the conclusions reached in the second of the studies we wish to highlight. In *"Heads! Tails! Or the Whole Coin?!* Contextual Method and Intertextual Analysis: Judges 4 and 5,"[84] Lawson Younger conducts a systematic investigation of comparative cuneiform and Egyptian texts to test the thesis, which he attributes to Athalya Brenner,[85] that Judges 4 and 5 are complementary, not contradic-

---

[83]An example would be the argument that Halpern builds on the occurrence of Hebrew '*āz* in 5:19. In Halpern's view, "the poem situates the tribal muster all in the stage before the battle (5:9–18, and the consecutive '*āz* 'then,' in v. 19)" and thus renders impossible Malamat's theory that the poem enumerates the tribes that participated in the pursuit, though not necessarily in the battle (p. 78). But this argument, in addition to exhibiting an overly rigid chronological expectation where poetry is involved, also assumes that '*āz* necessarily carries a temporal significance in this context. In fact, however, '*āz* can be used (and in this context probably is used) as a stylistic device for indicating the emphasized portion of a sentence (cf., e.g., Josh. 22:31; Isa. 33:23; 41:1; Hab. 1:11; Ps. 96:12; Mal. 3:16; cf. also W. L. Holladay, *A Concise Hebrew and Aramaic Lexicon of the Old Testament* [Grand Rapids: Eerdmans, 1971], p. 8; L. Koehler, W. Baumgartner et al., *Hebräisches und Aramäisches Lexikon zum Alten Testament*, 3d ed., 4 vols. [Leiden: E. J. Brill, 1967–1990], 1: 26; the latter explicitly cites Judges 5:19 and 22 under this usage).

[84]In *The Biblical Canon in Comparative Perspective: Scripture in Context IV*, ed. by K. Lawson Younger, Jr., William W. Hallo, and Bernard F. Batto, Ancient Near Eastern Texts and Studies (Lewiston, Me.: Edwin Mellen, 1991), pp. 109–46.

[85]"A Triangle and a Rhombus in Narrative Structure: A Proposed Integrative Reading of Judges IV and V," *VT* 40 (1990): 129–38.

tory. His engagement with a wide range of comparative ancient
Near Eastern literature in which a single event or episode is
represented in two or more texts of differing genres helps him
develop the ancient literary competence necessary for approaching
Judges 4 and 5 fairly. Younger concludes the first half of his essay,
a survey of the ancient Near Eastern parallel texts, with these
words:

> Ancient scribes could write different accounts about the same
> referents. But differences in purpose could determine differences in
> detail . . . , and in the selectivity of the events narrated. . . . If the
> scribes' purpose was to praise the king and/or the gods, poetry
> naturally offered a medium to heighten the emotions of the praise
> through rhetorical embellishment. Hence, divine activity and praise
> of the deities is encountered more often in the poetic versions. . . .
> But in most instances the poetic (or more rhetorical) text also added
> significant historical details so that the complementary nature of the
> accounts is manifest. (p. 127)

By taking seriously the prose-poetry distinction and, even more
importantly, by allowing the "ancient Near Eastern contextual
literary data" to provide "a means for evaluating and interpreting
Judges 4 and 5," Younger concludes that "neither account must be
dependent on the other." Rather, "both probably derive from a
common source (probably the historical referent itself) and possess
a complementary relationship" (p. 135).

I realize, of course, that it does an injustice to both Halpern
and Younger to treat their studies so briefly and selectively, and I
encourage the reader to weigh their respective arguments in their
full contexts. Younger's essay, as the latter of the two, is aware of
Halpern's treatment and is, overall, the more convincing. It
effectively demonstrates, on the basis of actual ancient Near
Eastern literature, that purpose affects selection and representation
and that it is not at all uncommon for complementary (though not
identical) portraits to be painted in the differing media of prose and
poetry. All of this illustrates and underscores the importance of
recognizing that the Bible comprises a library of various genres,
and that interpretation must never lose sight of this fact.

CONCLUSION

We began this chapter by asking if the Bible is a history book. We are now in a position to give a more nuanced answer. As we have seen, an affirmative answer cannot be given to this question if what is in view is the essential character of the Bible. But to give a negative answer is not entirely appropriate either. The Bible is in fact, as I have just stated, a library of books of diverse literary genres, so that no single description will suffice to characterize it, other than such very general labels as *religious book* or *Word of God*. Often the specific genres represented in the Bible are not employed in pure form, but are modified or blended by the biblical narrators and poets. Furthermore, the significance of smaller-scale literary forms within a larger textual discourse is necessarily affected by the larger entity. For this reason, we argued, study of the larger discourse unit, as in biblical poetics, for example, should be a priority in deciding questions of historical intent and import.

Classifying biblical texts according to genre categories derived from other literatures of the biblical world or even the modern world is sometimes enlightening, so long as we remain alert to the danger that such externally derived categories may be anachronistic or not quite suited to the biblical text. The comparative method, as useful as it often is, must not be allowed to become imperative—that is to say, we must not allow our genre classification to prescribe what a biblical text can and cannot contain.

We saw further that a historical impulse runs throughout the Bible, which, though not in every place and not always equally evident, is nevertheless pervasive. Hence, *lower-level* genre classification (as, for example, in form criticism) should not be regarded as a shortcut for determining the historical interest and significance of a given text. Above all, false dichotomies such as "the Bible is theology not history" or "the Bible is literature not history" must be avoided. The Bible evinces an interest in all three. In the next chapter we shall explore more fully the interrelationships of theology, history, and literary artistry as we ask, *What is history?*

2
HISTORY AND FICTION
What Is History?

"History . . . is all fictionalized, and yet history."[1] It may come as a surprise to readers unfamiliar with recent debates in biblical studies to discover the frequency with which the term *fiction* has begun to appear in discussions of biblical narrative. Alter, for example, in a provocative essay entitled "Sacred History and the Beginnings of Prose Fiction," emphasizes the vital role of fiction in biblical historiography. He even goes so far as to claim that "prose fiction is the best general rubric for describing biblical narrative."[2] It will be my aim in this chapter to argue that the concept of fiction, *if it can be properly defined and guarded against misunderstanding*, may be fruitfully employed in discussions of biblical historiography, but that it is in practice often applied in inappropriate and confusing ways, perhaps not least by Alter himself.[3] I shall suggest further that the confusion over fictionality derives in part from ambiguities within the term *fiction* itself. To complicate matters further, the term *history* is also ambiguous, being understood even by nonspecialists in at least two distinct senses.

Confusion over the role played by fictionality in history is

---

[1]Halpern, *First Historians*, p. 68.

[2]The essay constitutes chap. 2 of *The Art of Biblical Narrative*, and the quote is from p. 24.

[3]See Sternberg, *Poetics of Biblical Narrative*, pp. 23–30.

apparent since some are proclaiming fictionality as lying at the
heart of history-writing, while others are declaiming fiction as the
very opposite of history. Blomberg insists, for example, that "a
historical narrative recounts that which actually happened; it is the
opposite of fiction."[4] Similarly, Colin Hemer observes that "it is
no good raising the question of historicity if we are dealing with
avowed fairy-tale or fiction."[5] But Alter seems to have in mind
some other concept of fiction, for he insists that fictionality and
historicity are not antithetical. He writes:

> In giving such weight to fictionality, I do not mean to discount the
> historical impulse that informs the Hebrew Bible. The God of
> Israel, as so often has been observed, is above all the God of history:
> the working out of his purposes in history is a process that compels
> the attention of the Hebrew imagination, which is thus led to the
> most vital interest in the concrete and differential character of
> historical events. The point is that fiction was the principal means
> which the biblical authors had at their disposal for realizing history.[6]

A first step in coming to terms with the apparent disagreement is to clarify what the terms history and fiction can mean.
History, for example, as the term is commonly employed, can
refer either to the past or to the study of the past; or, to put it
another way, history can denote both events in the past and verbal
accounts of these events. Consider the following illustration
provided by David Bebbington.

> A visitor to the Tower of London may well buy a copy of its
> history. When 'history' is used in this way it means something
> different from 'history' in the claim that history repeats itself. A
> history of the Tower of London is its written history, a record of
> the past. The history that may or may not repeat itself, on the other
> hand, is the past itself, not a record but what really took place. In
> the English language the word history can mean either what people
> write about time gone by, that is historiography; or else it can mean
> what people have done and suffered, that is the historical process.[7]

[4]*Historical Reliability*, p. xviii n. 2.
[5]*Book of Acts*, p. 34.
[6]*Art of Biblical Narrative*, p. 32.
[7]*Patterns in History: A Christian Perspective on Historical Thought*, new ed.
(Leicester: Apollos, 1990), p. 1.

No doubt many disputes could be settled if the various terms of discussion were consistently defined and applied. If, for example, as Philip Davies suggests, the term *history* were reserved for "the events of the past as a *continuum*" and the term *historiography* for "the selective telling of those events," much confusion could be avoided.[8] But since such terminological consistency is frequently lacking in academic discussion,[9] about all one can do is to recognize that *history* is used in two quite distinct senses—to refer to the past itself and to interpretive verbal accounts of the past—and to discern in each context which is intended.[10] (It is perhaps also worth mentioning that much confusion and misunderstanding could be avoided if specialists would bear in mind that laypersons often have little understanding of the way *history* and *historical* are used as technical terms in professional discussions and, not surprisingly, are baffled when confronted by statements that both deny that some event is *historical* and at the same time insist that this does not mean it didn't happen.[11] To the layperson, history is what happened in the past.)

What about the term *fiction*? To the average person, who

[8]J. Rogerson and P. R. Davies, *The Old Testament World* (Englewood Cliffs: Prentice-Hall, 1989), p. 218.

[9]E.g., with respect to Old Testament studies, J. Van Seters (*In Search of History: Historiography in the Ancient World and the Origins of Biblical History* [New Haven: Yale University Press, 1983], p. 209) comments: "the subject of Israelite historiography has become highly diversified and the terminology increasingly ambiguous and confusing, [so that] the same terms are used in quite different ways."

[10]This discussion of *history* might easily be extended to cover such terms as *historic* and *historical*, *Historie* and *Geschichte*, and so forth, but what is important for our present purposes is the basic distinction between history-as-event and history-as-account. On the former pair, see Caird, *Language and Imagery*, p. 202; on the latter, see R. N. Soulen, *Handbook of Biblical Criticism* (Atlanta: John Knox, 1976), s.v. "Historie"; F. S. Leahy, "The Gospel and History," *Reformed Theological Journal* (Nov. 1985): 52–54.

[11]Cf. J. Barr, *The Scope and Authority of the Bible*, Explorations in Theology 7 (London: SCM, 1980), p. 9: "Again, it may be argued that the view just expressed assumes that God does not act in history and does not affect it. It assumes nothing of the sort. It simply observes that we do not apply the term 'history' to a form of investigation which resorts to divine agency as a mode of explanation."

tends to regard history and fiction as virtual opposites, a statement like the one by Alter quoted above—"fiction was the principal means which the biblical authors had at their disposal for realizing history"—will seem like nonsense. But Alter explains:

> The essential and ineluctable fact is that most of the narrative portions of the Hebrew Bible are organized on literary principles, however intent the authors may have been in conveying an account of national origins and cosmic beginnings and a vision of what the Lord God requires of man. We are repeatedly confronted, that is, with shrewdly defined characters, artfully staged scenes, subtle arrangements of dialogue, artifices of significant analogy among episodes, recurrent images and motifs and other aspects of narrative that are formally identical with the means of prose fiction as a general mode of verbal art.[12]

What Alter seems to be saying, in essence, is that literary shaping and artistry play no less significant a role in biblical historiography than in fiction. Halpern puts it succinctly when he states that "history [by which he means history as account] is fictional and employs the devices of all narrative presentation."[13]

The point in all this is that the word *fiction*, like the term *history*, may be used in two senses. Unfortunately, the two senses of fiction are not always clearly distinguished in discussions of narrative historiography. Alter, for example, sometimes speaks of "historicized fiction" and other times of "fictionalized history," without ever offering a clear articulation of the rather fundamental difference between the two.[14] The crucial term in each of these expressions, however, is the last one. In "historicized fiction," the weight of emphasis falls on *fiction*, suggesting that whatever bits of

---

[12]"How Convention Helps," p. 116.

[13]*First Historians*, p. 269.

[14]He does show awareness of the distinction on occasion; see, e.g., *Art of Biblical Narrative*, pp. 25, 33–34, 41. But his lack of clarity on this important point still leaves him open to criticism; e.g., D. Patrick and A. Scult (*Rhetoric and Biblical Interpretation*, JSOTS 82 [Sheffield: Almond, 1990], p. 50) write: "Alter has done much to open the Bible to serious reading by a wider audience, but by limiting himself to aesthetic judgments, he still does not integrate the Bible's truth-claims, as they are spoken, into his interpretative approach. He essentially reads the text as realistic fiction."

factual information may be included the story itself is nonfactual (as, for example, in a historical novel). In "fictionalized history," on the other hand, the weight falls on *history*, the claim being that the story is a representation of a real event in the past, whatever fictionalizing may be involved in the crafting of the narrative.[15] Only when this double sense of the term fiction is understood— fiction as *genre* and fiction as *artistry* or *craft*—does it become possible to agree with Blomberg that history "is the opposite of fiction" and at the same time to agree with Halpern that "all history . . . is fictionalized, and yet history."[16] Blomberg's focus is on history and fiction as distinct literary genres, whereas Halpern's point seems to be that any representation of the past, inasmuch as it is not (literally) the past, involves a "fictionalizing" aspect.[17] Halpern has in mind *form* (i.e., the way the story is told), while Blomberg is apparently thinking of *function* (i.e., for what purpose the story is told).

So long as we bear in mind this important distinction between form and function we may speak of a certain fictionality involved in all narrative discourse while still maintaining the common-sense differentiation between *historical* narratives, which "claim to tell us what really happened," and *fictional* narratives, which "portray events that of course by definition never happened, [though] they are often said to be true-to-life."[18] The point is simply that fictionality of a certain sort is as likely to be found in the historian's toolbox as in the fiction writer's.[19]

---

[15]For a similar distinction, cf. F. F. Bruce ("Myth and History," in *History, Criticism and Faith*, ed. Colin Brown [Leicester: IVP, 1979], p. 84), where he favors "mythologization of history" to "historicization of myth," but prefers "theological interpretation of history" to both.

[16]Both quotations occur at the beginning of this chapter.

[17]Cf. Powell, *What is Narrative Criticism?* p. 100: "The real world is never identical with the world of a story, even if that story is regarded as portraying life in the real world quite accurately."

[18]D. Carr, "Narrative and the Real World: An Argument for Continuity," *HTh* 25 (1986): 117.

[19]Sternberg *(Poetics of Biblical Narrative,* p. 28) illustrates this point well by citing an evaluation of historian Garret Mattingly's *The Defeat of the Spanish Armada* (1959) by a fellow professional historian and observing "how many of [Robert] Alter's *measures of fictionality* are invoked to define Mattingly's professional *excellence as a historian*" (insertion and italics mine).

Still, given the potential for (and indeed the presence of) much confusion resulting from the use of an ambiguous (bivalent) term like *fiction*, it would be far better, at least with respect to the perceptions of the average person, to substitute a term like *artistry* to describe the historian's literary technique, and reserve the term fiction for the nonfactual genre of that name. Since this is not likely to happen, however, it will be necessary when reading this or that scholar to discover how the term *fiction* is being used.

The issues raised so far can be elucidated by comparing historiography, which might be fairly described as a kind of a verbal representational art, with a visual type of representational art such as painting.[20]

HISTORY-WRITING
AS REPRESENTATIONAL ART

In his oil painting classes in Chicago, my former teacher Karl Steele would occasionally reflect on a criticism that he, as an impressionist painter, sometimes received from those more at-

---

[20]The analogy between historiography and art has a venerable history and continues to evoke interest today; see, e.g., F. R. Ankersmit, "Historical Representation," *HTh* 27 (1988): 205–28. No analogy is perfect, of course, and a criticism that could be made of this one is that a text should not be treated "as a static spatial form, like a painting, a sculpture, or a piece of architecture" (so R. M. Fowler, *Let the Reader Understand: Reader-Response Criticism and the Gospel of Mark* [Minneapolis: Fortress, 1991], p. 42), since reading is a "dynamic, concrete, temporal experience, instead of the abstract perception of a spatial form" (ibid., p. 25). I would argue, however, that the distinction between reading texts and viewing paintings should not be overpressed. While countless tourists may spend a few hours in the Louvre casting a glance this way and that to see the paintings, it can hardly be said that many of them have properly *viewed* the paintings. Time and dynamic interplay are as involved in giving a painting a "close viewing" as they are in giving a text a "close reading." If anything, the distinction between viewing a painting and reading a text is in the sequence of perception: with a painting, one generally begins with an impression of the whole, then proceeds to study individual *passages* of the painting, and finally returns to a greater appreciation of the whole in the light of its parts; with an unfamiliar narrative, one must generally begin by reading the individual passages in sequence, which leads eventually to an impression of the whole, and then finally to a greater appreciation of the parts in the light of the whole.

tracted by what is commonly called abstract or expressionist art. The basic criticism was that since his paintings were *representational*, or at least *realistic*[21] (primarily landscapes and seascapes), there was less *artfulness* in his craft—he simply *copied* nature. Steele's response was to challenge his critics to inspect at very close range any two-inch square of one of his canvases. Should the critics agree to the challenge, what they would find would not be nature, or even an exact copy of the appearance of nature, but a tiny abstract painting! In other words, each of Steele's *realistic* paintings consisted of a series of abstractions, which taken together and viewed from the proper vantage point gave a convincing and indeed realistic impression of the scene depicted. In one sense, then, Steele's paintings were *fictions* and not *literal* renderings of reality. There could be no question of counting blades of grass or leaves on trees; each brush stroke was an abstraction, just paint on canvas. In another sense, however, his paintings were very much representations of reality, imparting to receptive viewers a truer sense and appreciation of the scene, as Steele perceived it, than even the best color photography could have done.

The above illustration relates to the issue of historiography in the following manner. Common sense suggests that it would be a *reductio ad absurdum* to argue that since Steele's paintings at one level make use of techniques indistinguishable from those employed by abstract or expressionist painters, they therefore cannot be representational, or make reference to a reality outside themselves. One can find, however, among the writings of those who challenge the representational capacity of narrative discourse, statements that seem similarly reductionistic. Roland Barthes, for example, in drawing attention to what he calls "the fallacy of referentiality," writes:

---

[21]I am using the term in a general, not a technical sense, as a virtual synonym for *naturalistic*—i.e., concerned with depicting the world more or less as it appears. For a more technical description of these two terms, see, e.g., K. Reynolds with R. Seddon, *Illustrated Dictionary of Art Terms: A Handbook for the Artist and Art Lover* (London: Ebury Press, 1981), ad loc.

Claims concerning the "realism" of narrative are therefore to be discounted. . . . The function of narrative is not to "represent," it is to constitute a spectacle. . . . Narrative does not show, does not imitate. . . . "What takes place" in a narrative is from the referential (reality) point of view literally *nothing*; "what happens" is language alone, the adventure of language, the unceasing celebration of its coming.[22]

This sounds very much like saying that "what happens" in one of Steele's paintings is *paint alone*. Barthes's statement may be true of some narratives, but surely not all. If paintings can be broadly divided into representational and nonrepresentational varieties, into those that attempt to depict some aspect of the world outside and those that simply celebrate the potentialities of paint as a medium, then is it possible that narratives can be similarly classified? Of course, even representational (referential) painters enjoy considerable freedom in terms of how they choose to depict their subject—compositional and stylisitic decisions have to be made.[23] But this does not mean that a generic distinction cannot and should not be made between paintings that are representational and those that are not. By the same token, I would contend that a distinction can and should be made between narratives that are essentially representational (historiographical) and those that are not.

On what basis then are narratives to be classified? Form alone is not a sufficient criterion: "there are simply no universals of historical vs. fictive form. Nothing on the surface, that is,

---

[22]"Introduction to the Structural Analysis of Narratives" (1966), p. 124; quoted by Hayden White ("The Question of Narrative in Contemporary Historical Theory" *HTh* 23 [1984]: 14), which see for an extended critique of Barthes's position (pp. 12–15).

[23]E. H. Gombrich ("The Mask and the Face: Perception of Physiognomic Likeness in Life and in Art," in *Art, Perception, and Reality*, ed. Maurice Mandelbaum [Baltimore: The Johns Hopkins University Press, 1972], pp. 1–46) offers an extreme example of this in his description of a portrait painted by Picasso in which the subject's head is given a perfectly oblong shape, but then, in "a balancing of compensatory moves . . . to compensate for her face not being really oblong but narrow, Picasso paints it blue—maybe the pallor is here felt to be an equivalent to the impression of slimness" (p. 30). The interesting point is that despite the abstractions, the painting retains a referential function.

infallibly marks off the two genres. As modes of discourse, history and fiction make *functional* categories that may remain constant under the most assorted *formal* variations and are distinguishable only by their overall sense of purpose."[24] In other words, "there are no formal features, no textual properties that identify a given text as a work of fiction,"[25] yet history and fiction can still be distinguished on the basis of their overall purpose. Aristotle, writing more than two thousand years ago, came close to saying the same thing: "The difference between a historian and a poet is not that one writes in prose and the other in verse. . . . The real difference is this, that one tells what happened and the other what might happen."[26] This general point can be illustrated by observing the chiastic structure of the last four chapters of 2 Samuel.

21:1–14	A	Famine resulting from Saul's sin is stopped
21:15–22	B	Short list of Davidic champions
22:1–51	C	Long poetic composition: David's song of praise
23:1–7	C'	Short poetic composition: David's last words
23:8–39	B'	Long list of Davidic champions
24:1–25	A'	Plague resulting from David's sin is stopped

As Sternberg points out, chiasm is now widely recognized as "one of the indisputable literary devices" found in the Old Testament, and yet the chief goal of the epilogue to 2 Samuel "remains informational and memorial." The conclusion to be drawn from this is that while "form can produce or imply an artistic function, it still cannot enthrone one regardless of context."[27]

If, then, historical literature and fictional literature are "distinguishable only by their overall sense of purpose," *context* becomes one of the primary means of discovering this purpose.

---

[24]Sternberg, *Poetics of Biblical Narrative*, p. 30.

[25]Vanhoozer ("Semantics of Biblical Literature," p. 68), summarizing the view of J. R. Searle, "The Logical Status of Fictional Discourse," *New Literary History* 6 (1975): 319–32.

[26] *Poetics*, Loeb Classical Library (Cambridge, Mass.: Harvard University Press, 1982), chap. 9 (1451b).

[27]*Poetics of Biblical Narrative*, pp. 40–41.

We are reminded of one of the fundamental principles of discourse introduced in the preceding chapter—viz., that "each successively higher level of textual organization influences all of the lower levels of which it is composed." The question to be asked then is this: What is the apparent function of a particular narrative within its broader context? A sense of the purpose of a narrative is, as Sternberg puts it, "a matter of inference from clues planted in and around the writing."[28] Again let me illustrate with an example from the visual arts.

Imagine that we are viewing a painting of an old railroad depot. Imagine also that for the moment we are not allowed to look around to gain our bearings and to discover where the painting is hung. Without some knowledge of the painting's setting, we may be unable to decide whether the painting's primary function is a *historical* one—to be a lasting reminder of the appearance of an old landmark—or an *aesthetic* one—simply to be a pleasing work of art. Imagine that we are now allowed to look around. If we find that the painting is prominently displayed (with a bronze plaque beneath it) in the foyer of a brand new railroad terminal, we shall likely conclude that some *historical* function is being served (perhaps this was the old terminal that was demolished to make room for the new one). If, on the other hand, we find that the painting is displayed in an art gallery along with other paintings depicting various subjects, we shall be more inclined to assume that the aesthetic function is primary. Now, of course, the historical (or referential) purpose implicit in the first scenario does not exclude a concern with artistic quality. It is the greater aesthetic appeal of a painting over a photograph that will have prompted the railroad company to choose the more expensive option. The first scenario does imply, however, that the artist will have worked under some *referential constraints*. He will have been constrained by the actualities of the subject, at least to the point of making the subject recognizable. In the second scenario, though the artist may in fact fairly represent the appearance of the old depot, he will have been under no obligation to do so.[29]

---

[28]Ibid., p. 30.

[29]Illustrations of the continuum between referential and aesthetic interests might easily be multiplied: an architectural blueprint is referential, while an architectural

What is true of visual art (paintings) is true also of verbal art (narratives). The difference between a narrative whose primary purpose is representational (or referential) and one whose primary purpose is aesthetic is the degree to which the artist is constrained by the actualities of the subject matter. As Matt Oja puts it, "historians are constrained by the need to discover and work with a set of facts which already exist and which they look upon from without. Writers of fiction are not so constrained. . . . A fictional narrative does not have objective reality until the author creates it."[30] In some instances external evidence—material remains, eyewitness reports—may offer clues as to a narrative's purpose and its degree of adherence to the "facts,"[31] but in all instances our quest to discover a narrative's overall sense of purpose should begin with attention to clues in and around the narrative. If both the subject matter of the narrative itself and the nature of the surrounding context suggest a representational purpose, then we may assume that the writer has been in some measure constrained by the facts. I say "in some measure," because neither representational artists nor historians simply reproduce their subjects.

HISTORY-WRITING
AS A CREATIVE ENTERPRISE

I have argued that the chief difference between writers of history and writers of fiction is that the former are constrained by the facts of the past, while the latter are not. Does this disallow any creative input from the historian in the writing of history? Not at all, for as we have just noted, historians do not simply reproduce the past. Rather, they must contribute to the work they produce in at least a couple of ways. First, they must study all available

---

rendering of the planned construction combines representational and aesthetic interests in almost equal measure; a "mug shot" is referential, while a portrait combines representational and aesthetic interests, etc.

[30]"Fictional History and Historical Fiction: Solzhenitsyn and Kiš as Exemplars," HTh 27 (1988): 120; similarly, Sternberg, Poetics of Biblical Narrative, p. 29.

[31]For nuanced discussions of the slippery concept of "facts," see Stanford, Nature, pp. 71–74; R. H. Nash, Christian Faith and Historical Understanding (Grand Rapids: Zondervan, 1984), pp. 93–109.

evidence pertinent to their subject and develop their own vision of the past. Second, this vision must be encoded in a verbal medium in such a way that it can be shared with others. The first task, "the historian's construction of the past," is described by Stanford as "the pivot of historical knowledge" that stands between "history-as-event and history-as-record." The second task, the transposition of this construction into "written or spoken form," is equally important, since it "stands between the historian's mental construction and those of the audience."[32]

Few historians or philosophers would dispute the notion that writers of history make significant contributions in the ways mentioned above. What is hotly disputed, however, is the *nature* and *extent* of the historian's contribution. One of the major points of debate is whether *narrative form* as such is an aspect of reality itself or is a product solely of the historian's imagination. A narrative is characterized by having a plot, for example, with a beginning, a middle, and an end. Are such features aspects of reality itself or constructions created solely in the mind of the historian? Does the past present itself in narrative form, as a meaningful sequence, or is it a meaningless chaos, upon which the historian must impose a narrative structure?

Some historians and literary theorists today assume that "real events simply do not hang together in a narrative way, and if we treat them as if they did we are being *untrue* to life."[33] Others, however, disagree. David Carr, for example, strongly challenges the view that meaningful sequence is merely an invention of historians.[34] He sets the stage by quoting such notables as Louis Mink ("Life has no beginnings, middles and ends. . . . Narrative qualities are transferred from art to life") and Hayden White ("Does the world really present itself to perception in the form of

[32]*Nature*, pp. 143–44. Similarly, Axtell ("History as Imagination," p. 458) writes: "Since history at its best is shared discovery, the historian's final and most important task is to *translate* his vision, his 'achieved awareness' and understanding, of the past for the modern reader."

[33]Carr ("Narrative and the Real World," p. 117), who goes on to contest this view.

[34]Both in the article mentioned in the preceding note and in a book entitled *Time, Narrative, and History* (Bloomington: Indiana University Press, 1986).

well-made stories? Or does it present itself more in the way that the annals and chronicles suggest, either as a mere sequence without beginning or end or as sequences of beginnings that only terminate and never conclude?").[35] Carr himself maintains that "narrative is not merely a possibly successful way of describing events; its structure inheres in the events themselves."[36]

If Carr is correct, does this mean that the historian simply finds historical narratives rather than constructs them? I would contend that the answer lies somewhere in the middle, and that two extremes should be avoided: (1) that which denies the importance of the historian's vision and creative imagination and (2) that which denies to the past any inherent/coherent structure whatsoever. Historians, as verbal representational artists, find themselves in a position analogous to that of visual representational artists. The latter can paint a number of different pictures of a single subject, no two of which are alike, but this does not mean that the subject itself lacks inherent structure or that the artists are unconstrained by the facts. The production of a representational painting involves a coordination of creativity and constraint, the creativity of the artist under the constraint of the subject. The subject matter does not simply present itself to the artist as a painting waiting to be painted. The artist must make various kinds of choices. First, a subject must be chosen from among the multitude of possible subjects in the world around. Second, a vantage point must be chosen from which to view the subject. Third, compositional decisions must be made: what are to be the boundaries or limits of the painting? Do these boundaries result in an overall sense of balance? Depending on the purpose of the painting, the artist may have some freedom to arrange or rearrange elements of his subject. The portrait artist, for example, enjoys considerable freedom to rearrange objects in the setting but is rather constrained when it comes to rearranging the subject's face! Fourth, a paint medium must be chosen (oil, acrylic, watercolor, etc.), the palette of colors selected (will it include a limited or a full range of colors?), the style decided (will the painting be rendered

---

[35]"Narrative and the Real World," p. 118.
[36]Ibid., p. 117.

in intricate detail with small brushes or will it be executed boldly and rapidly with a palette knife?), and so forth.

Just as the physical world does not present itself in such a way that no creative choices are required of artists who would depict some aspect of it, so the past does not present itself in such a way that historians need make no creative choices in the construction of a historical account of some aspect of it. But if the past does have some inherent structure (as I believe it does), then the first task of historians is to seek to discern that structure. Beyond this, they must also choose a point of view—the most appropriate perspective from which to depict the subject and the "best light" in which to see it. And they must make aesthetic choices—how shall the work be composed, what degree of detail shall be included, what shall be the boundaries of their "picture" of the past, and so forth.

Constraint by the subject matter, point of view, aesthetic choices—our painting analogy can help us begin to understand how the three impulses mentioned in the preceding chapter might be coordinated in the biblical literature, not only its narratives but also in other genres (such as poetry) that may include historical reference. The *historiographical* impulse implies constraint by the subject, the *theological* implies point of view, and the *literary* implies aesthetic choices. But the fruitfulness of the painting analogy does not end here. So far, the creative choices required of painter and historian alike are but preliminaries to the actual execution of the work. When it comes to the latter, there are again a number of helpful parallels between the requirements of visual and of verbal representation.

CHARACTERISTICS OF SUCCESSFUL REPRESENTATION

Of the numerous points of advice that Karl Steele would customarily offer his painting classes, several stand out as particularly important. First, he would often instruct students at work on their paintings to blur their vision occasionally by half-closing their eyes; the effect of this was to eliminate the distraction of too much detail and to facilitate perception of the major contours and tonal relationships of the subject. Second, and as a corollary to this first point of advice, he would stress the importance of standing back from the canvas, or even walking backward, in order to view the subject and the canvas from a distance. Close proximity to the canvas, he would say, does not guarantee more accurate results but quite often the opposite, since the painter sometimes gets lost among the trees and loses sight of the overall shape of the forest. Third, he would contend that the most effective paintings are those that exploit the suggestiveness of visual ambiguities—lost edges, mysterious shadows, etc. He would point out that a common mistake of beginners is to attempt to record the great mass of detail exhibited by the subject, whereas the best way to achieve a realistic representation is to be very selective, limiting the depiction of details to a suggestive few so as to allow the mind of the viewers to fill in the rest.

These procedures of the visual artist—what we might call *creative means* to *representational ends*—find ready analogues in the work of the verbal artists we call historians. Since the "Ideal Chronicler"—viz., one who records everything that happens as it happens—does not exist, it is obvious that all historians must, to some extent at least, simplify their presentations of their subjects.[37] As Peter Ackroyd rightly observes, "the recounting of what happened, even a few moments later, inevitably introduces simplifications, selections, interpretations."[38] Indeed, one of the main tasks of historians, Axtell reminds us, is to discern and represent "the larger patterns, structures and meanings behind particular events and facts which contemporaries were not able to see."[39]

How do historians accomplish this? Where data are plentiful,

---

[37]For a critical evaluation of the concept of the "Ideal Chronicler," see P. A. Roth, "Narrative Explanations: The Case of History," *HTh* 27 (1988): 1–13; also L. O. Mink, "Narrative Form as a Cognitive Instrument," in *The Writing of History: Literary Form and Historical Understanding*, ed. R. H. Canary and H. Kozicki (Madison: University of Wisconsin Press, 1978), p. 140. Even if an exhaustive "Ideal Chronicler" existed, the resulting history would be so massive as to be useless.

[38]"Historians and Prophets," *Svensk Exegetisk Årsbok* 33 (1968): 21.

[39]"History as Imagination," p. 457.

historians must seek to discern the major contours of the subject by, as it were, half-closing their eyes so as to perceive the big picture. Alternatively, or additionally, they may enjoy the advantage of being able to view the subject from a distance, from across the room of time. As important as empirical evidence and eyewitness testimony are, historians standing at some remove from the subject are often in a favorable position to discern the major shapes and relations of the past. We often say of prominent contemporaries (presidents or prime ministers) that "it will be interesting to see how history treats them." Again, Ackroyd makes the point well: "the historian who writes at some distance from the events may be in a better position to give a true appraisal than one who is so involved as to see only a part of what makes up the whole."[40] One reason that the historian writing some time after the event may be at an advantage is that "the significance of a historial phenomenon is often recognized by its sequences or consequences, i.e., its posthistory."[41] Finally, historians, like painters, must avoid the temptation to include too much detail in their depiction. There must be an economy to their craft; if carefully selected, only a few suggestive details may be necessary to capture their subject (Esau's hairiness, Ehud's left-handedness, Eli's heaviness, etc.). "What matters most in history . . . is 'the great outline and the significant detail; what must be avoided is [a] deadly morass of irrelevant narrative' in between."[42]

THE ADEQUACY AND AUTHORITY OF REPRESENTATION

Simplification, selectivity, suggestive detail—these hallmarks of effective historiography are reminiscent of the kinds of features often highlighted in discussions of the *literary* artistry of

---

[40]"Historians and Prophets," p. 21.

[41]M. Tsevat, "Israelite History and the Historical Books of the Old Testament," in *The Meaning of the Book of Job and Other Biblical Essays* (New York: Ktav, 1980), p. 181; note also Tsevat's important qualification that "the significance is not bestowed by the latter upon the former; the consequences are indicators and not generators" (ibid.).

[42]Axtell, "History as Imagination," p. 459; quoting Lewis Namier.

biblical narrative. I hope that by now enough has been said to make the point that literary artistry and reliable historiography should not be set in opposition. But still the challenge might be raised: "In making a case that the Bible presents us with 'representational paintings,' have you not reduced our confidence in what the Bible can tell us about the past? Wouldn't photographs serve us better?" The answer to this question is that it very much depends on the artist! Admittedly, painting often involves a greater interpretive component than does photography (though even the latter requires that creative choices be made), but this is not necessarily a bad thing. As Carl F. H. Henry asserts, "Christian faith requires not simply the redemptive historical act but its meaning or significance as well; historical research alone is impotent either to guarantee any past event or to adduce its meaning or theological import."[43]

"But I'm just interested in the bare facts," the challenge might continue. Such a statement is both wrong-headed and a bit naive. Since the past is *past* and unrepeatable, it will never be possible to recover the "bare facts" pure and simple, at least not all of them; we are inevitably dependent on witnesses and evidences. As Caird explains, "History has a factual content, but it comes to the historian not as fact but as evidence, emanating from persons with whom he must engage in conversation."[44] Even if we could return to the past and record it on videotape, this would still not guarantee us an adequate understanding of the past. In the aftermath of the Persian Gulf War, I remember hearing a commentator on National Public Radio express a frustration he had felt while the war was in progress. It went something like this: "They kept sending us videotapes, but they didn't tell us what they meant. We had the video images, but no interpretation."

It is the greater interpretive capacity of painting over photography that makes it the generally preferred medium for portraiture (visual historiography). And it is the greater interpretive (explanatory) capacity of literary narrative over bare chronicle that makes it the preferred medium of biblical historiography.

---

[43]*God, Revelation and Authority* (Waco: Word, 1976), 2: 330.

[44]*Language and Imagery*, p. 202.

These preferences are only justified, of course, to the extent that
the narrators or painters are skillful and competent in their craft,
and they have adequate access to their subject. No one would
dispute that a portrait by an artist who is incompetent or who has
no clear notion of the character and appearance of the subject will
be inferior (on either artistic or referential grounds, or both) to
even a simple photograph of the subject. But recent studies are
increasingly demonstrating that the biblical narrators were con-
summate literary artists. And for those willing to accept it, their
claim to have written under divine inspiration more than adequately guarantees their access to their subject.[45]

There are, of course, many in today's world who dismiss any
notion of divine inspiration. In so doing, however, they find
themselves in a rather perplexing position. As Mink explains in
"Narrative Form as a Cognitive Instrument," many moderns
continue to embrace (consciously or unconsciously) a concept of
Universal History—the notion that "the ensemble of human
events belongs to a single story"—but they have no notion as to
"who devises or tells this story. In its original theological form, as
with Augustine, Universal History was the work of divine
Providence; but as the idea became secularized by the eighteenth
century, God the Author retreated, leaving the idea of a story
which is simply *there*, devised by no one . . . but waiting to be told
by someone" (pp. 136–137). Mink's proposed solution to this
rather unstable state of affairs brought about by modernism's
elimination of the Author but retention of the Story is, in the end,
to abandon altogether the residual belief that the past contains an
"untold story to which narrative histories approximate" and to
assert that only "individual statements of fact" are "determinate."
But since "the significance of past occurrences" cannot be grasped
except insofar as they find a place within a narrative, Mink
concludes that a story must yet be told, and it is *we* who must tell

---

[45]As Henry aptly puts it (*God, Revelation and Authority*, 2: 330): "Empirical
probability can indeed be combined with inner certainty when the meaning of
specific happenings is transcendently vouchsafed, that is, when that meaning is
objectively given by divine revelation." Cf. also Sternberg, *Poetics of Biblical
Narrative*, pp. 32–35.

the story; *we* must "make the past determinate in that respect" (p. 148). Having shown "God the Author" the door, modernism is left to tell the story itself. And though Mink does not address the issue, it would seem that since "we" denotes a plurality of persons, none of whom possesses more than a relative authority, the inevitable result of Mink's "solution" will be a thoroughgoing historical relativism.

The alternative to modernism's dilemma is to embrace a concept of biblical inspiration such that the authority of the Bible's pictures of the past (whatever may be the differences between them, and however incorrectly we may at times view them) is as secure as the authority of the One who inspired them.

AN EXAMPLE: SAMUEL-KINGS AND CHRONICLES

In the preceding paragraph, mention was made of differences that sometimes exist among the Bible's pictures of the past. Indeed, even biblical accounts of the same events often differ in various ways. Some might wish that these differences did not exist, but the fact of the matter is that our having different presentations of the same subject often puts us at an advantage! Multiple presentations enable us to view the subject from different angles and under various lights, and to benefit from the narrative artists' own interpretive contributions. However brilliantly a biography may be written, or however masterfully a portrait may be painted, our knowledge of the life and visage of a given individual is surely enhanced if we have access to more than one biography or portrait. When approaching the New Testament's four gospels, for example, or the Old Testament's two histories of the monarchy (Samuel-Kings and Chronicles), we do well to keep this perspective in mind.[46]

---

[46]The real question, of course, for those who are perplexed by differences among accounts of the same event(s) is whether or not these constitute *irreconcilable* differences—that is, contradictions—that would force us to call in question the narrative artists' competence, motives, control of the subject matter, or the like. While it would be obscurantist to deny that the Bible presents vexing difficulties for which solutions are not readily forthcoming, I would maintain (1) that a properly

To investigate how we might go about negotiating differences among biblical accounts purporting to cover similar historical terrain, let us look more closely at the *synoptic histories* of the
Old Testament. As Roddy Braun has observed, a comparative
reading of Israel's synoptic histories affords an opportunity "to
learn much about both the nature of historical writing in Israel and
the manner in which God used His inspired writers to speak a
message to their own day."[47] Even a quick reading discovers that
Samuel-Kings and Chronicles paint rather different pictures, not
only in points of detail but even in terms of their overall shape.
The Chronicler's history, for instance, has little or nothing to say
on matters that were of great concern in the earlier history of
Samuel-Kings: reference to King Saul (whose election, rejection,
and decline occupy much of 1 Samuel) is limited to a brief
summary of his death and its cause in 1 Chronicles 10;[48] nothing is
said of the Saulide opposition to David's rise to power (though this
opposition is a focus of interest in the second half of 1 Samuel and
the early chapters of 2 Samuel); no mention is made of David's
adultery with Bathsheba and his arranged murder of Uriah, nor of
the disastrous political and domestic consequences of these actions
(though 2 Samuel 11–20 are largely taken up with these matters);
no mention is made of Adonijah's threat to Solomon, or of
Solomon's palace, or of his apostasy (though these figure prominently in 1 Kings 1–11); no mention is made of the prophetic
ministries of Elijah and Elisha that occupy center stage in 1 Kings
17–2 Kings 8, save the report of a letter of judgment from Elijah
to Jehoram of Judah in 2 Chronicles 21:11–17 (which letter,

---

nuanced understanding of the nature and purpose of the biblical literature greatly
lessens the number of perceived difficulties and (2) that the remainder of stubborn
cases should be held in abeyance or, preferably, made the object of special study by
those whose technical training and theological orientation might place them in a
position to find, not strained harmonizations, but true solutions.

[47]"The Message of Chronicles: Rally 'Round the Temple," *Concordia Theological
Monthly* 42 (1971): 502.

[48]For a recent discussion of the significance of the brief treatment of Saul in
Chronicles, see Saul Zalewski, "The purpose of the story of the death of Saul in
1 Chronicles X," *VT* 39 (1989): 449–67; cf. also Achroyd, "The Chronicler as
Exegete," *JSOT* 2 (1977): 2–32.

curiously, is not mentioned in Kings);[49] no mention is made of the fall of the Northern Kingdom (an event of signal importance recounted in 2 Kings 17). The list could continue and be presented in much greater detail, but enough has been indicated to show that by virtue of its omissions the Chronicler's presentation of Israel's past is given a quite different shape than that of Samuel-Kings.

Not only does the Chronicler's picture omit much that is found in Samuel-Kings, it also includes much that is not found in the earlier corpus: extensive genealogical lists stretching back to Adam (1 Chron. 1–9); additional lists of David's mighty men (chap. 12); reports of David's Levitical appointments (chaps. 15–16); descriptions of his preparations for temple building and temple worship (chaps. 22–29); much additional material relating to the Kingdom of Judah (various additions in the stretch of text from 2 Chron. 11–32); and Cyrus's decree marking the end of the exile (36:22–23).

From this very general overview, we can see that the Old Testament's two histories of the monarchy present different pictures in terms of overall shape and composition. But the differences between them are not limited to such large-scale matters. The two histories often differ significantly even in the way they render the same event or in the way they portray the same person. As an example, we might compare the two accounts of God's dynastic promise to David as presented in 2 Samuel 7 and 1 Chronicles 17.[50] That "there is a clear literary relationship

---

[49]For discussion, see R. Dillard, *2 Chronicles*, WBC (Waco: Word, 1988), pp. 167–69.

[50]Other instructive examples would include, e.g., the Chronicler's depiction of King Abijah, which is comparatively more positive than that found in Kings (cf. 2 Chron. 13 and 1 Kings 15; for discussion see D. G. Deboys, "History and Theology in the Chronicler's Portrayal of Abijah," *Biblica* 71 [1990]: 48–62); the Chronicler's presentation of David's census as compared to the Samuel account of the same episode (1 Chron. 21 and 2 Sam. 24; see Dillard, "David's Census: Perspectives on 2 Samuel 24 and 1 Chronicles 21," in *Through Christ's Word: A Festschrift for Dr. Philip E. Hughes*, ed. W. R. Godfrey and J. L. Boyd [Phillipsburg, NJ: Presbyterian and Reformed, 1985], pp. 94–107; J. H. Sailhamer, "1 Chronicles 21:1—A Study in Inter-Biblical Interpretation," *TrinJ* 10 [1989]: 33–48); the depiction of Josiah and his reforms in Chronicles as compared to the presentation in Kings (see, on 2 Chron. 34:4–7 and 2 Kings 23:4–14; D. L. Washburn,

between the two" is beyond dispute.[51] But when we compare the two passages, we discover a number of differences between them. The chart on the next two pages basically follows the NIV, but with some adjustments to reflect more closely the Hebrew texts. In the chart, some (though not all) differences have been highlighted: material peculiar to one passage only is placed in italics and the location of this material is indicated by a dotted line in both texts; solid underlining identifies noticeable differences in phraseology; alternation of the divine names God and LORD (Yahweh) are in bold type. (See chart now.)

A side-by-side reading of these parallel texts discovers numerous divergences—some minor, others more major. What are we to make of them? In the present context we must limit ourselves to a few brief comments on some of the apparently more significant differences. But first a word of caution: it should not be assumed that all differences represent motivated changes by the Chronicler.[52] Some may simply reflect the Chronicler's freedom to paraphrase or generalize, as he does often in his composition.[53] Other differences seem to result from stylistic or lexical preferences.[54] In still other instances, the Chronicler may simply be repeating what he finds in his *Vorlage* (the text of Samuel with which he was familiar).[55]

"Perspective and Purpose: Understanding the Josiah Story," *TrinJ* 12 [1991]: 59–78); and many more.

[51]So H. G. M. Williamson, "Eschatology in Chronicles," *TynB* 28 (1977): 134.

[52]See Dillard, "David's Census," pp. 94–96; Williamson, "History," in *It is Written: Scripture Citing Scripture. Essays in Honour of Barnabas Lindars*, ed. D. A. Carson and H. G. M. Williamson (Cambridge: Cambridge University Press, 1988), pp. 31–32.

[53]This may be all that is involved in the Chronicler's "You are not the one . . ." (v. 4) instead of 2 Samuel's "Are you the one . . ." (v. 5).

[54]An example would be the Chronicler's preference for the shorter form of the first person singular pronoun (*'anî*) over the longer form (*'ānōkî*) that is prevalent in Samuel-Kings. Whereas in Samuel-Kings the ratio of shorter to longer is something like 3 to 2, in Chronicles it is more like 25 to 1.

[55]For example, 2 Sam. 7:7 has "tribes" (*šibṭê*), while 1 Chron. 17:6 has "leaders" (*šōpṭê*). Since the latter is contextually more appropriate and is attested also in 2 Sam. 7:11, it appears that the Chronicler's *Vorlage* may preserve the better reading. On this and other matters discussed in this paragraph, see R. L. Braun,

2 Samuel 7:1—17

After the king was settled in his palace and the LORD had given him rest from all his enemies around him, 2 the king said to Nathan the prophet, "Here I am, living in a palace of cedar, while the ark .... of **God** remains in a tent." 3 Nathan replied to the king, "Whatever you have in mind, go ahead and do it, for the **LORD** is with you." 4 That night the word of the **LORD** came to Nathan, saying: 5 "Go and tell my servant David, "This is what the LORD says: 'Are you the one to build me a house to dwell in? 6 I have not dwelt in a house from the day I brought the Israelites up out of Egypt to this day. I have been moving from place to place with a tent as my dwelling.

7 Wherever I have moved with all the Israelites, did I ever say to any of their tribes whom I commanded to shepherd my people Israel, "Why have you not built me a house of cedar?"' 8 Now then, tell my servant David, "This is what the LORD Almighty says: I took you from the pasture and from following the flock to be ruler over my people Israel. 9 I have been with you wherever you have gone, and I have cut off all your enemies from before you. Now I will make your name great, like the names of the greatest men of the earth. 10 And I will provide a place for my people Israel and will plant them so that they can have a home of their own and no longer be disturbed. Wicked people will not wipe them out anymore, as they did at the beginning 11 and have done ever since the time I appointed leaders over my people Israel. I will also give you rest from all your enemies. The LORD declares to you that the LORD will establish a house for you: 12 When your days are over and you rest with your fathers, I will raise up your offspring to succeed you, who will come from your own body, and I will establish his kingdom. 13 He is the one who will build a house for my Name, and I will establish the throne of his kingdom forever. 14 I will be his father, and he will be my son. When he does wrong, I will punish him with the rod of men, with floggings inflicted by men. 15 But my love will never be taken away from him, as I took it away from Saul, whom I removed from before you. 16 Your house and your kingdom will endure forever before me; your throne will be established forever."' 17 Nathan reported to David all the words of this entire revelation.

1 Chronicles 17:1—15

After Davi̲d̲ was settled in his palace, ...
.... Davi̲d̲ said to Nathan the
prophet, "Here I am, living in a palace of cedar, while the ark o̲f̲ t̲h̲e̲
c̲o̲v̲e̲n̲a̲n̲t̲ of the **LORD** i̲s̲ u̲n̲d̲e̲r̲ a tent." 2 Nathan replied to Davi̲d̲,
"Whatever you have in mind, ...do it, for **God** is with
you." 3 That night the word of **God** came to Nathan, saying: 4 "Go
and tell my servant David, 'This is what the LORD says: Y̲o̲u̲ a̲r̲e̲ n̲o̲t̲
the one to build me a house to dwell in. 5 I have not dwelt in a house
from the day I brought Israel up .... to this day. I have
moved from o̲n̲e̲ t̲e̲n̲t̲ s̲i̲t̲e̲ t̲o̲ a̲n̲o̲t̲h̲e̲r̲,̲ f̲r̲o̲m̲ o̲n̲e̲ d̲w̲e̲l̲l̲i̲n̲g̲ p̲l̲a̲c̲e̲ t̲o̲
a̲n̲o̲t̲h̲e̲r̲. 6 Wherever I have moved with all the Israelites, did I ever say
to any of their l̲e̲a̲d̲e̲r̲s̲ whom I commanded to shepherd my people
..........., "Why have you not built me a house of cedar?"' 7 Now then,
tell my servant David, 'This is what the LORD Almighty says: I took
you from the pasture and from following the flock to be ruler over my
people Israel. 8 I have been with you wherever you have gone, and I
have cut off all your enemies from before you. Now I will make your
name .... like the names of the greatest men of the earth. 9 And I
will provide a place for my people Israel and will plant them so that
they can have a home of their own and no longer be disturbed.
Wicked people will not o̲p̲p̲r̲e̲s̲s̲ them anymore, as they did at the
beginning 10 and have done ever since the time I appointed leaders
over my people Israel. I will also s̲u̲b̲d̲u̲e̲ all your enemies.
I̲ declare to you that the LO̲RD will b̲u̲i̲l̲d̲ a house for
you: 11 When your days are over and you g̲o̲ t̲o̲ b̲e̲ with your fathers, I
will raise up your offspring to succeed you, o̲n̲e̲ o̲f̲ y̲o̲u̲r̲ o̲w̲n̲ s̲o̲n̲s̲,
        and I will establish his kingdom. 12 He is the one who will
build a house for m̲e̲, and I will establish h̲i̲s̲ throne ....
.... forever. 13 I will be his father, and he will be my son. ....

.... I will never take my love away from him,
as I took it away from y̲o̲u̲r̲ p̲r̲e̲d̲e̲c̲e̲s̲s̲o̲r̲. .... 14 I̲
w̲i̲l̲l̲ s̲e̲t̲ h̲i̲m̲ o̲v̲e̲r̲ m̲y̲ house and m̲y̲ kingdom forever ...., h̲i̲s̲
throne will be established forever.'" 15 Nathan reported to David all
the words of this entire revelation.

(Return to p. 79, second paragraph.)

There are, however, some differences between the two
renditions that may require explanation on other grounds. Particularly striking are the Chronicler's omission in verse 13 of any
reference to the chastisement of David's royal descendant, should
he sin (contrast 2 Sam. 7:14), and his alteration of pronouns in the
succeeding verse from "your house and your kingdom" to "my
house and my kingdom." What are we to make of changes such as
these?

Perhaps the way to begin is to recognize that the Chronicler
presents a *second* painting of Israel's monarchical history, not an
*over*painting of Samuel-Kings. It is now widely acknowledged that
both the Chronicler and his audience were well familiar with the
Samuel-Kings material, and that the Chronicler's aim was to recast
and supplement, not repress or supplant, the earlier history.[56]
Thus, the Chronicler could feel free, for example, without pang of
historical conscience, to omit the warning of 2 Samuel 7:14 as of
little interest to his particular purpose for writing. After all, those
who had experienced the Babylonian captivity and could look
back on the checkered history of the divided monarchy did not
need reminding that wrongdoing leads to "floggings inflicted by
men." Moreover, in keeping with his overall purpose, the
Chronicler wished to highlight Solomon's obedience, not his
disobedience.

What then was the Chronicler's overall purpose for writing?
To answer this question adequately would require not only a
thorough study of the entirety of the Chronicler's work but also a

1 Chronicles, WBC (Waco: Word, 1986), p. 198. For speculation on the character of
the Chronicler's Hebrew *Vorlage,* see Dillard, "David's Census," pp. 94–95.

[56]B. S. Childs insists that "it is a basic error of interpretation to infer . . . that the
Chr's purpose lies in suppressing or replacing the earlier tradition with his own
account" (*Introduction to the Old Testament as Scripture* [Philadelphia: Fortress],
p. 646, which see for Childs's reasoning). Similarly, Dillard points out that "the
numerous points at which he [the Chronicler] assumes the reader's familiarity with
the account in Samuel/Kings shows that he is using the Deuteronomic history as a
'control' to an audience well familiar with that account" ("The Reign of Asa [2
Chronicles 14–16]: An Example of the Chronicler's Theological Method," *JETS* 23
[1980]: 214). On the Chronicler's many allusions to the earlier history, see also
Ackroyd, "The Chronicler as Exegete."

consideration of the Chronicler's intended audience. The former is, of course, out of the question here.[57] As regards the Chronicler's audience, 2 Chronicles 36:22–23 (along with the evidence of the genealogies in 1 Chron. 3) makes it clear that the Chronicler is addressing the postexilic, restoration community in Jerusalem. We must ask, then, in assessing the Chronicler's rendition of the dynastic promise, "What must have been the pressing theological concerns of those who had returned out of exile in Babylon, or their descendants?" The unthinkable had happened—Judah had fallen and God's elect people had been swept away into exile. The question as to why this calamity had befallen God's people had been answered already for the exiles by Samuel-Kings. But for those now back in the land of Israel the pressing questions must surely be not "Why the exile?" but, rather, "Is God still interested in us? Are the covenants still in force?"[58] The Chronicler's answer to these questions is affirmative: God still cares for his people and is bound to them in covenant.

In his rendering of the promise to David, the Chronicler seeks to underscore these truths by bringing into the light what could only be dimly perceived in the shadows of the earlier rendering. That is to say, the Chronicler draws forth and makes explicit what was only implicit in 2 Samuel 7.[59] Perhaps it is this

---

[57]If we were to attempt such an investigation, we might take our initial cues from the overall structure of Chronicles. It appears, for instance, that the Chronicler wishes to stress the continuity of Yahweh's dealings with (and interest in) his chosen people, as this is most strikingly expressed in the covenant with David. The Davidic kingdom is at a fundamental level the kingdom of Yahweh. And since this is so, events pertaining to the kingdom of Judah, where Davidic descendants once reigned, take on significance for "all Israel." Moreover, since in the Chronicler's day there is no Davidic king on an earthly throne, greater emphasis falls on the temple as the locus of Yahweh's continued rule. For more adequate appraisals, see the literature; e.g., Ackroyd, "Chronicler as Exegete"; Braun, "Message of Chronicles"; J. Goldingay, "The Chronicler as Theologian," *BTB* 5 (1975): 99–126; M. A. Throntveit, *When Kings Speak: Royal Speech and Royal Prayer in Chronicles*, SBLDS 93 (Atlanta: Scholars Press, 1987), pp. 77–88; Williamson, *Israel in the Book of Chronicles* (Cambridge: Cambridge University Press, 1977).

[58]Cf. Dillard, "David's Census," pp. 99–101.

[59]This is fully in keeping with the Chronicler's general practice; so, e.g., Childs: "Often the Chronicler spelled out in detail what was already partially implied in his source" (*Introduction*, p. 652; cf. p. 648). Cf. also Dillard, "Reward and Punish-

practice of making the implicit *explicit* that best explains the
Chronicler's alteration of the pronouns in verse 14. At the time of
the Chronicler's writing, there is no longer a Davidic kingdom,
literally speaking, but the kingdom of God, of course, remains.
Thus "your house and your kingdom will endure forever before
me" of 2 Samuel 7:16 becomes "I will set him over my house and
my kingdom forever." In underscoring the theocratic character of
the Davidic throne, the Chronicler is simply making explicit what
is already implicit in the promise of 2 Samuel 7:14: "I will be his
father, and he will be my son."

In other ways as well, the Chronicler renders the dynastic
promise so as to drive home its pertinence to his audience. Perhaps
his replacement of "the king" with the more personal "David" in
verses 1 and 2 is meant to evoke the thought that, though Israel no
longer has a human king on the throne, the Davidic line has not
vanished and neither has God's promise, which after all was made
personally to David. His addition of a reference to the "covenant"
in verse 1 may serve to remind his hearers that they are still bound
to God in covenant. His omission of "out of Egypt" in verse 5
tends to generalize the statement and make it perhaps more
immediately relevant to those who themselves have been delivered
out of bondage, though in a different land. A similar dynamic may
be involved in the Chronicler's replacement of "Saul" with "your
predecessor" in verse 13. Even his rephrasing of the reference to
God's dwelling in a tent may serve to take the focus away from the
tabernacle *per se* and to suggest the more general point that God's
presence is not confined to any particular locale or structure.
Could it also be that the change in terminology from "who will
come from your own body" (which recalls the promise to
Abraham in Gen. 15:4 and seems to suggest an immediate
descendant) to "one of your sons" (which allows reference to
future descendants; compare 2 Kings 20:18) is meant to hearten
the Chronicler's hearers with the thought that the Lord may yet
raise up a Davidic scion? In context, of course, the literal referent
remains Solomon (v. 12: "He is the one who will build a house for

ment in Chronicles: the Theology of Immediate Retribution," *WTJ* 46 (1984): 164–
72.

me"). But a future son of David is not thereby excluded, at least not if the significance of the "house for me" is allowed to extend beyond the physical temple of Solomon.

To the above considerations, more could be added,[60] but perhaps we had better stop and hear Williamson's caution that the Chronicler's "handling of the dynastic oracle in 1 Chronicles 17 is but one element of this larger whole [i.e., the 'larger narrative structure' of Chronicles], and rash conclusions concerning his *Tendenz* should thus not be drawn hastily from a single text without further ado."[61] For our immediate purpose, however, it does not so much matter that we discover the precise nature of the Chronicler's *Tendenz* as that we recognize that he had a *Tendenz*— a desire to present Israel's history in a certain light and for a certain purpose—and that this has influenced his depiction of the dynastic promise.

What then have we learned from this brief comparison of Israel's synoptic histories? Does the fact that 2 Samuel and 1 Chronicles present the dynastic promise to David in distinctive ways present a problem for those who wish to take seriously the historiographical character of each? If both texts are given a flat reading, as if they were verbatim transcripts of the event, then the answer would have to be yes. But as we have tried to show in this chapter, historical reportage is often more akin to painting than photography. That the Chronicler should explicitly present what is implicitly present in his source is entirely acceptable. After all, we do this sort of thing everyday. Imagine that in response to an invitation, we are told, "I'm afraid that we shall be busy that evening." If we then bring home the report, "They said they couldn't come," we will not be accused of fabrication—we have only made explicit what is implicit in the literal reply. The Chronicler's more interpretive presentation, focusing as it does on the inner significance of the promise, is all the more justified inasmuch as he seems to assume knowledge of the Samuel version

---

[60]We have not discussed, e.g., the Chronicler's avoidance of the term *rest* in his parallels to 2 Sam. 7:1, 11–12; see Dillard, "The Chronicler's Solomon," *WTJ* 43 (1980): 294.

[61]"Eschatology in Chronicles," p. 136.

on the part of his audience. In short, what the comparison of the two renderings of the dynastic promise illustrates is the extent to which historians may be creative in their presentations, while at the same time remaining constrained by the facts.

CONCLUSION

We began this chapter by asking the question *What is history?* In the opening paragraphs, we noted that the term *history* is used in at least two different senses: history-as-event and history-as-account. While never losing sight of the former, we focused primarily on the latter, which might better be termed *historiography*. Because there is so much talk nowadays of *fictionality* in narrative, it was necessary also to investigate whether and in what sense this term might legitimately be applied to historiography. The conclusion reached was that since an account of something (just like a painting of something) is not literally that something, one may legitimately describe the account or the painting as in one sense *fictional*. We noted, however, that because the term *fiction* is also used to designate a genre of literature that is not constrained by any "something" external to it (i.e., by any *referential* constraint), the term is not ideally suited to discussions of historiography and could profitably be replaced by less ambiguous terms such as *artistry* or *crafting*.

Having noted the analogy between historiography and representational painting, we went on to explore the place of *creativity* even in depictions whose essential purpose is referential. The analogy alerted us to some of the characteristics of successful representation such as selectivity, slant, simplification, suggestive detail, and so forth. As to the adequacy and authority of representation, we saw that these issues very much depend on the competence and credentials of the (visual or narrative) artists, as well as on their access to their subject.

Finally, we looked briefly at the synoptic histories of the Old Testament: Samuel-Kings and Chronicles. We saw that, though these cover much the same territory historically speaking, they are anything but identical. While a flat reading of the two might lead to the conclusion that they are mutually contradictory, we noted that many of the differences between them can be better explained on the basis of their distinct purposes and audiences. We noted also that the Chronicler is not only himself acquainted with Samuel-Kings but apparently assumes a similar acquaintance on the part of his audience. This frees him to present his didactic history in creative ways, sometimes making explicit what may have been only implicit in his sources.

We conclude then that historiography involves a creative, though constrained, attempt to depict and interpret significant events or sequences of events from the past. In this chapter we have considered some of what might be said in answer to the question *What is history?* In the next we shall take up the question *Is historicity important?*

3

HISTORY AND TRUTH
Is Historicity Important?

In an essay entitled "On Reading the Bible Critically and Otherwise," Alan Cooper makes the statement that "the historicity of the events described in the Bible is irrelevant; indeed, the idea that either the meaning of the Bible or its truth depends on its historical accuracy is probably the silliest manifestation of historical criticism."[1] To readers conversant with current debates over method in biblical studies, this statement may not seem all that unusual,[2] but it is certainly extraordinary when measured against the standard of classic Christianity. The traditional answer to the question whether the historicity of certain central events is necessary to the Christian faith has been a resounding *yes*! The following observation by Norman Anderson may be taken as representative:

> It seems to me inescapable . . . that anyone who chanced to read the pages of the New Testament for the first time would come away with one overwhelming impression—that here is a faith that 'does

---

[1]In *Future of Biblical Studies*, ed. Friedman and Williamson, pp. 65–66.

[2]Cf., e.g., J. J. Collins, "Is a Critical Biblical Theology Possible?" in *The Hebrew Bible and Its Interpreters*, ed. W. H. Propp, B. Halpern, and D. N. Freedman (Winona Lake, Ind.: Eisenbrauns, 1990), p. 11: the value of biblical narratives for theology "lies in their functions as myth or story rather than in their historical accuracy." See also Brown (*History and Faith*, p. 74), who observes that "the contemporary cultural and intellectual climate has encouraged numerous attempts to cut faith loose from history," and then proceeds to note several examples.

not understand itself to be the discovering and imparting of
generally valid, timeless truths,' but that is firmly based on certain
allegedly historical events—a faith which would be false and
misleading if those events had not actually taken place, but which, if
they did take place, is unique in its relevance and exclusive in its
demands on our allegiance.[3]

Anderson speaks of the New Testament, but what is true for the
New Testament is true also for the Old. Mattitiahu Tsevat
comments that "it should be evident that if Israelite history is
removed from the theological edifice of divine redemption coming
at the point of man's complete failure, God becomes whimsical,
toying with mankind, or even turns into a gnostic deity."[4] G. E.
Wright put it plainly when he said, "In biblical faith everything
depends upon whether the central events actually occurred." The
"central events," according to Wright, are "that there was an
Exodus, that the nation [of Israel] was established at Mount Sinai,
that it did obtain the land, that it did lose it subsequently, that
Jesus did live, that he did die on a cross, and that he did appear
subsequently to a large number of independent witnesses."[5]

As foundational as affirmations of this sort have been in
traditional Christianity, the trend in much modern theological
discussion has been in the direction indicated at the start of this
chapter—the disavowal of the importance of history in favor of,
say, *artistic* or *philosophical* truth. Already in 1906 Geerhardus Vos
lamented what he perceived as a growing tendency to depreciate
the importance of biblical historicity:

For some time past the assertion has been made, and it is being
made in our own day with greater confidence and insistence than
ever, that our Christian faith and historical facts have very little or
nothing to do with each other. Most frequently this assertion is
made with reference to some one particular event of Sacred History,
which has for the time being become the subject of debate from the
point of view of its historicity. Those who incline to doubt the

[3]*Jesus Christ: The Witness of History* (Leicester: IVP, 1985), p. 14. Cf. also Nash,
Christian Faith, pp. 11–12.
[4]"Israelite History," p. 178.
[5]*God Who Acts: Biblical Theology as Recital* (London: SCM, 1952), pp. 126–27.

historical truthfulness of some such narrative as, e.g., that of the supernatural birth or the resurrection of the Saviour, or at least incline to consider it an open question, are, when their skepticism awakens remonstrance from the conservative side, ever ready with the answer that Christianity is something too great and too deep, too inward, ideal and vital to be dependent in its essence on this or that single occurrence in the world of history.[6]

What Vos perceived as a developing trend in his day is even more in evidence in our own. Stephen Prickett, for example, commenting on Hans Frei's *The Eclipse of Biblical Narrative*,[7] draws attention to the current popularity of interpretative strategies that avoid asking the hard historical questions:

> Central to Frei's strategy is the notion that so far from trying to regard biblical narrative as "history" in our modern post-Rankean sense, and thinking of it as "factual" or "non-factual," we should rather think of it as, in his words, "fact-like". . . . We should not ask of it, therefore, did this actually happen to real people like this? but is this "true-to-life," is this artistically true? In the present crisis over biblical studies, this is proving a popular strategy in many quarters.[8]

What are we to make of this? Is the truth of the Bible somehow tied up with historical questions, or is it not? If we are convinced (by our study of truth claims) that the Bible presents certain events as having occurred, must they have *actually* occurred for the Bible to be true? Might not the essence of biblical truth lie in its "true-to-life" quality, its "artistic truth"? Or might not the Bible's truth lie simply in the ideas, the philosophical system, that it propounds? Couldn't it be that current debates over biblical historicity are nothing more than the dying gasps of a bygone era

---

[6]"Christian Faith and the Truthfulness of Bible History," *The Princeton Theological Review* 4 (1906): 289; I am indebted to my colleague David C. Jones for drawing my attention to this essay. See also J. Greshan Machen, "History and Faith," *PTR* 13 (1915): 337–51.

[7]Subtitle: *A Study in Eighteenth and Nineteenth Century Hermeneutics* (New Haven: Yale University Press, 1974).

[8]"Status of Biblical Narrative," *Pacifica* 2 (1989): 32. For a further critique of Frei's nonreferential theory of biblical literature, see Barton, *Reading the Old Testament*, pp. 158–79.

that should now be quietly buried? After all, Jesus himself often expounded theological truth through unhistorical parables. Couldn't the Bible be one big parable and still teach us truth about God?

"WHAT IS TRUTH?"

Having posed the question of truth, Pilate in John 18:38 did not wait for an answer. His "What is truth?" was intended to dismiss the issue, not to pursue it. And having dismissed it, Pilate went on to play his part (hand-washing notwithstanding) in the most infamous deed of all history. The question of truth is a serious matter. Fortunately, it is not necessary for our present purposes to tackle this question in a broad theological or philosophical sense. Because God's word comes to us in the form of Scripture, our concern, rather, is with the kinds of truth that literature, and particularly narrative literature, can convey. But even this more narrowly defined question cannot be answered adequately in the space available here. Happily, Kevin Vanhoozer has already provided a useful treatment of the issue in "The Semantics of Biblical Literature: Truth and Scripture's Diverse Literary Forms."[9] After arguing convincingly that the principles of *speech-act theory*[10] can be usefully applied also to units of discourse above the sentence level, Vanhoozer explains how these larger literary forms relate to the question of truth.

> Truth, like Reality, is in one sense One. However, Reality is so rich and multifaceted that it, like white light, can only be conveyed (verbally) by an equally rich "spectrum"—diverse literary forms. While Truth may be "about" Reality (what *is*), we only receive the full picture of Reality (*what* is) by contemplating "true" history, "true" parable, "true" song, "true" poetry. That Scripture has many literary forms is no impediment to the Truth; instead, it is the very possibility of Truth's expression. The diversity of literary

---

[9]In *Hermeneutics, Authority, and Canon*, ed. Carson and Woodbridge, pp. 49–104. Cf. also Oja, "Fictional History," esp. pp. 115–16.

[10]For brief summaries of speech-act theory, see, in addition to Vanhoozer, also Stanford, *Nature*, p. 69; M. H. Abrams, *A Glossary of Literary Terms*, 4th ed. (New York: Holt, Rinehart and Winston, 1981), pp. 181–83.

forms does not imply that Scripture contains competing kinds of Truth; it shows rather that Scripture is about various kinds of *fact* (i.e., historical, metaphysical, moral, etc.). A sentence or text is true if things are as it says they are, but as Aristotle observed, "Being may be said in many ways." (p. 85)

Thus the diversity of the Bible's literary forms does not imply a hierarchy in which some forms or genres are more revelatory than others, more truly the word of God. As Vanhoozer explains, "The Bible is divine discourse act. The 'divine' qualifies the literary forms of Scripture (the 'micro-genres,' as it were) and so renders them 'revelatory' (the *'macro-genre'*). Revealed truth may be said in many ways" (p. 93).

Every form of discourse makes its own *truth claims*, and the *truth value* of different discourses must be assessed in terms of the truth claims of each, that is, in terms of what each intends to communicate or accomplish. If parables, for example, are "stories designed to teach theological truth without reference to whether or not the events depicted within them actually happened,"[11] then it is incorrect to try to mine them for historical information and unfair to fault them if they fail to yield such. Parables are not to be read as history, for they imply no historical truth claim. This is an obvious point, and one that is universally acknowledged. But by the same token (and this point is not universally acknowledged), texts that do imply a historical truth claim must not be read as if they didn't, at least not if one's purpose is exegesis. The prologue to Luke's gospel (1:1–4), for example, offers the most explicit statement of intent of all the gospels. Noting that "many have undertaken to draw up an account of the things that have been fulfilled among us," Luke states his intention to write his own "orderly account," after having "carefully investigated everything from the beginning." That a historical truth claim is being made is unmistakable.[12] One may choose to deny the truth value of Luke's

[11]Blomberg, *Historical Reliability*, p. 238.

[12]So, e.g., T. Callan, "The Preface of Luke-Acts and Historiography," *New Testament Studies* 31 (1985): 580: "The stated purpose of Luke-Acts seems to mark it as a history . . . written to provide a true account of something." A historical truth claim is also implied in, e.g., John 20:30–31; 21:24–25.

account, but one is simply not free to read Luke as if no historical truth claim has been made.

To return then to the question posed earlier—"Couldn't the Bible be one big parable and still teach us truth about God?"—it would appear now that the question is moot, for the truth claims of the Bible simply do not allow us that option. In some of its parts—the so-called historical books of the Old Testament, for example, or the Gospels and the book of Acts in the New—the Bible makes fairly unmistakable historical truth claims.[13] The motive of its historiography as well as its standards of representation may differ from the political/sociological motive and minimalist approach of much modern historiography. But it can hardly be denied that it presents many of its stories—and, more particularly, the central thread of its one Story—as reflecting a real, and not simply a fictive, past. But still the question might be asked, *Is it not at least* hypothetically *possible that God could have taught us all we need to know about him without ever entering history?* After all, "Jesus' teaching in parables highlights how narrative prose can communicate theological truth by means of realistic but fictitious stories."[14] Could not biblical *faith* survive even if biblical *history* were destroyed? The answer of classic Christianity to this question is that it could not—and for good reason, as we shall see below.

THE IMPORTANCE OF HISTORY
FOR CHRISTIAN FAITH

Irrespective of questions of textual truth claims, in the current climate of biblical scholarship many voices are being raised to challenge the importance of history for Christian faith, as we noted at the beginning of this chapter. We shall discover below that some of the challenges are rooted in a worldview and a way of

---

[13]With respect to the Old Testament, see, e.g., Tsevat, "Israelite History," p. 184; Halpern, *First Historians*, pp. 97, 181; Smelik, *Converting the Past: Studies in Ancient Israelite and Moabite Historiography*, Oudtestamentische Studiën 28 (Leiden: E. J. Brill, 1992), p. 19; with respect to the New, see Trigg, "Tales artfully spun," pp. 129–30; Powell, *What is Narrative Criticism?* p. 3; Hemer, *Book of Acts*, p. 85.

[14]Blomberg, *Historical Reliability*, p. 255.

reasoning introduced by Enlightenment thinkers of the eighteenth and nineteenth centuries. Others find their impetus in modern trends in literary criticism (to be discussed in chapter 4), while some arise from a misapplication of valid insights into the multifaceted nature of truth, noted above. But this myriad of voices notwithstanding, history, or more precisely the historicity of certain core events recorded in the Old and New Testaments, is indispensable to the vitality and even validity of the Christian faith. This is especially true, as Vos forcefully argues, "in regard to the soteriological, or, if another more popular term be preferred, the evangelical character of Christianity."[15] One's assessment of the importance of history for faith will be a more or less direct reflection of one's understanding of the *essence* of Christianity. On this vital point, Vos's argument is worthy of quotation at some length.

> Let us suppose for a moment that our religion aimed at nothing more than the disclosure of a system of truth for the spiritual enlightenment of mankind—that there were no sins to atone and no hearts to regenerate and no world to transform. In that case its connection with historical facts would have to be regarded as a purely incidental matter, established for the sake of a more vivid presentation of the truth, and therefore separable from the essence of the truth itself. Obviously, further, it would on this supposition be of no consequence whether the historical mold into which the truth was cast consisted of a record of actual events, or of mythical and legendary lore having only a partial basis in facts, or of conscious literary fiction having no basis of facts at all. The same will apply to every view of religion which makes the action of truth consist exclusively in the moral suasion exercised by it on the human mind. It is plain, however, that both these conceptions of the function of Christianity, the intellectualistic as well as the moralizing, are tenable only from the standpoint of Pelagianism with its defective sense of sin. To the Christian Church, in the most catholic sense of the word, supernatural religion has always stood for something far more than a system of spiritual instruction or an instrument of moral suasion. The deep sense of sin, which is central in her faith, demands such a divine interposition in the course of natural development as shall work actual changes from guilt to righteous-

---

[15]"Christian Faith," p. 299.

ness, from sin to holiness, from life to death, in the sphere not merely of consciousness but of being. Here revelation is on principle inseparable from a background of historic facts, with which to bring man's life into vital contact is indeed the main reason for its existence. . . .

If what has been said be correct, it will follow that the proposal to declare the facts inessential betrays a lamentably defective appreciation of the soteriological character of Christianity. As a matter of fact, if one carefully examines the representations of those who claim that the results of criticism leave the religious substance of the Old Testament intact, one finds in each case that the truth left intact belongs to the sphere of natural religion and has no direct bearing on the question of sin and salvation. Such truths as monotheism and the ethical nature of God may still be found in the reconstructed Old Testament; what we look for in vain is the Gospel of redemption.[16]

For those, like the present author, who share Vos's view of the essence of Christianity, he makes a strong case that the central salvific events of the Gospel must be historical for Christian faith to be valid.[17] But what of the other, less central events recorded in biblical narrative? Need they too be historical? While it may be admitted that the validity of the Christian faith is not dependent on the historicity of events peripheral to the central flow of redemptive history, this does not mean that the question of historicity can simply be dismissed out of hand. The crucial question is again what *truth claims* are implied by each narrative within its broader context. Finding answers to this question is not always a simple matter, and some narratives (e.g., Gen. 1–11; the patriarchal narratives) or even whole books (e.g., Job; Jonah; Esther) will undoubtedly continue to elicit debate. But as Vos points out, the nature of God's work in Christ does create a certain presumption in favor of the historicity of other events in Scripture, even of those that by ordinary standards would seem quite fabulous: "If we can show that revealed religion is inseparably linked to a system of supernatural historical facts at its culminating epoch in

---

[16]Ibid., pp. 299–300.

[17]For a more recent defense of this basic position, see Blomberg, *Historical Reliability*, pp. 57–58.

Christ," then "it is certainly reasonable to assume that God will have adjusted the course of things that led up to Christ, to the fundamental character of the work of Christ—in the sense that He will have scattered over it great miraculous interpositions, to shadow forth the true nature of redemption, and, more than this, that He will have hung it not on the slender thread of legend or fiction, but on the solid chain of actual history."[18]

Again I must stress that the discernment of each text's truth claims is of primary importance, for it is no good defending a text with respect to claims that it never makes. For example, in the controversial matter of the historicity of the patriarchal narratives, George Ramsey is in principle correct that "a different form-critical analysis of the patriarchal narratives might be offered, with attendant implications for the historical reliability of the stories,"[19] and indeed Ramsey himself comes to a rather minimalist conclusion: "Figures like Abraham and Jacob became in time paradigmatic figures rather like the figures of the 'prodigal son' or the 'good Samaritan' of Jesus' parables; were they such from the beginning?"[20] But as we argued in the preceding chapter, such questions should not be decided without careful consideration of the overall purpose of the larger discourse in which the smaller plays a part. If Ramsey's last question were to be answered in the affirmative, then Abraham and Jacob would become not so much *sources* of faith as the *products* of faith. John Goldingay's consideration of the patriarchal narratives in the light of the broader sweep of the Bible leads him to the opposite conclusion—"not that faith creates Abraham, but that Abraham creates faith."[21] Like Ramsey, Goldingay sets out to discover whether the stories of the patriarchs are "more like a parable or a gospel" (p. 35). By this he means to ask whether or not the patriarchal narratives have an "implied

---

[18]"Christian Faith," pp. 301–2. Cf. J. Goldingay, *Approaches to Old Testament Interpretation*, rev. ed. (Leicester: Apollos, 1990), p. 81.

[19]*The Quest for the Historical Israel: Reconstructing Israel's Early History* (London: SCM, 1982), p. 12.

[20]Ibid., p. 44.

[21]"The Patriarchs in Scripture and History," in *Essays on the Patriarchal Narratives*, ed. A. R. Millard and D. J. Wiseman (Leicester: IVP, 1980), p. 37.

vested interest . . . in the historicity of the events they narrate." He
asks:

> Are they the kind of stories that could be completely fictional but
> still be coherent and carry conviction? A parable is fictional, but
> nevertheless carries conviction on the basis of who it is that tells it
> and of the validity of his world-view as it expresses it. A gospel,
> however, invites commitment to the person portrayed in it, and in
> my view this implies that it cannot be both fictional and true. The
> kind of response it invites demands that the events it narrates bear a
> reasonably close relationship to events that took place at the time.
> Without this it cannot be coherent and carry conviction. In the
> absence of reference, it cannot even really have sense. (p. 35)

In the course of his discussion Goldingay disputes in
particular T. L. Thompson's contention, in *The Historicity of the
Patriarchal Narratives*,[22] that these narratives need have no historical
value whatsoever to be true. While he grants some validity to
Thompson's criticism of the "Wright-Bright-Albright approach to
biblical history," which in its overstress on *event* tends to ignore
"the revelation in word or in language embodied in the Bible
itself," he points out that Thompson's view is equally guilty of
ignoring and even denying the *event aspect* of revelation. For
Goldingay, "Event and word are both part of revelation." This
truth can be most clearly seen when the patriarchal narratives are
"set in a subsequent literary and historical context." Goldingay
writes:

> First, Yahweh's words to the patriarchs constitute the divine
> undertaking fulfilled in the exodus and conquest. They constitute
> Israel's charter for her possession of the land of Canaan. They
> explain how this was Yahweh's gift rather than the Israelites' desert.
> They set Israel's position in the land in the context of the sweep of a
> divine purpose concerned with the destiny of the nations. If the
> patriarchal narrative is pure fiction (which Thompson suggests it
> may well be), is anything lost? Surely much is, because the exodus-
> conquest narrative grounds its statements of faith in these events. If
> the events did not take place, the grounds of faith are removed.
> (p. 36)

---

[22]Subtitle: *The Quest for the Historical Abraham* (Berlin: Walter de Gruyter, 1974).

Goldingay demonstrates how biblical writers viewed present faith as resting on prior events by citing Isaiah 51:1–2 and reflecting on the significance of the prophet's exhortation.

> Hearken to me, you who pursue deliverance,
> you who seek Yahweh,
> Look to the rock from which you were hewn,
> and to the quarry from which you were digged.
> Look to Abraham your father
> and to Sarah who bore you,
> for when he was but one I called him,
> and I blessed him and made him many. (Isa. 51:1–2)

Goldingay comments: "*on Thompson's thesis it does not matter that the call, the blessing, and the increase of Abraham are imaginative creations of faith!* The prophet's position seems to be the opposite." It is (if we may say it again) "not that faith creates Abraham, but that Abraham creates faith" (p. 37).

Is historicity important? Perhaps enough has been said, even in this very brief treatment, to suggest that without the historicity of the central events of the biblical story truly *biblical* faith cannot survive. Goldingay has argued this point convincingly from the Old Testament, and the same is of course true of the New. Roger Trigg concludes his essay on the centrality of historicity to the message of the New Testament with these words:

> To suggest that an account (or *logos*) can carry a meaning even if it is based on lying or mistaken witness is not in the spirit of the New Testament. We may wish to reject parts of what is written. What we cannot do is to suspend our belief in what actually happened and still be guided by the 'message' of the putative events. Keeping the message of a story while denying its truth, is to treat the accounts as *muthoi* and not *logoi*. It is like trying to hold on to the grin while the Cheshire Cat has long since departed.[23]

In the light of the truth claims of Scripture and the most widely agreed upon understanding of the essence of the Christian religion, it simply cannot be denied that the historicity of certain events is vitally necessary to true Christian faith. But, of course, simply to acknowledge this necessity in no way proves that the

---

[23]"Tales artfully spun," p. 132.

relevant events took place. Moreover, even could the bare events be conclusively demonstrated, this would still fall short of proof that they have been accurately interpreted by the biblical writers. In the end, one's acceptance of the biblical construal of events will very much depend on one's confidence in the biblical testimony, or (to use terms from the preceding chapter) on one's convictions regarding the adequacy and authority of the biblical representations.

One way to express the relationship of event and interpretation is to say that while the factuality of the core events of redemptive history is a necessary condition of the truth of the Christian faith, it is not a sufficient condition thereof.[24] This means that any faith that can properly call itself Christian can never entirely insulate itself from the findings of historical study. Faith does not require that the factuality of the biblical events be proven (such proof is, at any rate, seldom possible). On the other hand, should it be conclusively shown that the core events of redemptive history did not happen, not only would the veracity of the Bible be seriously undermined, but the fall of historicity would inevitably bring down Christian faith with it. It is imperative, then, that we consider carefully the challenges that have been issued against the historicity of the Bible's central events.

THE (POST-)ENLIGHTENMENT CHALLENGE
TO THE IMPORTANCE OF HISTORY FOR FAITH

Biblical scholarship is seldom unaffected by the intellectual currents and cross-currents of its own day. As Brevard Childs remarks in his *Introduction to the Old Testament as Scripture*, "The rise of the modern historical study of the Old Testament must be seen in connection with the entire intellectual revolution which occurred during the late sixteenth and early seventeenth centuries, and which issued in a radically different understanding of God, man, and the world" (p. 34). It was in the eighteenth-century Enlightenment in Europe that these radically new understandings came to full flower. Associated with such thinkers as Reimarus

---

[24]Cf. Goldingay, *Approaches to Old Testament Interpretation*, p. 77.

(1694–1768), Kant (1724–1804), Lessing (1729–1781), and Men-
delssohn (1729–1786) in Germany, Voltaire (1694–1778), Rous-
seau (1712–1778), and Diderot (1713–1784) in France, and Locke
(1632–1704), Newton (1642–1727), and Gibbon (1737–1794) in
England,[25] the Enlightenment (or Age of Reason) has been
characterized as a time when "increasing scientific knowledge gave
rise to the development of empiricist, naturalist, and materialist
doctrines and strong opposition to clericalism."[26] It was a time
when human reason, and human reason alone, was deemed
worthy of trust.

"Enlightenment," according to Kant, entails "man's release
from his self-incurred tutelage," a tutelage defined as "man's
inability to make use of his understanding without direction from
another."[27] This call to emancipate human reason from all external
constraints finds full expression in the writings of German-born
French *philosophe* Holbach (1723–1789). Beginning with the
premise that "Man is unhappy because he is ignorant of Nature,"
Holbach in his *Système de la nature* (1770) laid out an agenda for
addressing this problem. His main ideas have been summarized as
follows:

> Nature, he [Holbach] maintains, is knowable through human
> experience and thought, and explanations should not be sought in
> traditional beliefs or the alleged "revelations" of the Church. There
> is a fundamental continuity between man and the rest of nature,
> between animal and human behaviour; all natural phenomena,
> including mental ones, are explicable in terms of the organization
> and activity of matter. Religion and extranatural beliefs inculcate
> habits inhibiting enquiry and the acquisition of the knowledge that
> is necessary to achieve the fundamental aims of man: happiness and
> self-preservation.[28]

[25]The dates are as in *The Encyclopedia of Philosophy*, ed. P. Edwards, 8 vols. (New York: Macmillan, 1967), ad loc.
[26]*A Dictionary of Philosophy*, ed. A. Flew (London: Macmillan, 1979), p.106.
[27]The quote is from Kant's "Beantwortung der Frage: Was ist Aufklärung?" ("Reply to the Question: What is Enlightenment?"), cited by Brown, *History and Faith*, p. 13, q.v. for further bibliography.
[28]*Dictionary of Philosophy*, ed. Flew, p. 106.

Though characterized as "the foremost exponent of atheistic materialism and the most intransigent polemicist against religion in the Enlightenment,"[29] Holbach's views differed from those of many of his contemporaries more in degree than in kind.[30]

D. F. STRAUSS AND THE DEMOLITION OF BIBLICAL HISTORY

Of particular interest for the history of biblical studies up to the present are two other names—one the Enlightenment thinker Reimarus (already mentioned) and the other D. F. Strauss, a nineteenth-century German theologian who was deeply influenced by Reimarus. The literary offerings and intellectual impact of both of these men are well summarized by Robert Morgan in a chapter entitled "Criticism and the Death of Scripture."[31] Reimarus was a deist. He "believed in God, but not in revelation, miracles, or other supernatural interventions." In keeping with these beliefs, Reimarus was among the first to write "a non-supernatural, historical account of Christian origins in which he anticipated many of the insights of twentieth-century 'history of traditions' research on the Gospels" (p. 53). Many of Reimarus's views were subsequently adopted by Strauss, who, after correcting and refining them, set himself the task of, as he saw it, rescuing Christianity in an age when the central tenets of historic Christianity were no longer rationally viable or intellectually responsible. In this respect his program was more positive in intent, if not in result, than that of Reimarus. As Morgan explains, "Strauss thought he was doing Christianity a favour, Reimarus had no such illusions" (p. 54).

Strauss's rescue operation was to entail two phases: a "critical

---

[29] Aram Vartanian, "Holbach," in *Encyclopedia*, ed. P. Edwards, 4:49.

[30] To be fair, it should be noted that Holbach was one of the Enlightenment "minor thinkers" and, therefore, to be counted among the "terrible simplifiers" unworthy of the major figures of the period. Nevertheless, it was just such a simplified version of Enlightenment thinking that impressed itself on the "great audience of the enlightened"; see C. Brinton, "Enlightenment," in *Encyclopedia*, ed. Edwards, 2: 525.

[31] *Biblical Interpretation*, pp. 44–57.

destruction of the Gospel history" followed by a "theological reconstruction of Christian belief" (p. 45). It was to the former endeavor that Strauss dedicated more than seven hundred pages of his massive *The Life of Jesus Critically Examined* (first published in German in 1835),[32] while his program for theological reconstruction, which was meant to "re-establish dogmatically [i.e., at the theological level] that which has been destroyed critically [i.e., at the historical level],"[33] received only brief treatment in the final twenty-eight pages. Strauss's "philosophical theology," as distinct from the history-centered theology of traditional Christianity, was to have been worked out fully in a later volume, but this was never written. Not surprisingly, then, it was Strauss's massive assault on the historicity of the Gospels that had the greatest impact on his contemporaries and on subsequent biblical scholarship.

It is worth noting at this juncture that others in addition to Reimarus influenced Strauss in ways that facilitated his attack on biblical historicity. As Morgan explains,

> His critical aim of demolishing the historicity of the Gospel records was a first step in the programme of a theologian who had learned from Kant that the historical could serve only for illustration, from Lessing that there was a 'big, ugly ditch' between the truths of history and the truths of reason, and finally from Hegel how to get theological truth from these largely unhistorical Gospel records.[34]

Thus, Strauss formulated his ideas in an atmosphere in which the importance of history for faith was already diminished. If for Kant, history was useful only as illustration, might not *parable* or, as Strauss preferred, *myth* serve just as well? Lessing also viewed history as of limited value, as is evidenced by his oft-quoted assertion: "Accidental truths of history can never become the proof of necessary truths of reason." Henry Chadwick sheds light on this cryptic statement by pointing out that it

---

[32]The standard English edition is edited, with introduction, by P. C. Hodgson (New York: Fortress, 1972).

[33]Strauss, *Life of Jesus*, p. 757; cited with explanatory insertions by Morgan, *Biblical Interpretation*, p. 45.

[34]Ibid., p. 47.

presupposes on the one hand the epistemology of Leibniz, with its sharp distinction between necessary truths of reason (mathematically certain and known a priori) and contingent truths (known by sense perception), and on the other hand the thesis of Spinoza's *Tractatus Theologico-politicus*, that the truth of a historical narrative, however certain, cannot give us the knowledge of God, which should be derived from general ideas that are themselves certain and known.[35]

For Lessing then, as Gordon Michalson explains, "authentic faith is rational and potentially universalizable, meaning that it does not hang on the acceptance of any historical facts; and historical revelations do not introduce new and indispensable religious information but simply illustrate, or bring into our field of vision, what we are capable of knowing all along."[36]

Kant, Lessing, Hegel, Reimarus—against this background of influences it is apparent that Strauss was very much a man of his own time, a time when the underestimation of the importance of history was matched only by the overestimation of the potency and potential of autonomous human reason. Strauss differed from his predecessors not so much in theory as in the relentless energy with which he put theory to practice in the form of a frontal attack on the historicity of the Gospels and the "title-deeds" of the Christian faith. Not surprisingly, the publication of Strauss's *Life of Jesus* caused outrage in Christendom and proved very costly for Strauss's career,[37] for its "non-supernatural account of Jesus and early Christianity was inevitably an anti-supernatural account. If the historian had no need of that hypothesis (God), why should anyone else adopt it? Modern rationalism held a dagger to the heart of Christianity."[38]

---

[35]"Lessing, Gotthold Ephraim," in *Encyclopedia*, ed. Edwards, 4: 445.

[36]*Lessing's "Ugly Ditch": A Study of Theology and History* (University Park: Pennsylvania State University Press, 1985), p. 39.

[37]Morgan (*Biblical Interpretation*, p. 44) reports that "Strauss lost his post in Tübingen, and when in 1839 a liberal government in Zurich offered him a professorship the people rebelled, the government fell, and the young offender was pensioned off before he arrived."

[38]Ibid., p. 54.

After Strauss

Despite the furor that Strauss's *Life of Jesus* evoked, it is not inaccurate to say that his approach "opened a new era in Western religious thought."[39] Does this mean that Strauss's views won the day? A twofold answer is required. Strauss's theological program failed, but his exegetical method, with its systematic undermining of confidence in the historicity of the Gospels, endured among many scholars.[40] Again, Morgan's historical survey of scholarship in *Biblical Interpretation* (chaps. 3 and 4) is helpful. Contemporary with Strauss were two other scholars whose works were to prove highly influential in the history of biblical criticism: Old Testament scholar Wilhelm Vatke (1806–1882), who was to have a profound influence on Julius Wellhausen (1844–1918), and New Testament professor Ferdinand Christian Baur (1792–1860), known as the founder of the *Tübingen school* of radical historical criticism. All three, Strauss, Baur, and Vatke, "followed Reimarus in opting for a rational, historical, i.e. non-supernatural, account of Israel and of Christian origins" (p. 68). And all three were also in one way or another influenced by Hegel to believe that theological truth was not dependent in any essential respect on historical truth. Strauss, for example, credited Hegel with freeing "him for untrammelled academic work by convincing him that 'the essence of the Christian faith is perfectly independent' of historical criticism."[41] The sad irony in all this is that the brand of Hegelian theology by which Strauss and others thought to safeguard the Christian faith soon faded, leaving only their erosion of confidence in biblical historicity as their legacy.

The history of interpretation since Strauss is marked by a variety of responses to the wedge that had been driven between history and theology. In the mid to late nineteenth century, Baur and Wellhausen, for example, led a "shift away from synthesizing the new historical knowledge with philosophical and theological convictions to a new historical realism that was hostile to

---

[39]Ibid., p. 45.
[40]Cf. ibid., p. 47.
[41]Ibid., pp. 62–63 (citing Strauss, *Life of Jesus*, p. lii).

philosophical and theological speculation."[42] In the twentieth century, Gerhard von Rad (1901–1971), following the lead of Hermann Gunkel (1862–1932), tried to swing the pendulum in the other direction by reintroducing a theological focus in biblical interpretation. This attempt, however, did not include an effort to restore confidence in biblical historicity. What mattered for von Rad was not so much what actually happened in, say, the Exodus event, but how the Exodus had been theologically construed in Israel's traditions. Von Rad cared less for the event than for the tradition that arose about the event.[43] As Goldingay has observed, von Rad ultimately found himself "retelling the history of the development of Israel's faith in God's acts in history (contrary to his overt intention), not retelling the acts of God."[44]

The difference between von Rad's brand of salvation-history—a kind of traditio-historical idealism—and the history of salvation espoused by traditional Christianity is pronounced and problematic, as Morgan notes: "Taken at face value, the Old Testament depicts the history of Israel as a history of salvation, in the straightforward sense that God himself was the agent of all the great events which the Old Testament records" (p. 101). "How," then, "can we locate 'revelation' in the process that led Israel to develop and eventually to 'canonize' traditions, when the explicit content of these traditions states that revelation is actually located somewhere else, namely, in certain things that God has said and done?" The last phrase, "said and done," is key and is suggestive of how the relationship between event and tradition can be understood. Though he does not develop the point, Morgan notes that "it is quite consistent to claim that divine Providence both directed *events* in a certain way in Israel's history and controlled the *traditions* that grew up to interpret those events in such an unerring way that they were correctly interpreted: one can, that is, consistently locate revelation in both events *and* traditions" (p. 102).

This seems to me to be the most promising approach—*divine*

---

[42]Ibid., p. 93.

[43]Cf. ibid., pp. 99–100.

[44]*Approaches to Old Testament Interpretation*, p. 72.

*revelation should be located in both historical events and the interpretative
word which mediates these events to us.* It also seems to be the
approach that is most in keeping with the biblical witness itself.
Nevertheless, for some time now the hermeneutic pendulum in
biblical studies has continued to swing back and forth between the
two poles of *event* and *word*. One extreme position excites a
reaction, which then leads to the opposite extreme, which in turn
excites a counter-reaction, and on it goes. In the 1950s and 60s, for
example, the Albright-Wright-Bright school, reacting to the
depreciation of biblical history early in this century, laid great
stress on the historical events, the "mighty acts of God" in actual
history. More recently, as already noted, T. L. Thompson (among
others) has launched a counter-reaction. After charging Albright
and company (particularly G. E. Wright) with adopting "a deistic
and positivistic historicism" that leaves "very little room for any
theology of the word," Thompson has in essence tried to push the
pendulum back to the other extreme, stressing the importance of
the *word* irrespective of the *event*.[45] For Thompson, "salvation
history did not happen," and it doesn't matter! What matters is
"the reality and the truth of the human experience which
transcends the historical forms in which this experience has been
expressed."[46] And so the pendulum swings. Most recently the
trend in some quarters has been toward ahistorical varieties of
literary criticism, but I shall reserve discussion of this trend until
the next chapter.

What is needed, I would argue, is to bring the pendulum to a
halt in the middle, where it does not lose touch with either
historical event or interpretive word. Again to invoke an analogy
from painting, the question can be put this way, "What is of
essential importance in a portrait by a great master, the subject
itself as a historical person or the masterful interpretation of the
subject?" Surely both are important. Even to ask the question in
this way is to assume a false dichotomy. Art critics may tend to
focus on the artistry of the rendering, while historians may be

---

[45]*Historicity*, p. 327. For a critical evaluation of the Thompson vs. Wright debate,
see Goldingay, "Patriarchs," pp. 35–40.

[46]*Historicity*, pp. 328, 330.

more interested in what can be learned of the historical personage portrayed, but neither should mistake their particular interest for the full significance of the painting. If historians ignore the painterly aspect (that is, if they lack understanding and appreciation of the artistic medium), they may easily "misread" the portrait or unjustly criticize it as an inadequate representation of the subject. Or worse, if they discount the significance of the portrait simply because it is an *artistic interpretation*, they thereby cut themselves off from perhaps their only source of historical information about the subject. On the other hand, should art critics, in their appreciation of the artistic genius of the painter, lose sight of the painting's *referential character*, they would miss something of the painting's essential purpose and so prove themselves to be poor critics. A similar dynamic obtains in the study of biblical historiography. What is needed is the ability to do full justice to both the subject and the historian's (the artist's) particular interpretation. In other words, both event and interpretive word are important. This, at least, seems to be the Bible's own view of the matter. As G. B. Caird explains, after considering the Exodus and the crucifixion,

> the most important item in the framework within which the people of biblical times interpreted their history was the conviction that God was lord of history. He uttered his voice and events followed (Isa. 55:11–12). Thus the course of events was itself a quasi-linguistic system, in which God was disclosing his character and purpose. . . . The interpretation of God's history-language required the exercise of moral judgment (Jer. 15:19; cf. Heb. 5:14), and it was the task of the prophet to be the qualified interpreter. . . . The prophet thus discharged for his people the kind of responsibility which in this chapter we have been ascribing to the historian.[47]

God, the "lord of history"; the prophet, His "qualified interpreter"; the result: *authoritative testimony to event through the word*. Does this not solve the problem? Does not this combination provide a sound basis for a historically grounded Christian

---

[47]*Language and Imagery*, pp. 217–18. On the "rhetorical signification" of God's actions in history, see also Patrick and Scult, *Rhetoric and Biblical Interpretation*, p. 31.

theology? Some biblical scholars have consistently answered this question in the affirmative. Many others, however, encounter greater difficulties. As inheritors of the legacy of Strauss, many find themselves in the uncomfortable position of accepting some of Strauss's major tenets while denying others. They agree with Strauss's historical skepticism and assume a worldview that, if not identical to Strauss's in every respect, is at least closer to his than to the worldview evidenced in the Bible. But at the same time (and this is where the problem comes in), they no longer accept Strauss's ahistorical, philosophical theology. Though still largely convinced by the radical historical criticism promoted by Strauss, they are unable to share with him the view that the Christian faith can survive quite well without a foundation in history. Morgan puts it this way:

> Christian theology is reflection on a faith in God, which centres on the incarnate, crucified, and risen Lord Jesus. This faith is nourished by the Gospel story and stories. Such a faith does not need the historical reality of Jesus to be laid bare or fully disclosed. But it does need to know that it is based on that historical reality, and that it has nothing to fear from historical research.[48]

In short, Christianity needs a grounding in history, but the Bible, for the heirs of Strauss, appears inadequate to provide such grounding.

D. F. Strauss's Criteria for Detecting the Unhistorical: An Evaluation

From their first publication Strauss's ideas encountered strong opposition from some of Europe's most notable scholars. Bishop J. B. Lightfoot, for example, lauded as "the greatest English biblical scholar of the nineteenth century," voiced a sentiment that countless others from his own day to the present would echo: "I cannot pretend to be indifferent about the veracity of the records which profess to reveal him whom I believe to be

---

[48]*Biblical Interpretation*, p. 121.

not only the very Truth but the very Life."[49] Lightfoot was
certainly not alone in his insistence on the importance of the
historical accuracy of the Gospels. Indeed, "The outstanding
critical historians of the English Church, Thirlwall, Lightfoot, and
Stubbs, . . . were all," as Morgan puts it, " 'pre-critical' in their
attitudes to the Gospels."[50] That Morgan can speak of the English
church's outstanding *critical* historians as *pre-critical* suggests something of the ambiguity that inheres in the term *critical*. When
certain scholars are branded as pre-critical in their approach to
Scripture, is the implication that they have not yet developed the
capacity to *think critically* (a charge that would be unjustified in a
great number of cases) or that they are hesitant to *find fault* (their
conviction of the authority of Scripture disallowing commitment
to at least some principles of post-Enlightenment rationalism)? It
would further understanding if such distinctions were made
whenever the pre-critical charge is made.[51]

Lighfoot's emphasis was very much in line with the import
of the New Testament witness itself. Commenting on the First
Epistle of John, for example, G. B. Caird stresses the importance
that history held for the writers of the New Testament:

> According to John there is no Christianity apart from the solid
> reality of the earthly life of Jesus recorded in the apostolic
> tradition. . . . Eternal life remains an unsubstantial dream unless in
> one man's life it has become earthly reality. . . . Without the Jesus
> of history we know neither the Christ of faith nor the God he came
> to reveal.[52]

In view of the magnitude of the issues at stake, it will be
worthwhile to take a closer look at Strauss's own criteria for
detecting unhistorical materials in the Gospels. These he develops
in the Introduction to *The Life of Jesus* in a section entitled

---

[49]Ibid., p. 46.

[50]Ibid.

[51]There is clearly a need for a *criticism* of the sort described by Thistleton ("On
Models and Methods," p. 348)—viz. "critical detachment and checking [which]
follows the immediacy of engagement" with the biblical text. We shall return to the
question of *criticism* in our discussion of the historical-critical method in the next
chapter.

[52]*Language and Imagery*, pp. 215–16.

"Criteria by which to distinguish the unhistorical in the Gospel narrative" (pp. 87–92). Strauss divides his criteria into two kinds: *negative* criteria by which one can detect what is *not history*, and *positive* criteria by which one can detect what *is fiction*, i.e., "the product of the particular mental tendency of a certain community" (p. 87). The negative criteria are basically two, the first of which relates to worldview. An account is not historical, according to Strauss, when

> the narration is irreconcilable with the known and the universal laws which govern the course of events. Now according to these laws, agreeing with all just *philosophical conceptions* and all credible *experience*, the absolute cause [God] never disturbs the chain of secondary causes by single *arbitrary acts of interposition*, but rather manifests itself in the production of the aggregate of finite causalities, and of their reciprocal action. When therefore we meet an account of certain phenomena or events of which it is either expressly stated or implied that they were produced immediately by God himself (divine apparitions—voices from heaven and the like), or by human beings possessed of supernatural powers (miracles, prophecies), such an account is *in so far* to be considered as not historical. (p. 88)[53]

Strauss's argument can be reduced to the following syllogism:

1. All accounts irreconcilable with the known and universal laws that govern events are unhistorical.

2. All accounts in which God disturbs the natural course of events are irreconcilable with the known and universal laws that govern events.

3. Therefore, all accounts in which God disturbs the natural course of events are unhistorical.

---

[53]The insertion [God] and all italics, apart from the last, are mine. As subsidiary points, Strauss cites also the so-called "law of succession, in accordance with which all occurrences, not excepting the most violent convulsions and the most rapid changes, follow in a certain order of sequence of increase and decrease" and "all those psychological laws, which render it improbable that a human being should feel, think, and act in a manner directly opposed to his own habitual mode and that of men in general." These subsidiary criteria are to be "cautiously applied, and in conjunction only with other tests," since they may be less reliable when it comes of "men of genius" (p. 88).

This syllogism is logically valid, but its conclusion is sound only if each of its premises is true. In this regard, Strauss's argument is vulnerable. But we shall postpone discussion of *divine intervention* until the next chapter.

The second of Strauss's negative criteria relates to matters of *internal consistency* and *external noncontradiction*: "An account which shall be regarded as historically valid, must neither be inconsistent with itself, nor in contradiction with other accounts" (p. 88). This twofold criterion of consistency and noncontradiction is sound, so long as proper notions of consistency and contradiction are applied. But this is precisely where disagreements arise. What constitutes a genuine inconsistency or contradiction? The challenges inherent in making such judgments are highlighted by Walter Moberly in a discussion of Old Testament source criticism. He notes that while the "reconstruction of sources is . . . entirely dependent upon unevennesses and difficulties in the present text—doublets, contradictions, anachronisms, variant linguistic usages, divergent theological emphases, etc.," the challenge "is to determine what constitutes a genuine unevenness."[54] To illustrate the possibility of divergent assessments of the same textual phenomena, Moberly compares two quite different reactions to the description of the rising of the flood waters in Genesis 7:17–20. The text reads as follows:

> For forty days the flood kept coming on the earth, and as *the waters increased* they lifted the ark high above the earth. 18 The *waters rose and increased greatly* on the earth, and the ark floated on the surface of the water. 19 The *waters rose very greatly* on the earth, and all the high mountains under the entire heavens were covered. 20 The *waters rose* and covered the mountains to a depth of more than twenty feet.[55]

For Richard Simon, in his *Histoire critique du Vieux Testament*, the repetitions are indicative of multiple authorship: "Is it not

[54]R. W. L. Moberly, *At the Mountain of God: Story and Theology in Exodus 32–34*, JSOTS 22 (Sheffield: JSOT, 1983), p. 23.

[55]The English translation generally follows the NIV, though the italics are mine and a few phrases have been changed to approximate more closely the Hebrew text and to draw attention to the repetition of key phrases.

reasonable to suppose that if one and the same writer had been describing that event, he would have done so in far fewer words, especially in a history?" For Bernard W. Anderson, on the other hand, the repetitions constitute a dramatic literary device to convey a sense of the water's progressive ascent.[56] Thus, Simon's signal of disunity is Anderson's mark of aesthetic dexterity; one man sees composite authorship, while the other sees authorial competence. Who is right? In view of the now widely recognized use of repetition as a rhetorical device in Old Testament narrative, Anderson's interpretation seems by far the more ·convincing.

This simple example is indicative of the difficulties that can arise in attempting to apply the second of Strauss's negative criteria, which states that inconsistencies and contradictions prove a text unhistorical.[57] What constitutes a genuine inconsistency or contradiction is very much a matter of opinion and literary judgment. The insights being gained in the study of narrative poetics, for example, often call for reassessing negative historical judgments of the kind pioneered by Strauss. Advances in historical understanding and reconstruction will likely take place only as more readers of the Bible recognize the necessity of attaining sufficient literary competence to approach biblical texts fairly on their own terms. It may be hoped that the future will see increased dialogue taking place between those claiming to discover textual discrepancies and failures and those who see in the same phenomena narratorial dexterity and finesse.

In addition to the two negative criteria, Strauss in *The Life of Jesus* also proposes a positive criterion, namely, a text may be judged unhistorical if it exhibits characteristics of legend or fiction. According to Strauss, "The positive characters of legend and fiction are to be recognized sometimes in the form, sometimes in the substance of a narrative" (p. 89). As to form, he writes:

> If the form be poetical, if the actors converse in hymns, and in a
> more diffuse and elevated strain than might be expected from their

---

[56]For bibliographical information on Simon and Anderson, see Moberly, *At the Mountain*, pp. 29–30 nn. 51–52.

[57]For a more extended example, see the discussion of 1 Samuel 15:24–29 in Long, *Reign and Rejection*, pp. 37–38.

training and situations, such discourses, at all events, are not to be regarded as historical. The absence of these marks of the unhistorical does not however prove the historical validity of the narration, since the mythus often wears the most simple and apparently historical form: in which case the proof lies in the substance. (p. 89)

If what was said in the preceding chapter has any validity, then our response to the criterion based on *form* can be brief. In the section entitled "History as Representational Art," we concluded, in agreement with Sternberg and many others, that "there are simply no universals of historical vs. fictive form."[58] The biblical writers of course make choices in how their accounts are formulated, whether briefly or expansively, whether in straight narrative prose or in the elevated diction of poetry, and so forth. And Bible readers will need to give heed to these formal dimensions of the texts, lest poetry, for example, be read off as straight prose, or figurative speech be misconstrued literally. Still, the question of historicity cannot be decided on the basis of the narrator's preferred literary style (the form) but, as we have already argued, only in the light of the *overall purpose* of the broader discourse unit.

As to the matter of *substance*, Strauss writes:

> If the contents of a narrative strikingly accord with certain ideas existing and prevailing within the circle from which the narrative proceeded, which ideas themselves seem to be the product of preconceived opinions rather than of practical experience, it is more or less probable, according to circumstances, that such a narrative is of mythical origin. The knowledge of the fact, that the Jews were fond of representing their great men as the children of parents who had long been childless, cannot but make us doubtful of the historical truth of the statement that this was the case with John the Baptist; . . . (p. 89)

This criterion based on substance is notoriously slippery and raises several questions. Who is to say, for example, that John the Baptist was given a "barren-mother birth narrative" simply because the Jews were fond of such stories? And, more important-ly, whence came this fondness in the first place? If we assume that the birth narratives of the Old Testament are also only inventions

---

[58]Sternberg, *Poetics of Biblical Narrative*, p. 30.

reflecting the Jews' fondness for such stories, we have not
answered the question of origin but have only pushed it back to an
even earlier stage. If, on the other hand, we assume that at least
some unusual births did actually occur in Israel's history, and these
were recounted with delight, who is to say that another such birth
did not mark John the Baptist's entry into the world? To be sure,
there is often an element of *patterning* in the Bible's portrayal of
people and events, but this does not disprove the essential
historicity of those portrayals. The life of Abraham Lincoln can be
recounted according to the man-of-humble-origin-makes-good
pattern, but no one would cite this fact as evidence against the
historicity of Lincoln's career. On the contrary, it is Lincoln's
historical experience that has contributed to the fondness for such
stories.[59]

Before leaving Strauss, we should note how he extends his
skeptical approach to cover even texts that in and of themselves
show no sign of being unhistorical.

> It may be that a narrative, standing alone, would discover but slight
> indications, or perhaps, might present no one distinct feature of the
> mythus; but it is connected with others, or proceeds from the
> author of other narratives which exhibit unquestionable marks of a
> mythical or legendary character; and consequently suspicion is
> reflected back from the latter, on the former. (p. 90)

So certain is Strauss that "the absolute cause never disturbs the
chain of secondary causes" (p. 88) that he feels compelled not only
to label as unhistorical any text that would suggest otherwise but
to apply the same label to all texts that are in any way associated
with the first. But for those who do not embrace Strauss's
assumption regarding the impossibility of divine intervention, I
would suggest that where the larger discourse unit implies a
historical purpose (and in the absence of other indicators), the
burden of proof rests on those who would deny the historicity of a

---

[59]W. A. Bacon (*The Art of Interpretation*, 2nd ed. [New York: Holt, Rinehart and
Winston, 1972], p. 496) cites "the rise of the poor boy from log cabin to the White
House" as a typical "stock situation in American lore."

given text within the larger unit, whatever fabulous or miraculous elements it might contain.[60]

It should be apparent from the foregoing discussion how vitally one's view of the world, religion, and reality affects one's interpretation of the Bible. But herein lies a curious inconsistency in the history of biblical scholarship. As Morgan has observed, "Strauss destroyed history to make room for his kind of theology; his proposal, too, involved a theory of religion and reality. Those who later kept his history but ignored his theory and repudiated his theology had alternative theories of religion and reality as well as new theologies of their own."[61] But if scholars have largely rejected Strauss's view of religion and reality, by what right do they continue to accept his "destroyed" history, founded as it is on the very view of religion and reality now rejected? Of course, the issue is not quite as simple as this query suggests, for in fact it is only Strauss's first negative criterion, based on "all just philosophical conceptions and all credible experience," that is directly affected. But the other criteria—inconsistency and contradiction, characteristics of fiction or legend (whether in form or substance), guilt by association—are at least indirectly affected. At any rate, as we have seen, these other criteria are less than clear-cut in application.

As influential as Strauss has been in the history of modern scholarship, he was never without opponents among the ranks of biblical scholars. It can only be hoped that those who no longer share Strauss's view of religion and reality will proceed to a rethinking of the historical method he advocated and that, when the necessary adjustments have been made, a more positive

---

[60]Cf. Blomberg's similar observation with respect to the Gospels: "Once one accepts that the gospels reflect attempts to write reliable history or biography, however theological or stylized its presentation may be, then one must immediately recognize an important presupposition which guides most historians in their work. Unless there is good reason for believing otherwise one will assume that a given detail in the work of a particular historian is factual. This method places the burden of proof squarely on the person who would doubt the reliability of a given portion of the text" (Historical Reliability, p. 240).

[61]Biblical Interpretation, p. 188.

historical-critical practice may emerge. I shall have more to say about these matters in the chapters that follow.

AN EXAMPLE: "IF JERICHO WAS NOT RAZED, IS OUR FAITH IN VAIN?"

The aim of this chapter has been to explore the issue of whether questions of historicity are of significant import for Christian faith. Our deliberations have led us to answer the question in the affirmative. Far from being inconsequential, questions of history are of great importance to Christianity. Perhaps a good way to draw the chapter to a close is with a brief evaluation of a recent challenge to this view.

In his *Quest for the Historical Israel*, George Ramsey gives his final chapter the provocative title, "If Jericho Was Not Razed, Is Our Faith in Vain?" His clever play on Paul's confession, "If Christ was not raised, . . . your faith is vain" (1 Cor. 15:14), serves notice that serious issues will be at stake in his discussion of the relationship of historical study to Christian faith and makes it all the more curious that Ramsey never actually gets around to addressing the Pauline assertion directly. This raises a first question: Is it appropriate to base a discussion of the importance of history for faith on the razing of Jericho, to the neglect of the far more central and significant event to which Ramsey's phraseology so clearly alludes? In one respect, of course, Christian faith might well survive without the razing of Jericho, since it is not the razing of Jericho but the raising of Christ that saves us. But this evokes a further question. On what basis do we believe that Christ was raised? Surely an important part of the answer (in addition to, for example, the internal prompting of the Holy Spirit) is that we do so on the basis of trust in the scriptural testimony to that event. It is our confidence in the truth value (i.e., the trustworthiness) of Scripture that enables us to accept the otherwise astonishing truth claim that Christ was raised from the dead.

In this light, then, the question of the razing of Jericho appears to be of greater import than Ramsey allows. Were we to be absolutely certain that the book of Joshua claims unequivocally that Jericho was razed in space-time history, and were we likewise certain that archaeological study proves just the opposite, we would have a problem. Our confidence in the general trustworthiness of Scripture would not necessarily be destroyed, but neither would it be entirely unaffected. As regards the Jericho question, however, such certainties are elusive, despite the fact that Jericho is often cited as a parade example of irresolvable conflict between the "plain sense" of the Bible and the "proven results" of archaeology. On the one hand, given the powerful co-mingling of theological, literary, and historiographical impulses in the book of Joshua, discovery of the "plain sense" may not always be a simple matter. On the other hand, many are the "proven results" of archaeology that have subsequently been "*un*proven." Indeed, the case of Jericho itself provides an instructive example. After the excavations of Garstang in the 1930s, Jericho was put forward as a prime example of the close correlation of archaeology and biblical history. But as a result of the subsequent excavations of Kenyon in the 1950s, the site has come to be viewed as a prime example of just the opposite. In fact, however, there are indications that the archaeological verdict may still not be in.[62] We shall consider the nature of archaeological data as "objective" evidence in the next chapter.

Returning to Ramsey's question, "If Jericho was not razed, is our faith in vain?", the answer would now seem to be, "Not necessarily, but possibly." "Not necessarily," because the heart of the Christian gospel requires the raising of Christ, not the razing of Jericho. But "possibly," because we would be made less sure either of the trustworthiness of the biblical witness or of our ability to discover its basic sense. And in either case, the possibility that our faith might be in vain is increased. That is, our trust might well be misplaced or misguided. What is striking in Ramsey's discussion is that he does not appear to feel the force of these concerns. This may suggest, if we take our cue from Vos's words

---

[62]We note, e.g., B. G. Wood's recent attempts at a reassessment of Kenyon's excavation results ("Did the Israelites Conquer Jericho? A New Look at the Archaeological Evidence," *Biblical Archaeology Review* 16/2 [1990]: 44–59) and D. N. Pinaar's call for further excavation to be conducted at Jericho ("Die stad Jerigo en die boek Josua," *Journal for Semitics* 1 [1989]: 272–86).

cited earlier in this chapter, that Ramsey embraces a different notion of the essence of Christianity than we, for our part, have been assuming. Ramsey's last words in his *Quest for the Historical Israel* are these:

> If we can demonstrate, with our research tools, that parts of that tradition tell of events or persons that never were, or at least never were like the tradition describes them, this does not alter the fact that the tradition has spoken to believers for generation after generation with power and expressed things which they believed to be true. The tradition 'rang true' in their own experience and enabled them to develop a self-understanding and a lifestyle. It was the tradition as received which accomplished this, not the past-as-it-actually-was. (p. 124)

To be fair, I should point out that in the volume under discussion Ramsey nowhere explicitly articulates his understanding of the essence of Christianity. But insofar as it may be inferred from the general tenor of his book and these concluding words, it does appear to betray, as Vos predicted it would, a "defective appreciation of the soteriological character of Christianity."[63] Those whose understanding of the essence of Christianity approximates that implied by Ramsey's last remark may find his arguments for the inconsequentiality of the "past-as-it-actually-was" appealing. But Christian faith has classically stood for more than a "self-understanding and a lifestyle." For the majority of those who call themselves Christians, the historicity of the core events of redemptive history, precisely because it is *redemptive* history, can never be dismissed as insignificant considerations.

CONCLUSION

Living near the end of the fast-paced twentieth century and looking to a new millennium that promises to move even faster, most of us share an aversion to endless debate. This chapter's consideration of post-Enlightenment controversy over the historicity of the Bible, though selective and abbreviated perhaps to a fault, can nevertheless give the impression of endless debate. So we

---

[63]"Christian Faith," p. 300; quoted already above.

ask ourselves the question: Might it not be better simply to stay out of it? Shouldn't we heed the warning of Proverbs 26:17: "Like one who seizes a dog by the ears is a passer-by who meddles in a quarrel not his own"? For those who regard the Bible as God's inspired word for us to read and obey today, is it all that important to concern ourselves with questions of the past? Can't we simply enter imaginatively into the world that the Bible creates and let that imaginative identification mould our thoughts and actions— even if that world itself, like Tolkien's Middle Earth, should turn out to be purely imaginary?

Such questions and the pragmatic sentiments that prompt them have been around for a long time. "The present religious mind has a veritable dread of everything that is not immediately practical or experimental," wrote Vos of his own generation in the first decade of this century. "Thus the whole theoretical side of faith has fallen into neglect, and this neglect involves, besides other things, the historic basis of facts." In Vos's day, as in ours, there was even a sense that interest in questions of history was a sign of a deficient faith:

> the peculiarity of the present situation is not merely that the facts are neglected, but that in the name and for the sake of the integrity of the Christian faith itself the non-essentialness of the facts is clamorously insisted upon. It is held that where the facts play a central and necessary part in the psychological process of religious trust, that there faith must lose its purity and power.[64]

I hope that enough has already been said about the importance of history as it pertains to both soteriology and divine disclosure to suggest the unacceptability of the above line of thinking. Few persons in the New Testament display a more practical turn of mind than the first missionary to the Gentiles, and yet Paul insists that if certain events that lie at the heart of the Gospel did not happen—specifically, "if Christ has not been raised"—then there really is no Gospel to preach, and faith itself is ultimately futile (1 Cor. 15:14–19).

---

[64]"Christian Faith," pp. 294–95.

4

HISTORY AND MODERN SCHOLARSHIP
Why Do Scholars Disagree?

Assuming that most scholars mean well and are seeking to be as fair and objective as possible in their assessments, why is it that they come to such widely differing opinions regarding the historicity of various portions of the Bible? As we saw in the preceding chapter, part of the answer lies in what individual scholars themselves bring to the historical task, for as Stanford has observed,

> How a historian sees the past is only a part of how he or she sees the world. The final colour and shape of a historian's construction is bestowed by his or her own *Weltanschauung* (assuming that this world-view is not merely a copy of someone else's). Dominating all technical considerations of evidence, method, interpretation and construction is the individual human being.[1]

In other words, the individual historian's basic intellectual and spiritual commitments ("how he or she sees the world") exercise an inevitable, even "dominating," influence over which historical reconstructions will appear plausible to that historian. Some historians are theists, others nontheists; some believe in an open universe, others in a closed universe; some regard material forces as the prime motors of historical change, others accord this role to personal (whether human or divine) agency. All of these basic beliefs influence how historians read the biblical texts and at least

---

[1]*Nature*, p. 96.

in part determine whether the Bible's accounts of the past appear plausible or not.

A second part of the answer to the question why well-meaning scholars disagree on matters of biblical historicity is closely related to the first. Just as the historian's worldview, (or *model* of reality) influences how he or she perceives the past, so also the *model* influences his or her preference for certain *methods* of investigation and the manner in which these methods are applied. In the final analysis, the historian's *model* of reality, expressing itself through the historian's preferred *methods* of investigation, inevitably affects the historian's historical conclusions/constructions. Thus it is not so much the data in themselves—textual, artifactual, comparative, etc.—that account for the wide diversity of opinion among scholars. Most well informed scholars have access to essentially the same data. It is, rather, in the assessment of the data that differences arise.[2] Ernst Troeltsch, whose writings have been very influential in modern conceptions of historical method, seemed himself to recognize this, as Michalson reminds us: "Troeltsch appreciated that the real problem for theology was not that biblical critics emerged 'from their libraries with results disturbing to believers,' but that the historical-critical method itself was 'based on assumptions quite irreconcilable with traditional belief.' "[3]

In this chapter we shall look at some of the different methodological approaches to biblical interpretation, the models of reality that underlie them, and the ways in which each of these affects historical conclusions. Our aim will not be to discover "the correct method," for Barton is in a sense correct that "much harm has been done in biblical studies by insisting that there is, somewhere, a 'correct' method which, if only we could find it,

[2]For some telling illustrations of how "interpreters of the past reflect their underlying assumptions by what they select to serve as evidence," see Henry, *God, Revelation and Authority*, 2: 318–19.

[3]*Lessing's "Ugly Ditch,"* p. 94; citing V. A. Harvey, *The Historian and the Believer: A Confrontation Between the Modern Historian's Principles of Judgment and the Christian's Will-to-Believe* (New York: Macmillan, 1966).

would unlock the mysteries of the text."[4] The biblical texts are more likely to yield their fruits when approached from various angles with a diversity of questions in mind. Thus, distinctive methodological approaches should not be viewed as mutually exclusive,[5] *so long as each is compatible with a consistently held worldview, or model of reality.* Our aim, therefore, will be to explore some of the assumptions and affirmations that underlie prominent trends in contemporary biblical scholarship. There will be no attempt, of course, to offer an exhaustive survey of methods. We shall focus, rather, on those methodological approaches that tend to influence assessments of Scripture as a historical source and which, in turn, account for some of the scholarly disagreements on questions of biblical historicity. Specifically, we shall look at (1) anti-theological tendencies in the historical-critical method as traditionally practiced, (2) anti-literary tendencies in some of today's social-scientific and archaeological approaches to historical reconstruction, and (3) anti-historical tendencies in some forms of modern literary and reader-response criticism. If this plan sounds too negative, we might recall the words of A. E. Housman, who said, "I have spent most of my time finding faults because finding faults, if they are real and not imaginary, is the most useful sort of criticism."[6] More positively, however, it should be emphasized that the unfortunate tendencies evident in many studies are not, in fact, *necessary* aspects of the approaches themselves. As we shall see, if the various approaches are properly understood and qualified, the historically interested biblical scholar may gain useful insights from all of them.

---

[4]*Reading the Old Testament,* p. 5; cf. pp. 196–97 and *passim.* A. C. Thiselton (*New Horizons in Hermeneutics: The Theory and Practice of Transforming Biblical Reading* [Grand Rapids: Zondervan, 1992], p. 502) points out that there is a "tantalizing half-truth" in this statement by Barton. I am taking it in the "correct and healthy" sense mentioned by Thiselton, namely, that various methods "make some positive contribution to textual elucidation, and that one method should not be judged in terms of the reading-competence appropriate to another" (ibid.).

[5]See, e.g., Brett, "Four or Five Things," pp. 357–77.

[6]*Selected Prose* (Cambridge: Cambridge University Press, 1961), p. xii; cited by D. R. Hall, *The Seven Pillories of Wisdom* (Macon, GA: Mercer University Press, 1990), p. viii.

ANTI-THEOLOGICAL TENDENCIES IN SOME HISTORICAL-CRITICAL APPROACHES

What Is the Historical-Critical Method and Who Can Use It?

It is often asserted that those who study the Bible as a source of history must, if they wish to merit the title *historian*, acknowledge and adhere to the same canons of historical research as those espoused by their secular counterparts. In principle, this assertion is valid. In practice, however, difficulties are encountered because the canons of historical research are still a matter of some debate and, at any rate, are often misunderstood and misapplied.

For example, Halpern has recently asserted that "confessional" scholars (the "faithful" as he also calls them) simply cannot be critical historians. He writes:

> The straightjacket of doctrinal conservatism . . . prohibits critical historical analysis of the Bible. . . . The confessional use of the Bible is fundamentally anti-historical. . . . Worshipers do not read the Bible with an intrinsic interest in human events. Like the prophet, or psalmist, or, in Acts, the saint, they seek behind the events a single, unifying cause that lends them meaning, and makes the historical differences among them irrelevant. In history, the *faith*ful seek the permanent, the ahistorical; in time, they quest for timelessness; in reality, in the concrete, they seek Spirit, the insubstantial.[7]

After what was said in the preceding chapter about the importance of history for faith, Halpern's "anti-historical" charge leveled at the "*faith*ful" comes as something of a surprise and raises a number of questions.[8] The validity of his basic claim, however—that

---

[7]*First Historians*, pp. 3–4.

[8]E.g., is not Halpern assuming false oppositions here? May not a past, *historical* event have a continuing significance for the present and the future and, in that sense, be timeless? And what is wrong with following the precedent of prophet, psalmist, and saint in seeking the unifying meaning that ties disparate events together? At least for the theist, who believes that the past constitutes more than a meaningless chaos of isolated events, this would seem to be a fair procedure. And does Halpern really mean to equate "reality" with "the concrete" and oppose these to the "Spirit," as if the latter were not only "insubstantial" but also unreal?

confessional scholars cannot engage in historical-critical analysis—
hinges on how one defines the terms *historical* and *critical*. Paul
Achtemeier, for instance, defines *historical* as implying the "continuing necessity to recognize that the Bible is the product of another
time, and that this must be taken into account whenever we
attempt to use it to solve contemporary problems." *Critical* he
defines as implying a "critical attitude to what *we* think a given
passage means. We are not to assume that what seems obvious to
us as modern people is necessarily the meaning of the passage
when seen in its total historical and literary context."[9] If this were
all that is involved in the historical-critical method, it would be
hard to imagine why it should ever have encountered resistance
from confessing scholars. Surely, they are as prepared as any to
admit that the Bible is the "product of another time" and that
"what *we* think a given passage means" is open to criticism.

But this is not, in fact, what has traditionally been understood as the historical-critical method. James Barr, for example,
offers a rather different description:

> 'Historical' reading of a text means a reading which aims at the
> reconstruction of spatial-temporal events in the past: it asks what
> was the actual sequence of the events to which the text refers, or
> what was the sequence of events by which the text came into
> existence. This constitutes the 'historical' component. Such histori-
> cal reading is, I would further say, 'critical' in this sense, that it
> accepts the possibility that events were not in fact as they are
> described in the text: that things happened differently, or that the
> text was written at a different time, or by a different person. No
> operation is genuinely historical if it does not accept this critical
> component: in other words, being 'critical' is analytically involved
> in being historical.[10]

Whether confessing scholars can be historical critics of Barr's
variety depends on what is meant by the somewhat ambiguous
phrase, "accepts the possibility." When functioning strictly as
historians, they may leave open the hypothetical possibility that

---

[9]"The Authority of the Bible: What Shall We Then Preach?" *TSF Bulletin*
(November–December 1986): 21–22.

[10]*Scope and Authority of the Bible*, pp. 30–31.

the text may be wrong, but their tendency will be to approach the text expectantly, assuming its reliability until proven otherwise. Secular biblical critics, on the other hand, who regard the Bible as a *merely* human composition, will approach the text assuming not only the possibility but the probability (if not certainty) that the text has erred in places, since "to err is human."

Who then can make use of the historical-critical method? Until clarity of definition is achieved for the terms *historical* and *critical*, a firm answer cannot be given. As traditionally practiced, at least, the historical-critical method rests on certain assumptions that the "faithful" scholar, to use Halpern's designation, will not wish to embrace. We may illustrate this point by quoting Maxwell Miller's description in *The Old Testament and the Historian* of three basic ways in which the modern "critical" historian differs from his "pre-critical" counterparts.[11]

> The contemporary historian's approach tends to differ from that of his earlier counterparts in three ways: (1) he generally takes a critical stance toward his sources; (2) he is inclined to disregard the supernatural or miraculous in his treatment of past events; (3) he is very much aware of his own historicity and, accordingly, of the subjective and tentative character of his own historical conclusions. (pp. 12–13)

Because of its second element, such an approach naturally encounters difficulties in dealing with the

> frequent references in the ancient texts to divine involvement in human affairs . . . , especially when the involvement is depicted as direct and overt. The historian of today may not specifically deny the supernatural or miraculous. But it is obvious from the history books which he writes that he disregards overt supernatural activity as a significant cause in his history and that he is skeptical of claims regarding supposedly unique historical occurrences which defy normal explanation—i.e., the miraculous. (p. 17)

Where reports of miracles or of divine involvement in human affairs do occur, the historian's first reflex, according to Miller, is to ignore them or to *re-explain* them in naturalistic terms. As an

---

[11]Philadelphia: Fortress, 1976.

example, Miller cites the Mesha Inscription (Moabite Stone), in which it is reported that after the defeat of Moab by Omri of Israel and after some years of Israelite domination, king Mesha finally succeeded in regaining Moab's independence. The initial oppression, according to the inscription, came about because "Chemosh was angry with his land," and the deliverance was accomplished when "Chemosh drove him out before me."[12] Historians have little trouble accepting the essential political assertions of the inscription, but as Miller observes, "they ignore Mesha's insistence that these turns of events were the doings of Chemosh and seek to re-explain them without reference to the supernatural. If Chemosh enters into this 're-explanation' at all, he enters only as an element of Mesha's theology" (p. 17).

Now unless Mesha's *theological* explanation be dismissed as no more than a conventional manner of speaking, a meaningless religious overlay believed by no one even in Mesha's day, then the modern scholar must at least acknowledge that some ancient Moabites believed in a god Chemosh who involved himself in human affairs.[13] Of course, few if any modern scholars will share this belief in the existence and activity of Chemosh, and so it is understandable that they seek to re-explain the events described without reference to a god whose existence they deny. Confessing biblical historians are not likely to raise much objection to this procedure, since they are no more inclined to believe in a god called Chemosh than are their secular counterparts (though they may, in principle, be more open to the possibility of a metaphysical dimension in the story). But does it follow that "Biblical sources [should] receive essentially the same treatment" (p. 17)? For those at least who claim to believe in the reality and sovereignty of the God of the Bible, such a move would be illogical. Why should the possible activity of the God whose existence they affirm be limited to that of the false god whose

[12]Lines 5 and 19 of the Mesha Inscription; available *inter alios* in John C. L. Gibson, *Textbook of Semitic Inscriptions. Vol. I: Hebrew and Moabite Inscriptions* (Oxford: Clarendon Press, 1971), pp. 71–83.

[13]On the issue generally, see A. R. Millard, "The Old Testament and History: Some Considerations" *Faith and Thought* 110 (1983): 34–53.

existence they deny? Surely a Christian or Jewish historian is free
to believe that the one true God is sovereign above history and also
active in its processes, without at the same time having to allow
that a god called Chemosh ever occupied such a position. Or put
the other way, surely Jewish or Christian scholars may dismiss or
re-explain claims about Chemosh's purported role in historical
events without subjecting the God whom they confess to similar
treatment.[14]

Beyond the tendency described above, there is a fundamental
principle of the historical-critical method that tends to bring its
results into direct conflict with the biblical testimony. As Miller
describes it, this *principle of analogy* assumes that "all historical
phenomena are subject to 'analogous' explanation—i.e., explanation in terms of other similar phenomena." By virtue of this
methodological criterion, "the modern historian appears to be
presuming in advance that there are no truly miraculous or unique
occurrences in history." This presumption creates a point of
tension between the modern historian and the biblical witness.
Miller puts it succinctly: "The obvious conflict between the
biblical claims regarding God's overt and unique actions in Israel's
history on the one hand, and the presuppositions of the historical-
critical method of inquiry on the other, lies at the heart of much of
the present-day theological discussion" (p. 18).

Why, then, do biblical scholars disagree in their historical
conclusions? In practice, the answer often depends on which side
of the above conflict enjoys their greater loyalty—"the biblical
claims" or "the historical-critical method" as traditionally practiced. But this raises a further question. Must the issue be cast in
terms of such an opposition? Must one either discount the biblical
claims or else commit the apparent *sacrificium intellectus* of rejecting
the historical method? Van Harvey in his influential book *The
Historian and the Believer: A Confrontation between the Modern
Historian's Principles of Judgment and the Christian's Will-to-Believe*,
seems to suggest as much when he sets in opposition "the morality
of historical knowledge" and the traditional, orthodox "ethic of

---

[14]On the issue generally, cf. Goldingay, *Approaches to Old Testament Interpretation*,
pp. 77–79.

belief."[15] But is it not possible to embrace a sound historical method and still maintain that God has intervened decisively in history? In *Divine Revelation and the Limits of Historical Criticism*[16] William Abraham argues compellingly that it is. Not only does he maintain that the "theologian who would turn his back on this [the historical discipline] is a fool, however much he may feel that his work has been in bondage to a discipline whose experts threaten to swallow up the riches of faith" but, even more importantly, he contends that "the theologian need have no fears that the historian must pronounce his commitment to divine intervention as hostile to the critical canons of the historian's trade" (p. 188). In the next section we shall investigate how Abraham arrives at these convictions.

The Historical-Critical Method and the Question of Divine Intervention

Abraham sets two tasks for himself in *Divine Revelation and the Limits of Historical Criticism*. First, in chapters one to four he seeks to demonstrate that the "traditional understanding of divine revelation" necessarily entails a "commitment to divine intervention of a substantial sort." Second, in chapters five to eight he argues that "it is possible to believe in special divine revelation without any sacrifice of critical judgement in either history or science" (p. 7). A full summary of Abraham's argumentation is not possible here, but we may at least focus on the crucial issue addressed in the second half of his book.

The question, as Abraham puts it at the beginning of chapter five, is whether "the traditional claims as set forth in the first four chapters [should] be abandoned because of the character of critical historical investigation" (p. 92). To help describe what is involved in critical historical investigation, Abraham turns to the writings of German theologian, historian, and social scientist Ernst Troeltsch (1865–1923), already mentioned above. According to Troeltsch, a true historian must be committed not only to the

[15]See esp. his chap. 4.
[16]Oxford: Oxford University Press, 1982.

principle of *analogy*, but to two other principles (or presuppositions)[17] as well: *criticism* and *correlation*. As Abraham explains, the principle of *criticism* means that

> the historian is to offer his conclusions in the form of probability judgments of a greater or lesser degree. His conclusions, that is, do not take the form of necessary truths, as in mathematics, but are contingent in character and can be ranged on a scale of truth so that some conclusions may be claimed to be more likely to be true than others. Given this, there will be differences in the inner attitude of the historian to his claims. Concerning some claims he will feel very sure, concerning others less sure, etc. Further, his conclusions will always be open to revision should fresh evidence emerge, and thus they cannot be treated as absolute or final. (p. 100)

This description of *criticism*, or what it means to be a *critical* historian, comes closer to Achtemeier's concept than to Barr's (both mentioned above). Historians' claims must remain open to criticism, that is, review and revision (so Achtemeier). But there is no insistence that source documents must, as a point of principle, be systematically doubted (Barr). Troeltsch's second principle, *analogy*, is related to the first in the following manner, as Abraham again explains:

> As the historian seeks to determine what happened in the past he guides his work by his convictions about what is taking place in his own time, and uses this as a scale for judging the probability of claims about the past. 'Harmony with the normal, familiar or at least repeatedly witnessed events and conditions as we know them is the distinguishing mark of reality for the events which criticism can recognize as really having happened or leave aside.' (p. 100)

As noted earlier, this principle can seem to be assuming in advance that the unique cannot occur, that miracles do not happen, and that

---

[17]For Abraham's defense of his use of the not altogether happy term *presupposition*, see *Divine Revelation*, pp. 98–99. Note well also Harvey's warning against too undifferentiated a notion of *presuppositions* (*Historian and the Believer*, esp. chap. 3). In Harvey's view, "the assertion, 'Every historian has his presuppositions' is both true and misleading," since it tends to mask the fact that presuppositions are of many different types and are operative on various levels of inquiry (p. 84).

God never intervenes in history. Indeed, in practice this is often the way the principle of analogy is applied, with the result that the *theological* presentation of history in the Bible is rejected out of hand by "critical" historians and replaced with an *atheological*, nonmetaphysical reconstruction. When this happens, scholars are again placed in the uncomfortable position of choosing between the biblical testimony to the past and "real" history as critically reconstructed. But must the principle of analogy be applied so woodenly? Must it entail a dismissal of the unique or miraculous in history? Abraham contends that it need not, and he charts a pathway out of the impasse by refining the notion of analogy.

He begins by noting that the principle of analogy "can be understood in either a narrow or wide sense." Depending on the sense, the historian is limited to what is "normal, usual, or widely attested" in his own personal experience (the narrow sense) or in the experience of people currently living (the wide sense). The narrow sense is clearly too restrictive, for historians regularly accept the reality of events and practices that lie outside their immediate experience.[18] The wide sense is less "hyper-restrictive" but is still open to several objections: (1) "it is quite impossible to put into effect," since historians could never travel widely enough, consult enough encyclopedias of *normalcy*, etc. to ascertain what in fact is normal, usual, or widely attested; and even if they could, they would be left with little time or energy for historical research; (2) even "with respect to what is claimed to have happened in the present," historians exercise "critical judgement" that is derived in part, at least, from their knowledge of the past (thus, one might on occasion reverse the standard adage that "the present is the key to the past" and say that "the past is the key to the present"); (3) "in some cases historians would be prepared to allow as happening events that are not normal, usual, or widely attested"—e.g., "the climbing of Mount Everest or the first human landing on the moon" (pp. 101–103).

---

[18]To underscore this point, Abraham (p. 101) cites Collingwood's telling remark: "That the Greeks and Romans exposed their new-born children in order to control the numbers of their population is no less true for being unlike anything that happens in the experience of contributors to the Cambridge Ancient History."

To illustrate how the principle of analogy may properly function in determining the historicity, or factuality, of a claim about the past, Abraham describes two imaginary scenarios. The first involves the discovery in an ancient document of a claim that Plato wrote *The Republic* when he was only two years old. The immediate reaction of historians will be to dismiss such a claim, since, as everyone knows, "children of two years of age do not write books like *The Republic*" (p. 103). The second scenario involves a primitive tribe confronted for the first time with the claim that man has landed on the moon. Again, on the principle of analogy, this claim will be immediately dismissed by the tribe. Nevertheless, a historian may succeed in convincing the tribe that a moon landing did in fact occur if he does three things: (1) bring corroborating testimony, "e.g., from fellow westerners who are trusted by the tribe," (2) "initiate the members of the tribe into the theories and concepts of natural science," especially as these relate to space flight, and (3) explain "the purposes and intentions of those who planned and carried out the moon landings." If the tribe still refuse to believe on the grounds that "this event is not normal, usual, or widely attested even in the west" (p. 104), the historian will need to bring further arguments. He might explain the infrequency or even uniqueness of the event on the basis of cost, government restrictions, safety concerns, and so forth. In the end, the tribe may be led to believe in an occurrence that finds no analogy in their own experience.

What becomes clear in all of this is that "the principle of analogy is a principle that operates within a wider context." There is "an intimate relation between analogy and its context or network of background beliefs" (p. 105). As the example of the tribe illustrates, *conclusions drawn from an application of the principle of analogy are only as sound as the background beliefs held by those drawing the conclusions.* How then do we discern the background beliefs of this or that historian or, for that matter, how do we examine our own? The key, according to Troeltsch (and Abraham), is to investigate what each of us thinks about the third basic principle of the historical-critical method, the principle of *correlation.*

The principle of correlation maintains that "events are interdependent and interrelated in intimate reciprocity" (p. 105).

In other words, events do not simply happen unprompted. They are caused either by the choices and actions of personal agents or by natural forces, or by some combination of the two. As regards personal agency, the decisive question is, as Abraham puts it, whether the historian adopts a *formal* conception of correlation (which would allow both human and divine agency) or a *material* conception of correlation (which would limit causation to the terrestrial sphere and disallow divine agency).

For those like Troeltsch and so many after him who are committed to a material conception, any record of events that expresses or implies divine agency must, in that regard at least, be discounted as history. Indeed, to those steeped in Troeltschian thinking any appeal to direct divine activity in earthly affairs will appear to be the epitome of "an uncritical and even superstitious mentality" (p. 110).

But such thinking must be challenged. Abraham argues forcefully that "direct actions of God are not bolts from the blue or random events, but are related to a wider conceptual scheme that gives point and intelligibility to their occurrence" (p. 111).[19] This being the case, to admit discourse about divine intervention as an acceptable component of historical explanation is not to abandon the principle of correlation but to widen it. If one's network of background beliefs includes belief in a personal God, one may affirm that this God has acted in history—for example, that he has spoken, that he has become incarnate in Christ, that he has performed miracles—and still remain true to the principle of correlation: the belief that events do not simply happen unprompted.

At times, of course, for the sake of dialogue with those who do not share the same background beliefs, theistic historians may legitimately adopt a qualified material conception of correlation, but only as a temporary *methodological* constraint. In other words,

---

[19]The resurrection of Jesus from the dead, for example, is not an arbitrary abrogation of the laws of nature but is "one part of a complex and sophisticated story of divine action that stretches from eternity to eternity and involves in a unique way the person of Jesus" (Abraham, *Divine Revelation*, p. 132; see also pp. 116–35 for a full discussion of this very important point).

theistic historians may choose not to talk about *all* they believe in order to talk profitably, even if on a minimalist level, with those who believe less. As Bebbington explains, "the Christian historian is not obliged to tell the whole truth as he sees it in every piece of historical writing. He can write of providence or not according to his judgment of the composition of his audience. So long as his account accords with the Christian vision of the historical process, he will be fulfilling his vocation."[20] The last sentence above is key. It recognizes that, whatever limitations may be set on the terms of discussion, Christian historians, if they are to be consistent, must take care that what they do say is compatible with their full set of background beliefs. To safeguard this compatibility, they must remain aware of two dangers that typically attend lowest-common-denominator discussions.

First, whenever talk of divine agency is methodologically excluded, there can be a real temptation to seek an exclusively *natural* explanation for each and every occurrence in the past, even for those occurrences that the Bible presents as involving direct divine action. This temptation must be resisted, for succumbing to it may lead to an endorsement of historical reconstructions at odds with the Christian historian's full set of background beliefs.[21] In contexts where explicit affirmation of divine activity would be a "conversation stopper," Christian historians should at least refrain from endorsing historical reconstructions that explicitly deny such activity, for that too is a conversation stopper, or should be. As an example of appropriate restraint, John Bright remarks regarding the events surrounding the Israelite exodus from Egypt, "If Israel saw in this the hand of God, the historian certainly has no evidence to contradict it!"[22]

A second, equally grave danger is that biblical historians may unwittingly allow the *minimalist* method, adopted for the sake of

---

[20]*Patterns*, pp. 187–88.

[21]As Bebbington (*Patterns*, p. 186) warns, "If a Christian historian tries to write without a thought for providence, he is likely to succumb to some alternative view or blend of views that happens to be in fashion. He will probably grow accustomed to the current assumptions of the academic world, positivist, historicist, Marxist or whatever."

[22]*A History of Israel*, 3d ed. (Philadelphia: Westminster, 1981), p. 122.

dialogue, to begin to infect their model of reality. Methodological procedure can all too easily slide into metaphysical profession. Such a shift is a logical and procedural error of the first order, for it is one's model of reality that should suggest what methods are appropriate in approaching a given subject, and not the reverse. I am not suggesting that one's model of reality should be immune from challenge. But the fallacy of unthinkingly allowing a chosen method to determine one's model of reality is like that of the fisherman who is convinced that his fishing hole contains no fish smaller than five centimeters in length simply because he has never caught any. When a bystander points out that the fisherman's net has a mesh too large to catch fish smaller than five centimeters, the fisherman insists, mistakenly, that what his net (method) cannot catch does not exist (model of reality).[23]

In summary, while the historical-critical method (as traditionally practiced) systematically and insistently excludes the notion of divine intervention, the method itself, if applied in the context of a theistic set of background beliefs, need not exclude talk of divine intervention. For those willing to embrace a historical-critical method of the type developed by Abraham and advocated above, Miller's "obvious conflict between the biblical claims . . . and the presuppositions of the historical-critical method"[24] disappears. The historian may believe that God is the "lord of history,"[25] sovereignly at work behind the scenes and even intervening on occasion, and still remain a competent historian. Indeed, unless theists are badly mistaken in their theism, then surely it is the denial of any place for God in the historical process that is the mark of bad history.

Why do scholars disagree on historical questions relating to the Bible? One reason, as we have seen, is the common though unnecessary tendency of the historical-critical method to exclude from the realm of history any notion of direct divine intervention.

---

[23]Cf. Hans Peter Dürr's more elaborate parable of the ichthyologist and the metaphysician, described by J. Spieß, "Die Geschichtlichkeit der Heiligen Schrift," *Jahrbuch für Evangelikale Theologie* 4 (1990): 117.

[24]*Old Testament and the Historian*, p. 18.

[25]So Caird, *Language and Imagery*, p. 217.

This tendency leads to an a priori dismissal of many events recorded in the Bible and, in some cases, to a general skepticism towards the biblical text as a historical source. It is perhaps this skepticism that contributes to the popularity of approaches to historical reconstruction that seek to minimize the importance of literary, or textual, evidence. Among such are the social-scientific approaches to which we now turn.

ANTI-LITERARY TENDENCIES IN SOME SOCIAL-SCIENTIFIC APPROACHES

Sociology: The New Handmaid?

As Carolyn Osiek observes in "The New Handmaid: The Bible and the Social Sciences," now that the once-dominant influence of nineteenth-century-style historical criticism is in decline, it is social study of the Bible that has staked its claim to being "the scientific investigative mode."[26] A fundamental difference between historical study, as traditionally conceived, and sociological analysis is that while the former tends to stress the importance of the "individual and particular," the latter is more concerned with the "general and typical."[27] This is often referred to as the distinction between an *idiographic* and a *nomothetic* approach. These terms were apparently first introduced by Wilhelm Windelband, rector of the University of Strassburg, in

---

[26] *Theological Studies* 50 (1989): 260. Osiek provides a convenient historical survey of the growth of sociological approaches to the Bible, from the planting of the seeds in the last century by, e.g., J. Wellhausen and W. Robertson Smith, to their subsequent cultivation by Gunkel, Mowinckel, Pederson, Weber, and others, and finally to the current burgeoning of interest in such approaches, as evidenced by the attention given, e.g., to the writings of Norman Gottwald. For other evaluative surveys, see A. D. H. Mayes, "Sociology and the Old Testament," in *The World of Ancient Israel*, ed. R. E. Clements (Cambridge: Cambridge University Press, 1989), pp. 39–63; Morgan, *Biblical Interpretation*, chap. 5; C. S. Rodd, "Sociology and Social Anthropology," in *Dictionary*, ed. Coggins and Houlden, pp. 635–39. And for an up-to-date treatment of sociological investigations of the New Testament, see B. Holmberg, *Sociology and the New Testament: An Appraisal* (Minneapolis: Fortress, 1990).

[27] Morgan, *Biblical Interpretation*, p. 139.

his inaugural address in 1894 entitled "History and Natural Science."[28] Windelband's distinction between the natural sciences and the historical disciplines is summarized by McCullagh as follows:

> Natural scientists . . . proceed by quantification and abstraction to formulate, as precisely as they can, general laws of nature, true of many individual sequences of events. Historians, on the other hand, are forever seeking a particularity and uniqueness. Windelband called the natural sciences 'nomothetic' (lawgiving) and the historical disciplines 'idiographic' (describing the separate, distinct, individual).[29]

Broadly speaking, this distinction is valid. Traditional histories tend to focus on significant individuals as shapers of history, while the social sciences, insofar as they strive to be "scientific," seek to discover general "laws" about the way large-scale societal forces influence historical change. This does not mean, of course, that historians have no interest in generalizations. "If they are to describe what life was like for groups of people in the past, they must generalize." Moreover, they need to become familiar with "the conventions of a society" if they are to "understand documents relating to it." Generalizations play a big part in the historian's development of what we have earlier referred to as an ancient literary and cultural competence. "Historians must know the general significance within a society of certain words and actions if they are to make sense of the evidence they have of that society, and of the deeds to which that evidence relates."[30]

There is, then, a place for nomothetic investigation in historical study as traditionally practiced. Its chief function is to describe "the abiding institutions and patterns of culture, against which the quicker movements that catch the scholarly eye are visible."[31] Nomothetic study, in other words, seeks to present the general cultural, material, and historical background against which the specific actions of individuals and groups are to be viewed.

---

[28]See McCullagh, *Justifying Historical Descriptions*, p. 129.

[29]Ibid., p. 129.

[30]Ibid., p. 130.

[31]So Halpern, *First Historians*, p. 122.

Some of the best sociological approaches to the history of ancient cultures acknowledge the complementarity of nomothetic and idiographic forces in the processes of history. Unfortunately, however, this is not always the case. Many (though certainly not all) social scientific treatments of biblical issues are explicitly or implicitly Marxist in perspective, and this inevitably influences the way in which the actions of past individuals, and the texts that report them, are assessed. In Marx's view, individuals play a very minor role in history. At best, they may affect specific details of historical transformation, but they have no power, as individuals, to bring about major changes.[32] For Marx, it is not individuals but material/economic forces that drive history. In *A Contribution to the Critique of Political Economy* he writes: "The mode of production of material life determines the general character of the social, political and spiritual processes of life. It is not the consciousness of men that determines their being, but, on the contrary, their social being determines their consciousness." In other words, as he puts it in *The German Ideology*, it is the "process of production" that ultimately accounts for "the different theoretical productions and forms of consciousness, religion, philosophy, ethics, etc."[33]

What does all this have to do with the claim that some social-scientific approaches exhibit an anti-literary, or anti-textual, tendency? It is this. Denials of the significance of individuals, such as we have noted above, almost inevitably lead to a depreciation of texts (particularly narrative texts such as are found in the Bible) in which individuals and their actions are portrayed as vitally important in "making history." Hayden White provides a nice illustration of this point in a discussion of the place of narrative discourse in historical theory. He observes that "certain social-scientifically oriented historians, of whom the members of the French *Annales* group may be considered exemplary . . . regarded narrative historiography as a non-scientific, even *ideological repre-*

---

[32]See McCullagh (*Justifying Historical Descriptions*, pp. 225–26), who cites as counter-evidence to the Marxist perspective the impressive case that can be made in support of the view "that the Russian Revolution of 1917 would not have occurred without Lenin's leadership, and that there was no chance of anyone else bringing it about in his absence."

[33]Both quoted in ibid., pp. 157–58.

sentation strategy, the extirpation of which was necessary for the transformation of historical studies into a genuine science."[34] The explicit charge brought against narrative history by the *Annalistes* was that "narrativity is inherently 'dramatizing' or 'novelizing' of its subject-matter, as if dramatic events either did not exist in history or, if they did exist, are by virtue of their dramatic nature not fit objects of historical study."[35] White maintains, however, that what actually underlies the depreciation of "narrative history" is not the supposed antithesis between the "dramatic" and the "scientific" but, rather, "a distaste for a genre of literature that puts human agents rather than impersonal processes at the center of interest and suggests that such agents have some significant control over their own destinies."[36]

The issue then is between a nomothetic view of historical change, which ascribes primary significance to impersonal processes, and an idiographic view, which allows individual personalities to exercise significant influence. Wherever the former viewpoint holds sway, narratives in general and biblical narratives in particular (in which individual persons, to say nothing of a personal God, play so large a part) will receive little respect as sources of historical information. In a recent essay addressing questions of historical method, Keith Whitelam argues that "the whole concept of the study of the history of Israel needs to be enlarged and reformulated in order to overcome the constraints and limitations, *for the historian*, of the traditions preserved in the Hebrew Bible."[37] To be sure, historians may wish to overcome the "limitations" of the biblical evidence by investigating, for example, sociological or cultural or economic or political questions that the text *does not address*. But if they insist also on escaping the "constraints" of the text on matters to which it does speak, then what is to provide the basis of historical reconstruction?

Whitelam defends his dismissal of the text with the observa-

---

[34]"Question of Narrative," p. 7.

[35]Ibid., p. 9.

[36]Ibid., p. 10.

[37]"Recreating the History of Israel," *JSOT* 35 (1986): 55; cf. Thompson, *Early History of Israel*, p. 169.

tion that "the text is not a witness to historical reality, only to itself. It is a witness to a particular perception of reality."[38] But surely we are always limited to a particular perception of reality— if not the text's, then our own. Having jettisoned the former, Whitelam is left with only the latter, and this leads him to conclude that "all [historical] reconstructions [of the history of Israel] are contingent." He writes:

> As our perspective or vantage point shifts, a frequent occurrence in the present age, so our view of the history of Israel must be readjusted. This is not to suggest that what happened in the past or the reasons why it happened change, but our perspective of these two aspects of the past radically changes with adjustments in our own situation, new discoveries, or fresh perspectives on the interrelationship of various pieces of data.[39]

There is a sense in which Whitelam is correct, of course. Our own perceptions of the past do change as we gain new data and see the past in new lights. The social sciences can be useful, as we have already suggested, in pursuing questions that the text does not address, or does not address directly. But are we well advised to seek to escape the *constraints* of the text in matters that it *does* address? Should not the text at least be included among the available data?

The anti-textual, or anti-literary, error of some sociological approaches is all too easily compounded by an anachronistic error. As Charles Tilly observes in *As Sociology Meets History*,[40] sociological theory is grounded in "one piece of history: the piece their formulators are currently living. . . . The mistake is to extrapolate backwards, without attempting to place the small contemporary strip of history into the broad band of social transformation to which it belongs" (p. 214).

What is needed, it would seem, is a properly balanced perspective on both the *nomothetic* and the *idiographic* forces at work in history. Exclusively idiographic, text-based reconstructions of history may well capture the soul of past events but have little

---

[38]"Recreating the History of Israel," p. 52.
[39]Ibid., p. 64.
[40]New York: Academic Press, 1981.

understanding of their embodiment. Exclusively nomothetic reconstructions, on the other hand, easily fall into a kind of reductionism and determinism that loses sight of the very soul of past events.[41] Morgan stresses the importance of coordinating the emphases: "Anyone wanting to understand past or present societies will use both [history and sociology]. Whether or not either can 'explain' a society, both offer partial explanations of particular features."[42]

Finding the balance between the nomothetic emphasis of the social sciences and the idiographic emphasis of the historical discipline is a desideratum. But there is a further aspect to the problem, as is perhaps suggested by Morgan's last statement above. Sociology, like the nineteenth-century-style historical criticism discussed above, is ill-equipped to treat the religious dimension in human experience without becoming reductionistic. This may not be too surprising if, as Cyril Rodd asserts, "many of the early anthropologists and sociologists were atheists."[43] The tendency of some social scientists to overbalance the equation in the direction of nomothetic forces must be resisted by historians of the Bible, since, as Stanford insists, every culture is the product not only of "human volition and adaptation, as well as of physical energies" but also of "spiritual energy." He explains: "Religious

---

[41]Gottwald himself (*The Hebrew Bible: A Socio-Literary Introduction* [Philadelphia: Fortress, 1985], p. 33) acknowledges that "anthropological and sociological categories deal with the typical and thus provide 'average' descriptions and general tendencies which by themselves may miss the momentary oddities and exceptions of historical figures and happenings." Cf. also Holmberg, *Sociology*, p. 157. For an insightful critique of sociology's tendency toward positivism, relativism, reductionism, and determinism, see G. A. Herion "The Impact of Modern and Social Science Assumptions on the Reconstruction of Israelite History," *JSOT* 34 (1986): 3–33. To catch something of the flavor of the nomothetic vs. idiographic debate that is going on in the field of secular history, see C. Parker's review of recent writers in "Methods, Ideas and Historians" *Literature and History* 11 (1985): 288–291; cf. also F. K. Ringer, "Causal Analysis in Historical Reasoning." *HTh* 28 (1989): 154–72.

[42]*Biblical Interpretation*, p. 140.

[43]According to Rodd ("Sociology," p. 636), "Only W. Robertson Smith, among the circle of early anthropologists, retained his firm Christian faith up to his death. . . . It is curious, therefore, that the early theories were accepted so uncritically by OT scholars."

experience in many different ages and cultures seems to have borne witness to a power that rules the universe yet can be found within the individual man or woman."[44]

Even among sociological approaches that are less directly influenced by Marxist materialism, there is a tendency to downplay the significance of individuals and their religious commitments. As Bengt Holmberg observes,

> The tendency of modern sociological theory is to minimize the part played by cognitive interests in social actions, such as generating and sustaining religious commitments. The religious viewpoint of the actors is registered but not accorded any validity or effect, which is reserved for social factors (level of education, family background, relative deprivation, etc.). Thus the implicit claim of the sociologists is that they understand the basis of religious belief and action better than religious people do.[45]

Andrew Hill and Gary Herion likewise lament sociology's "innate deficiency to properly address the role of personal faith in the socio-political process." They point out that "the application of modern social science concepts to the OT often fails to disclose adequately the true nature of the relationship between politics and religion in ancient Israel. This is due in large measure to the inability of such concepts to account fully for the dynamic variable of individual faith in Yahweh."[46]

Is it any wonder then that scholars who employ methods that share this "innate deficiency" arrive at historical reconstructions radically different from those employing methods that do not? Only time will tell whether the application of social-science analysis will ultimately clarify or cloud our perception of the history and culture of the people of the Bible. Much depends on making the necessary adjustments to give not only nomothetic, but also idiographic and religious influences their due. While the social sciences have great potential for increasing our understanding, particularly of the background against which the events of

---

[44]*Nature*, pp. 39–40.

[45]*Sociology*, pp. 147–48.

[46]"Functional Yahwism and Social Control in the Early Israelite Monarchy," *JETS* 29 (1986): 277.

biblical history played themselves out, they are inadequate to predict specific courses of events.[47] For purposes of *historical* reconstruction, the social sciences must resist the anti-literary tendency and remain in some measure dependent on written sources.

Archaeology: A Discipline in Flux

The present century has witnessed a dramatic increase in archaeological knowledge of the lands of the Bible, and some of this new knowledge has proved very helpful in the interpretation of biblical texts. Yet when it comes to the matter of historical reconstruction, archaeology is subject to some of the same limitations and potential abuses as described above with respect to the social sciences. To complicate matters further, the very nature and proper function of archaeological investigation has in recent years been hotly debated. As the late D. Glenn Rose observed, not only are "archaeological method and associated methods of interpreting the data . . . in flux," but "the relationship of this changing archaeology to the Bible is . . . also in flux."[48] What for years was called *biblical archaeology* has today generally been displaced in favor of *Syro-Palestinian archaeology* or what is called the *new archaeology*, and there are signs that even these terms may fall into disfavor and be replaced by others.[49]

But what is this *new archaeology* that has enjoyed popularity in recent decades? Philip King describes it as a "model of interdisciplinary archaeology" in which "natural and social scien-

---

[47]Halpern ("Biblical or Israelite History?" in *Future of Biblical Studies*, ed. Friedman and Williamson, p. 122) rightly warns that "we cannot deterministically 'predict' on this basis [i.e., knowledge of background] developments the sources do not register. But *Kulturgeschichte* and sociology can afford us what they did classical history: a means to evaluate specific reports about specific events."

[48]"The Bible and Archaeology: The State of the Art," in *Archaeology and Biblical Interpretation*, ed. L. G. Perdue, L. E. Toombs, and G. L. Johnson (Atlanta: John Knox, 1987), p. 57.

[49]See, e.g., W. G. Dever, "Biblical Archaeology: Death and Rebirth?" in *Proceedings of the Second International Congress on Biblical Archaeology* (Jerusalem, 1990), forthcoming.

tists and archaeologists" work side-by-side at a particular site. He attributes the early cultivation of this brand of archaeology in Palestine to the influence of G. Ernest Wright's dream of "ecological archaeology."[50] Lawrence Toombs further elucidates the nature of the new archaeology by comparing it with traditional archaeology, which embraced three principle aims: to reconstruct "cultural history," to reconstruct the "life-ways of the people who left the archaeological record," and to study "cultural process."[51] To illustrate these three aims, Toombs compares them to various aspects of the work of excavating a tell. The chronological concerns of reconstructing history he compares to the stratigraphic trench, the interest in life-ways to the "area of exposure of a single level or stratum," and the interest in cultural process to the "interstices between the levels." The primary goal of the new archaeology, according to Toombs, is the "processual" one. That is, it is most concerned with discovering "the laws of cultural change" (p. 46). In keeping with this concern, the new archaeology is "not primarily a revision of methodology but rather a profound reexamination of philosophy and theory. . . . The movement is from theory to praxis, not the reverse" (p. 42). And what is the theory? In broad terms, it is the notion that archaeology belongs to the sciences and not to the humanities. So conceived, archaeology is constrained to "develop its theories and procedures in ways congruent with those of the physical sciences" (p. 43). The result is that "archaeological knowledge" becomes limited to "confirmed generalizations" (p. 44) or purely "materialistic" explanations, to the unhappy exclusion, for purposes of historical reconstruction at least, of any proper recognition of the "role of ideology" (or theology) or of "individual creativity and imagination in producing cultural variability" (p. 48).

As with the social sciences, these nomothetic tendencies of the new archaeology can lead to a reductionism and environmental determinism that discounts the significance of individuals in

---

[50]"The Influence of G. Ernest Wright on the Archaeology of Palestine," in *Archaeology and Biblical Interpretation*, ed. Perdue et al., p. 22.

[51]"A Perspective on the New Archaeology," in *Archaeology and Biblical Interpretation*, ed. Perdue et al., p. 45.

making history and thus encourages a downplaying of the historical import of the Bible's admittedly idiographical narratives. As Rose aptly puts it, because of the new archaeology's theoretical framework, in which culture is conceived as "the product of human adaptation to environmental change" rather than as the "shaping agent of that environment," the approach sometimes becomes "very deterministic as it is handled through statistics and systems theory."[52]

In view of the fact that much current archaeological practice downplays or denies the significance of textual evidence, the question that must be addressed is whether archaeology alone, independent of literary evidence, is an adequate basis for *historical* reconstruction. Several observations suggest that it is not.

First, with the exception of inscriptional evidence, most of what archaeology can discover (artifactual remains and stratigraphic sequence) speaks of life conditions in general and not of specific events. As Miller notes, "Although it is a good source for clarifying the material culture of times past, artifactual evidence is a very poor source of information about specific people and events."[53]

Second, and again with the exception of inscriptional evidence, the material remains unearthed by archaeology do not in fact *speak* at all, but *must be interpreted* on some basis. Frederic Brandfon has recently drawn attention to the fallacy of assuming that archaeological evidence, whether artifactual or stratigraphic, is somehow more *objective* than other types of evidence: "once the researcher begins the necessary task of grouping the evidence into typologies of artifacts on the one hand, or charts of comparative stratigraphy on the other, theoretical concerns begin to transform the archaeological evidence into an historical account. In this sense, archaeological evidence, despite its brute factuality, is no more objective than any other type of evidence."[54] He explains:

[52]"Bible and Archaeology," p. 56.

[53]"Old Testament History and Archaeology," *Biblical Archaeologist* 50 (1987): 59.

[54]"The Limits of Evidence: Archaeology and Objectivity," *Maarav* 4/1 (1987): 30. Cf. Miller's assertion that archaeological investigation "involves highly subjective judgments on the part of the interpreter" ("Reflections on the Study of

I can experience a given ash layer by touching it, seeing it and even tasting it; but this immediate experience is not history until I talk about it or write about it to someone else. The minute I do that, however, I begin to interpret the facts. I have to choose the words which will describe that layer, e.g. 'destruction debris' or 'burnt debris.' This interpretation transforms the individual facts into 'general concepts' by grouping them with other facts and other ideas. This transformation is the creative process of historiography.[55]

Third, the archaeological evidence available to the historian is both partial and constantly changing. It is partial, since not all significant sites nor all sections of given sites have been excavated (to say nothing of the fact that only a small percentage of material remains from the past will have survived anyway). And it is constantly changing, since continuing archaeological investigation is regularly bringing new evidence to light.

All of these factors indicate that archaeology alone does not provide an adequate foundation for historical reconstruction, at least not in terms of traditional history's interest in particular events and individuals. As with the social sciences discussed earlier, archaeology's greatest potential is in the delineation of the general milieu (cultural, material, etc.) within which specific events may have taken place. Archaeological evidence may form part of a cumulative case suggesting the plausibility of a specific event, but it is hardly adequate to prove it (or, in most instances, to disprove it). As Boling and Campbell aptly state, "only rarely will archaeology settle an issue and only rarely is it of total irrelevance."[56] We do well, then, to go slowly when advised on the basis of archaeological discussion (for example, the continuing controversies over the site of Ai) to "redirect our thinking about Bible."[57] Surely, we should recall how often the assured archaeo-

Israelite History," in *What Has Archaeology to Do With Faith?* ed. J. H. Charlesworth and W. P. Weaver [Philadelphia: Trinity Press International, 1992], p. 67).

[55]"Limits of Evidence," p. 30.

[56]"Jeroboam and Rehoboam at Shechem," in *Archaeology*, ed. Perdue et al., p. 264.

[57]So J. A. Callaway, "Ai (et-Tell): Problem Site for Biblical Archaeologists," in *Archaeology*, ed. Perdue et al., p. 97.

logical results of one generation have been overturned in the next.[58]

If, then, archaeology alone is an inadequate basis for historical reconstruction, and if, as Brandfon has argued, "theoretical concerns" inevitably come into play whenever archaeological evidence is marshalled in the service of historical reconstruction, the crucial question becomes: what provides our theoretical grid? As Brandfon points out, "An historian may use any number of theories in order to transform evidence into history, e.g., Marxist theory, Freudian theory, or a combination; possibly literary or religious theories. Some of these theories we may judge apt or applicable and others not."[59] Certain of these theories, as we have already seen, will by virtue of their generalized, nomothetic tendencies downplay the significance of texts (especially the biblical text) in reconstructing history. But we must not forget that for many aspects of Israelite history, the Bible is our *main*— and sometimes even our *only*—source.[60] Admittedly, scholars wishing to prove the veracity of the Bible have sometimes been guilty of wittingly or unwittingly misconstruing archaeological results. But this does not mean that archaeologists are well advised to bracket out the biblical evidence entirely.[61] Where the Bible, with its particular view of reality, is excluded from the archaeologist's interpretive grid, some other theory will fill the void, with

---

[58]One thinks, e.g., of N. Glueck's contention, based on surface-surveys of Transjordan, that the region was lacking in settled population between the 19th and 13th centuries B.C.; more recent archaeological work in the area suggests otherwise (see R. G. Boling, *The Early Biblical Community in Transjordan* [Sheffield: Almond, 1988], pp. 11–35).

[59]"Limits of Evidence," pp. 30–31.

[60]Clines (*What Does Eve*, p. 101) notes that what he calls the "Primary History" (i.e., Genesis–2 Kings) is "for most of the period it covers . . . the only source we have for knowing anything at all about what actually happened in ancient Israel"; cf. Miller, "Reflections," pp. 65–66; Garbini, *History and Ideology*, p. 16.

[61]As D. W. J. Gill notes in a review article of Robin Lane Fox's *The Unauthorized Version: Truth and Fiction in the Bible* (London: Viking, 1991), "Just because biblical archaeologists have made some 'howlers' . . . that with hindsight look ridiculous does not mean that biblical archaeology (or the Bible) is wrong. The same strawman arguments could be used against the classical historian Herodotus" ("Authorized or Unauthorized: A Dilemma for the Historian," *TynB* 43/1 [1992]: 194).

no less potential for distortion. Individual archaeologists will quite naturally be attracted to those theories whose views of reality most closely resemble their own set of background beliefs. These various considerations lead to the following conclusions with respect to the place of archaeology in the reconstruction of history.

First, historians should recognize archaeology's innate limitations (i.e., its partial, ever changing, and generalized character). Where this is done, two results will follow: historians will be less likely to attempt to establish specific courses of events on the basis of archaeological evidence alone, and they will be more cautious about accepting without qualification what some might regard as archaeology's "proven results."

Second, since the archaeological data are neither purely objective nor self-interpreting, historians should remind themselves that as soon as they begin to talk about the data, they are doing so on the basis of an interpretive grid that they themselves bring to the task.

Thus, third, where archaeological evidence is used in building a cumulative case for the likelihood or unlikelihood of a specific historical scenario, historians should openly acknowledge, to themselves and to their audience, the extent to which their own background beliefs influence their judgments. To put the matter another way: clarity would be served if archaeologists and historians would be more self-conscious and explicit about their own belief systems, since theory plays such a large part in the interpretation of archaeology's limited, changing, and essentially mute data. Awareness of one's own presuppositions and predispositions is, of course, also the first step toward avoiding special pleading and the distortion of evidence.

Fourth, far from dismissing the literary (biblical) evidence as little more than a hindrance to historical reconstruction, historians should seek a closer coordination of archaeological and literary studies, despite the difficulties and dangers that attend such an enterprise. Admittedly, as Ephraim Stern has observed,[62] this task is made more difficult by the "information explosion" of recent decades and the consequent "narrow specialization" of scholars.

---

[62]"The Bible and Israeli Archaeology," in *Archaeology*, ed. Perdue et al., p. 37.

The rigors of mastering the various technologies that are employed by the new archaeology have cut sharply into the time that scholars can find "to devote themselves to the literary sources, whether biblical or external." But this, as Stern rightly notes, is a "genuine loss," and one with which historical and archaeological scholarship can ill afford to rest content.

Finally, whenever scholars begin to reflect on the relationship of archaeology and the Bible, they should give some indication not only of their general attitude toward the Bible but also of their level of competence in dealing with its literature.[63] In the end, biblical archaeology is, according to Philip King, "a Biblical, not an archaeological, discipline. It is the responsibility of Biblical scholars, not archaeologists, to ferret out pertinent material evidence and apply it to the Bible." King cites the "crying need for synthesizing works that bring archaeological data to bear on the Biblical text."[64]

Where scholars are willing to proceed cautiously, with such issues as these in mind, archaeology has much to contribute to the historical study of the Bible. Indeed, as Darrell Lance maintains, "Archaeology helps to keep vital biblical scholarship as a whole. When all is said and done, few tasks in the study of the Bible can match it in excitement and importance, for it is the source of ever-new data to increase our ability to read the Bible with understanding and appreciation."[65]

So then, what can archaeology contribute to the task of historical reconstruction? It can supplement, but should not be allowed to supplant, written sources, including the Bible. It can suggest the plausibility, or otherwise, of specific events, but it can seldom prove or disprove them. Even where it can render probable the *occurrence* of an event, it is ill-suited to pronounce on the *interpretation* of that event. As we turn now to consider literary approaches to the Bible, we shall discover that the tendency of some of them is to err in a different direction—viz., so to stress

---

[63]Cf., e.g., Gill's comments in "Authorized or Unauthorized," pp. 199–200.

[64]"The *Marzeaḥ* Amos Denounces," *Biblical Archeology Review* 14/4 (1988): 34.

[65]*The Old Testament and the Archaeologist* (Philadelphia: Fortress, 1981), p. 96.

the interpretive word as to deny, or at best disavow interest in, the occurrence of any underlying event.

ANTI-HISTORICAL TENDENCIES IN SOME LITERARY APPROACHES

Literary Approaches: A Mixed Blessing?

After well over a century of domination by *historical* criticism, biblical studies has welcomed, hesitantly at first but then more readily, the arrival of *literary* approaches to the Bible. The quickening of interest in adopting explicitly literary approaches to biblical interpretation can be attributed in part to "a sense of disappointment and disillusionment with the traditional historical-critical methods" and in part to a desire of biblical scholars to apply trends in secular literary theory to their own discipline.[66] A further motivating factor is the simple fact that the Bible is, after all, a literary work. If the Bible comprises a library of literary genres (as I argued in the first chapter of this book), then a literary approach is not a luxury, but a necessity. Even the Bible's historiography, which I described in chapter 2 as a kind of verbal representational art, requires that we seek to become as competent as possible in the conventions of ancient literature. Without some understanding and appreciation of the literary medium of the Bible, we are likely to misperceive its messages (historical, theological, or whatever).[67] Self-consciously literary approaches often shed new light on the workings of biblical texts, and this new light frequently calls for revision, or even reversal, of previously held opinions about the nature of these texts.[68] Thus, as Thiselton insists, "literary theory in biblical interpretation has

---

[66]Barton, *Reading the Old Testament*, pp. 105–6. The results achieved by historical criticism were deemed by many as theologically rather sparse, if not detrimental. Even among those who did not think "that historical criticism had failed or that its goals were invalid," there was a sense that "something else should also be done" (Powell, *What is Narrative Criticism?* p. 3).

[67]For fuller remarks, see the section "Genre Criticism and Biblical Interpretation" in chap. 1 above. Cf. also Alter, *The World of Biblical Literature*, p. 56.

[68]Cf., e.g., Hall, *Seven Pillories*, p. 110; Powell, *What is Narrative Criticism?* pp. 86–87, 96–98; Polzin, "1 Samuel," p. 305; Long, *Reign and Rejection*, pp. 10–20.

nothing to do with 'icing on the cake' or with 'fluff.' "[69] It is essential.

Essential though it be, the adoption of a literary approach to biblical interpretation is not without attendant dangers. Indeed, Thiselton warns that the application of literary theory to the Bible "provides the most radical challenge to traditional hermeneutical models which has yet arisen."[70] The benefits of becoming acquainted with the literary workings of biblical texts are manifold, to be sure,[71] and this not least for Bible readers interested in historical questions. But under the general rubric *literary approach* is to be found an astonishing diversity of methods, not all of which are well suited for dealing with the Bible. "Literary theory, for good or for ill, brings into biblical studies an intimidating and complicated network of assumptions and methods which were not in origin designed to take account of the particular nature of *biblical* texts. These carry with them their own agenda of deeply philosophical questions about the status of language, the nature of texts, and relations between language, the world, and theories of knowledge."[72]

Surveys of the assumptions and methods of the various literary approaches that have enjoyed some influence in biblical studies—New Criticism, formalism, rhetorical criticism, structuralism, narrative criticism, deconstruction, and the like—are readily available, so that I need not attempt one here.[73] Of more

---

[69]*New Horizons*, p. 473.

[70]Ibid.

[71]See, e.g., ibid., pp. 471–79; Powell, *What is Narrative Criticism?* pp. 85–90; Longman, *Literary Approaches*, pp. 58–62; W. W. Klein, C. L. Blomberg, and R. L. Hubbard, eds., *Introduction to Biblical Interpretation* (Dallas: Word, 1993), pp. 432–38.

[72]Thiselton, *New Horizons*, p. 471.

[73]See, e.g., Barton, *Reading the Old Testament*; Longman, *Literary Approaches*, chap. 1; P. R. House, *Beyond Form Criticism: Essays in Old Testament Literary Criticism*, Sources for Biblical and Theological Studies 2 (Winona Lake: Eisenbrauns, 1992); Powell, *What is Narrative Criticism?* chap. 2; Thiselton, *New Horizons*, chaps. 13–14; as well as the glossaries of literary terms and literary theory by, e.g., Abrams (*Glossary*), C. Baldick (*The Concise Oxford Dictionary of Literary Terms* [Oxford: Oxford University Press, 1990]), J. A. Cuddon (*A Dictionary of Literary Terms and Literary Theory*, 3rd ed., [Oxford: Basil Blackwell, 1991]), J.

pertinence to our present concern with the issue of why scholars disagree over historical questions is the fact that certain of the "literary approaches" tend in *ahistorical*, or even *anti-historical*, directions.[74] In some instances the anti-historical bias simply reflects philosophical assumptions—that is, some of the newer literary approaches "incorporate concepts derived from movements in secular literary criticism that repudiate the significance of historical investigation for the interpretation of texts."[75] In other instances, however, the anti-historical tendency may stem from a lack of clarity over just what the terms *literature* and *history* mean and over how the two interrelate. Recent studies have made it ever more apparent that the Bible's narratives, even those regarded as historiographical, exhibit markedly *literary* traits. Does this mean that they should no longer be considered *historical*? I think not, not only for the reasons presented earlier (especially in Chap. 2) but also for those given in the next paragraph.

The assumption that literature and history constitute mutually exclusive categories is a distinctly modern one, as Lionel Gossman has argued: "For a long time the relation of history to literature was not notably problematic. History was a branch of literature. It was not until the meaning of the word literature, or the institution of literature itself, began to change, toward the end of the eighteenth century, that history came to appear as something distinct from literature."[76] As *literature* increasingly came to be associated with poetry and fiction, and as *history* came to be thought of in positivistic terms as needing to draw "as close

Hawthorn (*A Glossary of Contemporary Literary Theory* [London: Edward Arnold, 1992]).

[74]See Longman, *Literary Approaches*, pp. 54–58; Sternberg, *Poetics*, chap. 1; Gunn, "New Directions in the Study of Biblical Hebrew Narrative." *JSOT* 39 (1987): 73; Geller, "Through Windows and Mirrors into the Bible: History, Literature and Language in the Study of Text," in *A Sense of Text: The Art of Language in the Study of Biblical Literature* (Winona Lake: Eisenbrauns, 1983), p. 39.

[75]Powell, *What is Narrative Criticism?* p. 7; cf. Whitelam, "Between History and Literature: The Social Production of Israel's Traditions of Origin" *SJOT* 2 [1991]: 64.

[76]"History and Literature: Reproduction or Signification," in *The Writing of History: Literary Form and Historical Understanding*, ed. R. H. Canary and H. Kozicki (Madison: University of Wisconsin Press, 1978), p. 3.

as possible, epistemologically and methodologically, to the natural sciences," the gap between literature and history widened. "Finally," continues Gossman, "in our own times, the very idea that the historian's activity consists in discovering and reconstituting, by whatever means, a past reality conceived of as something objectively fixed, has begun to be questioned. The old common ground of history and literature—the idea of mimesis and the central importance of rhetoric—has thus been gradually vacated by both. The practicing historian is now rarely a practicing literary artist."[77]

Whatever may be the modern trend, if the line that we have been taking in this book is at all leading in the right direction, there are grounds for rebridging the gap between literature and history, at least when our concern is with *ancient* historiography.[78] Perhaps one way to accomplish this is to be more circumspect in our definition of literature. As David Robertson points out in *The Old Testament and the Literary Critic*,[79] literature can be subdivided into two general types: *pure* (imaginative, nonutilitarian) literature and *applied* (utilitarian) literature. Much in the Bible "was originally written as applied literature: as history, liturgy, laws, preaching, and the like" (p. 3). This needs to be borne in mind whenever we speak of the Bible as literature, lest we wrongly assume that it will display only the characteristics of pure literature.[80] If literature, broadly conceived, involves "an interpretive presentation of

---

[77]Ibid., pp. 5–7.

[78]It may be noted in passing that many modern historians are calling for renewed attention to the relationship between historiography and literature; see, e.g., A. Rigney, *The Rhetoric of Historical Representation: Three Narrative Histories of the French Revolution* (Cambridge: Cambridge University Press, 1990); A. Cameron, ed., *History as Text: The Writing of Ancient History* (London: Duckworth, 1989).

[79]Philadelphia: Fortress, 1977.

[80]For a fuller discussion of Robertson's own approach and his curious decision to view the Old Testament as pure or imaginative literature, see Long, *Reign and Rejection*, p. 13. On the general point that *literature* includes both referential and non-referential varieties, we may note New Criticism's adoption of T. S. Eliot's coinage *autotelic* to describe literature which has "no end or purpose beyond its own existence" and which is distinguishable from "works that involve practical reference to things outside themselves" (Baldick, *Dictionary of Literary Terms*, p. 19).

experience in an artistic form"[81] and is distinguished by "artful verbal expression and compelling ideas,"[82] then a history may qualify as literature and merit a literary interpretive approach no less than a novel or a poem.

The problem with some modern literary approaches to the Bible is that they tend to dismiss historical questions as either uninteresting or illegitimate. But to bracket out forever or to banish historical questions is to do an injustice to the biblical literature. Much of the Bible presents itself as applied literature—literature meant to serve a communicative function.[83] And literary communication, as analyzed in the now familiar diagram first developed by M. H. Abrams, involves four constituent elements, or "co-ordinates."[84] The central element in Abrams' diagram is the *work* (the text), but it is not the only element. Around it are arranged three others: the *universe* (i.e., the *subject*, which may include "people and actions, ideas and feelings, material things and events, or supersensible essences"[85]), the *artist* (the author or authors), and the *audience* (the reader or reading community). The *text* rightfully belongs in the middle because this is where the other three elements meet in the act of literary communication, as the author presents the universe (subject matter) via the text to the reader. Historical criticism, in its preoccupation with questions of authorship and textual *pre*history, frequently fails to give the "text as it stands" adequate consideration in its own right and on its own terms before moving to extratextual issues. Literary criticism seeks to redress the balance by emphasizing the text and, more recently,

---

[81]L. Ryken, *The Literature of the Bible* (Grand Rapids: Zondervan, 1974), p. 13.

[82]A. Berlin, "On the Bible as Literature," *Proof* 2 (1982): 324.

[83]Cf. Thiselton, *New Horizons*, p. 502: "Many, perhaps most, of the biblical writings at one level remain 'literary'; but it is even more fundamental to their *raison d'etre* that they reflect what human beings say and do, and how, in turn, they are addressed, *in everyday life*. This is not to deny that these texts are often also literary products, which are designed to produce certain *effects*, but *it is to deny that this latter aspect provides the primary, only, or supposedly most comprehensive model of meaning.*"

[84]*The Mirror and the Lamp: Romantic Theory and the Critical Tradition* (New York: Oxford University Press, 1953), pp. 3–29. Cf. also Barton, *Reading the Old Testament*, pp. 199–203; Longman, *Literary Approaches*, p. 18.

[85]Abrams, *Mirror*, p. 6.

the reader (as we shall see below). Attentiveness to text and reader can be welcomed, *but not if it becomes excessive to the point of excluding the other coordinates of author and universe.* "Text-immanent exegesis" is of great value, as Barton has stressed, but only if "counter-intuitive tendencies" (such as an "unreasonable hatred of authorial intention, referential meaning, and the possibility of paraphrase or restatement") are kept in check.[86]

If the last several decades have witnessed a shift of interest in biblical studies from historical concerns with author, historical event, and textual prehistory to a (sometimes myopic) focus on the text, the last decade or so has witnessed a shift to the last remaining co-ordinate in Abrams's diagram, the *reader.* In the next section we shall consider reader-response criticism, which, like some of its literary cousins, can (but need not necessarily) tend in an anti-historical direction.

Reader-Response Criticism: Where's the Meaning?

No less than the literary approaches discussed in the preceding section, reader-response criticism is characterized by great variety. Robert Fowler, in *Let the Reader Understand: Reader-Response Criticism and the Gospel of Mark*, comments that "the spectrum of reader-response critics is so broad that whether they can all be categorized under that one heading is questionable."[87] Fowler is nevertheless able to highlight two common features shared by "most varieties of reader-response criticism": "(1) a preeminent concern for the reader and the reading experience and (2) a critical model of the reading experience, which itself has two major aspects: (a) an understanding of reading as a dynamic, concrete, temporal experience, instead of the abstract perception of a spatial form; and (b) an emphasis on meaning as event instead of meaning as content" (p. 25).

The first feature of reader-response criticism can be cautiously welcomed. In the discussion of the "Characteristics of Success-

---

[86]*Reading the Old Testament*, p. 191.
[87](Minneapolis: Fortress, 1991), p. 25; cf. p. 23. For a summary of the diversity among reader-response approaches, see Thiselton, *New Horizons*, p. 529.

ful Representation" in chapter 2, we noted the way in which representational painting achieves its goal by "limiting the depiction of details to a suggestive few so as to allow the mind of the viewers to fill in the rest." The same is true of representational narrative, so that focusing on the way in which readers are active in *filling in* or *completing the picture* on the basis of promptings embedded in the text can be illuminating.[88] That Fowler should describe concern for the reader as "preeminent," however, is disquieting. It hints at what in fact turns out to be the case for many reader-response approaches: in their desire to correct the imbalance resulting from neglect of the readerly element, some reader-response theories themselves end up neglecting the other vital elements in the act of literary communication—viz., text, author, and universe (e.g., for historiographical texts, the people and events referred to).

As for the "critical model of the reading experience" described by Fowler, the most perplexing aspect is its "emphasis on meaning as event instead of meaning as content."[89] This seems to me to involve a blurring of the distinction between *meaning* and *perception of meaning* or, as speech act theory would put it, between *illocution* (what the speaker wishes to accomplish in uttering a *locution*) and *perlocution* (the effect the speech act actually has on the hearer). Fowler is not unaware of the problematic status of *meaning* in reader-response theory: "Concerning meaning, is its locus in the text or in the reader?" (p. 34). But on at least one occasion in his discussion he evidences the kind of confusion over the locus of meaning that typifies many reader-response approaches. He writes:

> The obverse of the illocutionary force set in motion by the speaker is the hearer's apprehension or uptake of that illocutionary force (see chap. 1). Both illocutionary force and its *uptake* are functions of the context of the utterance, which is to say that the meaning of an

---

[88]Cf. Thiselton's comments (*New Horizons*, p. 515) on Wolfgang Iser's use of "a theory of perception to establish the role of readers in *filling in or completing* a textual meaning which would otherwise remain only potential rather than actual."

[89]I have already commented on the inadequacy of Fowler's assumption that "perception of a spatial form" is *not* "a dynamic, concrete, temporal experience" (see p. 63, n. 20).

illocution in speech act theory has the nature of dynamic event rather than static content. Thus does speech act theory teach us not to seek meanings in locutions alone but in the exercise and uptake of the illocutionary force of utterances. *In brief, an utterance means what it does, not what it says.* (p. 48; my italics)

Fowler is quite correct to insist that the meaning of a speech act rests not only in the locution (the words themselves) but in the illocutionary force behind them (e.g., the intent to inform, persuade, threaten, console, etc.). But his inclusion of "uptake" in the definition of meaning is troubling and runs counter to common-sense and everyday experience. "Don't forget to write," John reminds Mary as she boards the airplane. "Why didn't you write me?" he chides her upon her return. "Oh," she responds, "the speech act we shared didn't mean that I should write *to you*. That's not the way I took it. Your exact words (your *locution*) were 'don't forget to write,' and I did write a few things: a shopping list, a letter to my mother, my name on the hotel register. Your utterance couldn't have meant that I should write to you, an utterance means what it does, not what it says." Is John likely to find Mary's construal of the meaning of his speech act convincing? She has wrongly (con)fused *his* illocutionary intent and *her* perlocutionary "uptake" as the standard by which the meaning of his speech act is to be measured.

Fowler's inclusion of "uptake" in his definition of "meaning" is all the more curious in the light of what he has to say in the paragraph immediately preceding the above quotation. He explains that locutions "refer just to the utterances themselves," while "*illocutions* are what a speaker intends to do by uttering a particular locution, and *perlocutions* are what the speaker actually accomplishes through uttering the locution." Further, he asserts that perlocutions can be "laid aside" as "ultimately beyond anyone's control" (pp. 47–48). Why then does he fuse "uptake" (perlocution) to the concept of illocution? Again, it seems to me that this illicit *fusion* typifies the *confusion* found in some reader-response theories of meaning.

I have intentionally chosen to focus on Fowler's work because his reader-response approach is on the whole insightful, moderate, and useful. Unlike some of the more radical reader-response critics, Fowler recognizes that "the text imposes power-ful constraints upon the reading experience, constraints that to this point have been acknowledged only sporadically and unsystemati-cally" (p. 15). In this moderate stance, which allows the text a vital role in constraining readers' perceptions of meaning, Fowler is joined by others such as Wolfgang Iser and Umberto Eco. But within the reader-response camp there are also those (Stanley Fish, for example, in his later writings) who divest texts (and so, of course, also authors of texts) of virtually all authority in the establishment of meaning. "The reader's response is not *to* the meaning: it *is* the meaning," writes Fish.[90]

In such extreme versions of reader-response criticism, the text becomes little more than a Rorschach ink blot; how you "read" the ink on paper, whether text or blot, may reveal much about *you* (or your interpretive community), but little indeed about anything else (thus the recent emphasis on the "ethics of ideological reading"—*you, not the text or its author, are responsible for what you read out of the text*). Where biblical texts are read in this extreme fashion, questions of authorial intent and historical reference either will never be asked or will be dismissed as inappropriate. No longer will the Bible have any power to address readers or to change them "from outside."[91] Ultimately, as Thiselton warns, Fish's brand of reader-response criticism can disintegrate "into the anarchy in which *the most militant pressure-group actually carries the day about what satisfies their pragmatic criteria*

---

[90]Quoted in Thiselton, *New Horizons*, p. 474. For a full discussion of the weaknesses of Fish's approach, especially his insistence that one must choose between a formalist approach in which the text absolutely determines reader perceptions and a socio-pragmatic approach in which readers themselves (or more properly the reading community) autonomously determine what counts as "right reading," see ibid., pp. 535–50. Thiselton insists rather that "*it is not the case, as Fish suggests it is, that we must choose between the sharply-bounded crystalline purity of formalist concepts and the unstable concepts of contextual pragmatism. Concepts may function with a measure of operational stability, but with 'blurred edges.'* Differences of social context and practice may *push or pull them into relatively different shapes*, but do not necessarily change their stable *identity*" (p. 541).

[91]Ibid., pp. 503–50 *passim*.

of 'right' reading."[92] As to its consequences for Christian faith, such a "socio-pragmatic hermeneutics transposes the meaning of texts into projections which are *potentially idolatrous* as instruments of self-affirmation. *Such a model transposes a Christian theology of grace and revelation into a phenomenology of religious self-discovery."*[93]

Equally in vogue among some contemporary biblical scholars, and similar in effect to the more radical reader-response theories in its denial that meaning resides in authorial intent as this comes to expression in texts, is the literary theory of *deconstruction*, sometimes referred to as *post-structuralism*. As "a philosophically skeptical approach to the possibility of coherent meaning in language," deconstruction quite naturally challenges "the status of the author's intention or of the external world as a source of meaning in texts."[94] Indeed, for deconstructionists, "a text does not have a meaning in the sense of something that is 'signified,' that is meant, by the configuration of the words of which it consists." Rather, "the text is said to practice 'the infinite deferral of the signified.' "[95] Because of the ceaseless play of language, meaning is ultimately indeterminate, or undecidable. And since "the author is no longer seen as the source of meaning, . . . deconstruction is guilty of being an accessory after the fact with regard to the death of the author."[96] Having dispatched the author (and therewith also any notion of an author's illocutionary intent), deconstruction "invites us instead to read any writing 'creatively,' as a play of systemic 'differences' which generate innumerable possibilities of meaning."[97]

Clearly, a deconstructionist approach to textual meaning will not prove fruitful for those wishing to discover what a text may have to say about times past. An historical approach requires a degree of confidence in the ability of texts to serve as a medium for

---

[92]Ibid., p. 535, cf. 515.

[93]Ibid., p. 550.

[94]Baldick, *Dictionary of Literary Terms*, p. 51.

[95]P. D. Juhl, "Playing with Texts: Can Deconstruction Account for Critical Practice?" in *Criticism and Critical Theory*, ed. Jeremy Hawthorn (London: Edward Arnold, 1984), p. 59.

[96]Hawthorn, *Glossary of Contemporary Literary Theory*, p. 49.

[97]Abrams, *Glossary*, p. 150.

communication between writer and reader. But, as Juhl points out, if the deconstructionist theory "is even roughly correct, it is clear that anything like a speech act model of literary interpretation cannot be right." The converse, however, is also true, as Juhls goes on to observe: "if there is such a thing as understanding a text and if that is essentially like understanding a person's speech act and hence necessarily involves reference to the speaker's intentions, then not much remains of the theory of the text sketched above."[98]

So, what does the future hold? The deconstructionist wave will presumably continue to play itself out on the beach of scholarly fashion, and some of its insights may leave a lasting mark. But since even the most ardent deconstructionists tend to assume a more traditional concept of meaning in their own critical practice (e.g., they expect their audiences to "get their drift"), Wright is correct that "deconstructive criticism probably will go away: it is in the nature of sudden reflex-movements of absurdist cognitive skepticism to be short-lived."[99] Reader-response criticism may enjoy a longer tenure, provided that common sense prevails and the less radical forms of reader-response theory are adopted (i.e., those that, while giving attention to the often neglected *readerly* aspect of literary communication, nevertheless also take account of *text, author*, and *universe*.)[100] Modern literary approaches to the Bible, at least those that can avoid falling into a counter-intuitive, anti-historical bias, may well develop a "symbiotic relationship" with "historical approaches to the text."[101] After all, careful literary reading is a prerequisite of responsible historical

---

[98]"Playing with Texts," p. 60. For a critique of deconstruction's "anti-historical," "ultra-relativist," "reader's liberationist" hermeneutic and a qualified commendation of a dialogue model of textual communication in which texts are treated as persons who address us from outside and with whom we may agree or disagree, see I. Wright, "History, Hermeneutics, Deconstruction," in *Criticism*, ed. Hawthorn, pp. 83–98.

[99]Ibid., p. 88.

[100]An example would be Powell's approach in *What is Narrative Criticism?*; Powell (p. 16) classifies his own method as a kind of reader-response criticism at the opposite end of the spectrum from deconstruction.

[101]Ibid., p. 98.

reconstruction. That is to say, a conscientious, fair-minded attempt to understand a biblical text on its own terms is logically prior to any historicizing about it. Therefore, the more skilled biblical interpreters become in reading texts *literarily*, the more competent they will become in assessing them *historically*.

We may bring this section to a close by observing that, as in so many areas of life, beatitude in biblical interpretation comes in finding balance and avoiding one-sided extremes. The problem with approaches that go so far wrong is often simply that they go so far. To the extent that biblical literature comprises *communicative* texts,[102] what is needed in biblical interpretation is an integrative approach that gives due attention to all the co-ordinates of Abrams' model of literary communication—author, reader, and reference as these meet on the ground of text.

AN EXAMPLE: THE EMERGENCE OF ISRAEL IN CANAAN DEBATE

My intent in this chapter has been to address the question of why it is that biblical scholars often disagree profoundly in their historical assessments of the biblical traditions and the biblical periods. In pursuing this question, I have explored several prominent approaches to biblical interpretation and historical reconstruction (though of course I have not attempted anything like a comprehensive survey). We are now in a position to look at a specific example, and the much-debated question of the emergence of Israel in Canaan comes to mind. It is hard to think of any period in Israel's history about which opinions differ more widely and over which more ink has been spilt in recent years. To attempt a survey of the literature that has appeared on this subject even during the last decade would require far more space than I can spare here. My intent, rather, will be simply to mention some of the main lines of approach and, more particularly, to ask how the tendencies of the various criticisms discussed above might bear on the kinds of questions asked and the results achieved.

---

[102]On the "Functions of Biblical Literature," see the section by that name in Longman, *Literary Approaches*, pp. 68–71.

Until the modern period, the general understanding of how Israel came to be in Canaan was that it entered from the outside by means of conquest, as described particularly in the book of Joshua. In this century, however, a number of other scenarios have been proposed, such as Alt's *infiltration theory*, Mendenhall's *peasant revolt theory* (revived and modified in Gottwald's *social revolution theory*), and a variety of more recent theories in which Israel is thought to have been formed from nomadic or displaced populations already indigenous to Canaan (see the works of Fritz, Finkelstein, Callaway, Lemche, Coote and Whitelam, etc.).[103]

The preference for alternatives to the conquest model may be accounted for in several ways. One predisposing factor (which relates to our earlier discussion of the presuppositions of traditional historical criticism) is the modernist assumption that texts in which divine agency plays any part are to be considered historically suspect. By this measure, of course, both Joshua and Judges would hardly be deemed trustworthy as historical sources. But quite apart from this modern a priori, which not all will share, there is also a general sense that the conquest model simply does not square with recent archaeological findings. Specifically, archaeology has failed to provide evidence of the extensive destruction commonly associated with the conquest model. Moreover, there is the perception that Joshua and Judges present rather different, even conflicting, pictures of the conquest, and this quite naturally leads some to doubt the historical plausibility of the one or the other, or both. Finally, increased literary sensitivities and recognition of the challenge of properly discerning textual truth claims has caused some scholars to be more open to the possibility that the book of Joshua, for instance, does not even *intend* to be taken historically.

How are we to assess these considerations? Having already noted the inappropriateness of the anti-theological tendency of traditional historical criticism, we may now focus on the other concerns. Each of these, in its own way, has to do with the way

---

[103]For a convenient summary and critique of these various positions, plus a proposal of his own, see J. J. Bimson, "The origins of Israel in Canaan: an examination of recent theories," *Them* 15/1 (1989): 4–15.

the biblical texts are *read*. First, then, let us consider the apparent conflict between the biblical tradition and the archaeological data. In the popular (and, indeed, scholarly) imagination there has crystallized over the years a picture of the Israelite conquest of Canaan as an event of almost unprecedented violence and destructiveness.[104] But is this in fact the *biblical* picture? Has the *literature* been properly read before turning to archaeology? In our discussion of the anti-literary tendency of some sociological and archaeological approaches, we noted the proclivity of such approaches to bracket out or even to ban literary considerations in the assessment of material evidence. Whatever may be the pros and cons of this attempt at methodological purity, the deficit is that experts in biblical literature and indeed literary expertise in general are sometimes lacking from the archaeological team.[105] This in itself need not be so bad, provided that field archaeologists are careful always to consult with experts in the biblical literature before beginning to speculate about the import of their discoveries for questions of biblical history or, failing that, are willing simply to refrain from such speculation. But sometimes archaeologists who exercise the greatest of care and rigor in their own discipline fall into the trap of giving the biblical text a rather flat, unnuanced reading and then, on the basis of this reading, pronouncing on the "fit" or "lack of fit" between the Bible and the archaeological data.

But this brings us back to the important question: does the Bible, properly understood, depict a violent conquest involving great destruction of persons and property? The answer is yes and no. *Yes*, because both Joshua and Judges attest that Israel entered Canaan from outside and that this involved much loss of life to the indigenous populations, but *no*, because property damage is said to

---

[104]E.g., W. S. LaSor et al. (*Old Testament Survey* [Grand Rapids: Eerdmans, 1982], p. 214) write: "A careful reading of Joshua would give the impression that the Israelites had 'devoted' every city and destroyed every pagan altar. The story of the Conquest stresses that side."

[105]For a balanced approach that seeks to respect the individual integrity of both archaeological and literary studies while at the same time taking care to bring the two together in a "dialogical method," see J. F. Strange, "Some Implications of Archaeology for New Testament Studies," in *What Has Archaeology*, ed. Charlesworth and Weaver, pp. 23–59.

have been much more minimal. Specifically, the Book of Joshua testifies that the populations of numerous cities were placed under the ban and totally destroyed (e.g., Makkedah, Libnah, Lachish, Eglon, Hebron, and Debir [10:28–39]), but of only three sites is it explicitly said that property, too, was utterly destroyed: Jericho (6:24), Ai (8:28; 10:1), and Hazor (11:12–14). The latter instance is particularly instructive, for while the report of Joshua's defeat of Jabin's coalition (11:1–5) states that "Joshua took all these royal cities and their kings and put them to the sword. He totally destroyed them, as Moses the servant of the LORD had commanded" (v. 12), it immediately adds that "Israel did not burn any of the cities built on their mounds—except Hazor, which Joshua burned" (v. 13). Clearly, then, to "take a city," "put it to the sword," and "utterly destroy it" (that is, place it under the ban) implies the decimation (or, at least, driving out) of its population but may say nothing of property damage. The picture presented in Joshua is that destruction of property was the exception, not the rule. Indeed, 24:13 finds Israel living in "cities you did not build" (see also Deut. 6:10–11).[106]

In the light of the *literary* evidence, then, it is a mistake to look for extensive *archaeological* evidence of the conquest, as scholars across the theological spectrum have tended to do.[107] And it is a double error to assume that if archaeology fails to yield evidence of wide-spread destruction in this or that time period, then the conquest could not have taken place at that time, or did not take place at all.[108]

---

[106]The book of Judges reports the destruction of several other cities—Zephath by the men of Judah (Judg. 1:17), Shechem by Abimelech (9:45), and Laish by the Danites (18:27)—but the basic pattern is the same, populations were destroyed or displaced but cities remained.

[107]On this point, see B. K. Waltke, "Palestinian Artifactual Evidence Supporting the Early Date of the Exodus," *Bibliotheca Sacra* 129 (1972): 34–35; E. H. Merrill, "Palestinian Archaeology and the Date of the Conquest: Do Tells Tell Tales?" *Grace Theological Journal* 3 (1982): 107–21; *idem*, "The LB/EI Transition and the Emergence of Israel: An Assessment and Preliminary Proposal" (forthcoming).

[108]Unfortunately, this error is all too common. For instance, M. D. Coogan ("Archaeology and Biblical Studies: The Book of Joshua," in *Hebrew Bible*, ed. Propp et al., pp. 22–23), denies the "essential historicity" of the list of conquered kings in Joshua 12:9–24 on the basis of a supposed conflict between archaeology

This is not to say, of course, that archaeology may not shed significant light on the Israelite *settlement* in Canaan. In a recent volume of the *Scandinavian Journal of the Old Testament* dedicated to the question of the emergence of Israel in Canaan, the volume's editor, Diana Edelman, points to four areas of growing consensus: (1) that beginning in the Late Bronze Age and continuing throughout the Iron I period "population shifts and displacements" were taking place in Canaan, the net result of which was "the growth of new settlements in the Cisjordanian highlands"; (2) that "the Merneptah Stele indicates the existence of some entity called Israel somewhere in Palestine in the late 13th century"; (3) that "Israel is somehow to be related to the surge in small settlements in the highlands during the end of the Late Bronze–Iron I periods," though "how this relationship is to be understood remains problematic"; (4) that "the biblical texts must be used with great caution in reconstructing the history of Israel's origins and prestate conditions."[109] The issue, of course, is how these archaeological results are to be interpreted and applied to the questions of Israel in Canaan. The predominant contemporary approach is to associate these transformations with Israel's initial *emergence* in Canaan and as a consequence to dismiss the possibility of a conquest in favor of one of the other models. But as Bimson has recently argued, the Merneptah (or Merenptah) Stele presents something of a problem for this view, and it is equally possible to

and text. Noting that the archaeological evidence suggests that the city of Lachish was destroyed "at least a century after the destruction of Late Bronze Age Hazor," Coogan concludes that this "contradicts the plain sense of the biblical narrative in Joshua, namely that the cities, or at least their populations, were destroyed within a generation." But Coogan's statement of the "plain sense" is imprecise; were the *cities* themselves destroyed or just their *citizens*? Only if it were the former could we expect to find much evidence in the archaeological record. But as we have already seen, destruction of cities was the exception, not the rule. Thus, the date of the destruction of the *city* of Lachish is irrelevant to the list of kings in question. Coogan's implicit reading of the textual witness is in fact better than his explicit statement of the "plain sense," for he recognizes that the biblical narrators did *not* in fact claim that many of the cities themselves were destroyed.

[109] *Toward a Consensus on the Emergence of Israel in Canaan*, Papers Read at the SBL/ASOR Hebrew Bible, History and Archaeology Section (New Orleans, 18th November 1990), *SJOT* 2 (1991): 4–5.

regard the proliferation of Iron I highland sites as evidence of the
sedentarization (settling down) of Israel towards the end of the
Judges period.[110] Which explanation one favors will depend in part
on how seriously one is willing to take the "biblical texts"
mentioned in item 4 above and the care with which one reads
them.

This brings us to the next reason that many contemporary
scholars have moved away from the conquest model as an
explanation of Israel's emergence in Canaan. This is their sense
that Joshua and Judges mutually undermine one another's historical credibility by painting conflicting pictures of the conquest—the
former a hugely successful *Blitzkrieg* and the latter a much more
protracted, complex affair.[111] It is quite true, of course, that the
two books present different pictures, but are they in fact
contradictory? While the question cannot be adequately addressed
in the space available here, it may at least be observed that the
sense of tension between the two books is greatly lessened when
each is understood on its own terms and in the light of its own
purposes. At the risk of oversimplification, it could be said that the
book of Joshua stresses God's faithfulness in *giving* his people the
land (i.e., in giving them the upper hand by not allowing any of
their adversaries to withstand them),[112] while Judges stresses the
people's failure to act faithfully in *occupying* it.[113] The introductory
section of Judges (1:1–3:6), for example, describes how "after the
death of Joshua" (1:1) the people of Israel gradually lost their grip
on the land until, instead of having the upper hand, they found
themselves living among the Canaanites, intermarrying with them

[110]"Merenptah's Israel and Recent Theories of Israelite Origins," *JSOT* 49 (1991):
3–29.

[111]E.g., a flat reading of Josh. 21:43–45 in comparison with Judg. 2: 21–23 might
create such an impression. For a brief summary of this view and a response, see L.
K. Younger, *Ancient Conquest Accounts: A Study in Ancient Near Eastern and Biblical
History Writing,* JSOTS 98 (Sheffield: JSOT, 1990), pp. 241–47.

[112]See, e.g., Josh. 21:43–45; 23:9. References to the Lord giving the land (of
Canaan) to his people are at least five times as frequent in Joshua as in Judges.

[113]Younger (*Ancient Conquest Accounts,* p. 246) aptly distinguishes between
subjugation and *occupation.*

and worshipping their gods (3:5–6).[114] But even the book of Joshua, amidst its stress on Joshua's success in taking the land (11:16, 23), acknowledges that the war was a protracted affair (11:18), that there was much to be done even after the land was "subdued" (18:1; see also v. 3), and that the tribes of Israel sometimes failed to occupy fully their allotted territory (e.g., 13:13; 17:12). Thus Joshua can speak in the same breath of Israel having "rest from all their enemies round about" (23:1) and yet needing still to contend with "these nations that remain among you" (23:7). In sum, it seems that the pictures presented by the books of Joshua and Judges, though different in their emphases, are ultimately compatible and complementary.

We come then to a final reason why the conquest model is sometimes rejected in favor of one of the other theories. Simply put, this has to do with the anti-historical tendency that characterizes some modern literary approaches to the Bible. A literary approach can, of course, be of great value in establishing the character and historical import of a book like Joshua.[115] But for those interpreters who take their cue from trends in secular literary criticism that are essentially ahistorical in orientation, historical questions can easily be seen as uninteresting and even unwelcome interruptions to the enjoyment of a *good story* such as the book of Joshua presents. Of course, if a convincing case were to be made that the book of Joshua means to present itself as nothing more than a good story, that it doesn't at all intend to make any sort of historical truth claim, then it would not only be permissible to dismiss historical considerations from the interpretive enterprise, but mandatory. But so long as an historiographical impulse is felt to be present, valid interpretation must take this into account and seek to explore the precise nature of the claims made. In the case of the book of Joshua, it is difficult to escape the conclusion that,

---

[114]Of particular interest is the way in which the section 1:16–36 conveys a sense of progressive decline in Israel's ability to displace the Canaanites; see B. G. Webb, *The Book of Judges: An Integrated Reading*, JSOTS 46 (Sheffield: JSOT, 1987), pp. 88–101.

[115]Again, we may mention as an example Younger's ground-breaking semiotic analysis of ancient Near Eastern conquest accounts, including the accounts in Joshua and Judges (*Ancient Conquest Accounts*).

whatever simplifications, idealizations, and hyperbole may be present, a historiographical claim is being made that military conquest played a significant role in Israel's emergence in Canaan.

CONCLUSION

In the first chapter of this book, and often thereafter, I noted that biblical literature tends to exhibit three basic impulses: theological (or ideological), historical (or referential), and literary (or aesthetic). The presence of the one or the other may be more pronounced in some biblical passages than in others, but there are relatively few places in the Bible, at least in the Bible's narratives, where one of the three is entirely absent. An example of biblical narratives lacking in the historical impulse would, of course, be parables, but even parables generally function within a larger narrative framework that itself exhibits an historical impulse.

In this chapter, I have asked why scholars so often come to very different conclusions regarding the historical import of biblical passages. The results of our exploration of this question suggest that the answer has much to do both with the models of reality held by different scholars and with their consequent preference for certain types of methods, or approaches. As this chapter now draws to a close, it is worth noting that each of the several approaches discussed above appears deficient precisely to the degree that it downplays or dismisses one of the three characteristic impulses of biblical narrative. Some historical-critical approaches methodologically exclude divine agency (the theological impulse), some social-scientific and archaeological approaches downplay the value of texts (the literary impulse), and some literary approaches systematically ignore the possibility that texts may be referential (the historical impulse). Where biblical scholars adopt one or the other of these deficient approaches in seeking to reconstruct (or deconstruct) biblical history, it is not surprising that they should come to radically differing results.

But to end on a more positive note, I would add that each of the approaches, if properly conceived and incorporated into a synthetic methodological symbiosis, can serve a very useful function. A proper literary approach helps us to read texts on their

own terms and thus to come to more accurate conclusions
regarding textual truth claims (historical and otherwise). The fruits
of sociological and archaeological study provide much-needed
flesh to the bones of biblical history. And historical criticism's
three principles of criticism, analogy, and correlation, if conceived
in terms appropriate to the object of study (in this instance the
Bible), offer helpful guidelines for assessing evidence and drawing
historical conclusions.

5

HISTORY AND HERMENEUTICS
How Then Should We Read the Bible
"Historically"?

We come now to that point in our journey when we may begin to draw some conclusions about how the traveler interested in historical questions should traverse the biblical landscape. The basic question we face is this: can we develop an approach that will help us discover the historical import of the various stages in our journey through the Bible? How can we know, for example, when reading this or that biblical narrative, whether we are to read it as historiography—viz., an account claiming to represent and interpret events of the past—or as some other literary genre? What about books like Jonah and Job? Masterful literature with unmistakably didactic intentions, these books are among the most debated with respect to their historiographical intentions and are likely to remain so.[1] Some scholars extend the uncertainty regarding historiographical intentionality to cover much, or even most, of the biblical testimony. Reflecting recently on the study of Israelite history, Maxwell Miller laments that some scholars "regard the Bible as essentially useless for the historian's purposes. It is 'a holy book that tells stories.' "[2]

While wishing to remain far from such a reductionistic

---

[1]The relative independence of these two books from a larger literary context may also contribute to their debated status; we have already discussed the importance of *context* for determining the primary *purpose* of a work of literature (chap. 2, section "History as Representational Art").

[2]"Reflections," p. 74.

approach to the biblical narratives, we must nevertheless admit that, with our present state of knowledge, there may be times in our reading of Scripture when we are simply not sure whether, or to what precise degree, a biblical story means to be taken as a historical account. This admission will seem as obvious as it is necessary to some students of the Bible, but it will likely make others uneasy. Silva has noted, for example, that "for some conservative Christians, certainty about historical details appears to be inseparable from a high view of Scripture." But as Silva rightly goes on to argue, "such a connection [i.e., between the historicity of a scriptural account and the veracity of scripture itself] is valid . . . only where Scripture speaks directly and unambiguously on the historical question involved."[3] In other words, only where a text's *truth claims* involve historicity does a denial of historicity become a denial of the *truth value* of the biblical text, and thus become a problem for those holding a high view of Scripture.

Understanding the matter in this way, we may freely admit to the presence of some border cases where we are uncertain whether or to what degree a text's truth claims involve historicity. It would be a grave error, however, to extend this uncertainty respecting *some* passages of Scripture to cover *all* passages of Scripture. And it would be an equally grave error to cite our occasional historical uncertainties as grounds for treating the whole Bible as if its overall truth value could somehow stand apart from historical questions.[4] If, as Halpern has recently argued at length, the writers of the Bible's historiographical portions "had authentic antiquarian intentions"—that is, if "they meant to furnish fair and accurate representations of Israelite antiquity"—then valid interpretation must recognize these intentions and the truth claims implied by them and admit that the truth value of the Bible stands or falls, in part at least, on questions of history and historicity.[5]

---

[3]"Historical Reconstruction," p. 111.

[4]The vital relationship between biblical historicity and authentic Christian faith was discussed in chap. 3 above.

[5]*First Historians*, p. 3. For a compelling case for the antiquarian intentions of, e.g., the writer of Luke-Acts, see C. Hemer, *Book of Acts*, esp. chaps. 1–3. New Testament references suggestive of the high value placed on giving an accurate

Having encountered the concepts of *truth claim* and *truth value* at numerous junctures in our discussion so far, we may now build on them in what follows. Part of the aim of the present chapter will be to show how these concepts provide the basis of a procedure for exploring the historical import of biblical passages as we encounter them. My aim will not be to discuss specific methods in any detail but, rather, to suggest how the various methods associated with Bible study can be fruitfully arranged under the rubrics *truth claim* and *truth value* as we seek to read the Bible historically. Before we can discuss methods, however, I must address the prior question of models. As we have already seen (particularly in the preceding chapter), there is a close correlation between one's model of reality (that is, one's worldview or fundamental set of background beliefs) and the methods of study that one deems appropriate. Since much confusion and even harm can result where methods are adopted and employed without adequate reflection on the model(s) of reality underlying them, it is to the question of models that we must first turn in preparing to explore the historical import of a biblical passage.

PREPARATION: CONTEMPLATING MODELS

In an essay entitled "The Role of Theory in Biblical Criticism,"[6] E. L. Greenstein observes that "in biblical studies we often argue as though we all shared the same beliefs and principles, as though the field were all built upon a single theoretical foundation. But it is not" (p. 167). Greenstein acknowledges the link between one's model (one's "theoretical foundation") and one's methods, and he insists that "if we have different models, and then of necessity different methods—and we do—we can only understand each other in the terms of each other's theories" (p. 173). In other words, proper evaluation of a specific interpretation (one's own or someone else's) of a given biblical passage must

---

account of past events could be multiplied: e.g., in addition to the prologue to Luke, also John 20:30–31; 21:24–25; Acts 4:20; 2 Pet 1:16; 2:3; 1 John 1:1.

[6]In *Proceedings of the Ninth World Congress of Jewish Studies: Jerusalem, August 4–12, 1985* (Jerusalem: World Union of Jewish Studies, 1986), pp. 167–74.

have at least two foci—viz., the truth of the fundamental assumptions (model of reality) behind the interpretation and the appropriateness of the means (methodological steps) by which the interpretation is arrived at. Greenstein puts it this way: "I can get somewhere when I challenge the deductions you make from your fundamental assumptions. But I can get nowhere if I think I am challenging your deductions when in fact I am differing from your assumptions, your presuppositions, your premises, your beliefs" (p. 167).

The issue of fundamental assumptions, presuppositions, premises, beliefs, worldview, model of reality, and so forth (the terms are many but the concept is the same) must be approached on several levels. Not only must I, as an interpreter, seek to gain a more conscious awareness of my own worldview,[7] but I must also seek to discover the worldview embodied in the text I am studying, the worldview undergirding the method I am applying, and the worldviews held by other interpreters whose writings I am consulting. Where there are differences at the fundamental level of worldview, tensions and disagreements on the levels of interpretation and/or application are inevitable. If the interpreter's model of reality is distinctly different from that embodied in the text, there will be tension. If a method is applied to a text whose fundamental assumptions about the world and reality run counter to the assumptions underlying the method, there will be tensions. If interpreters approaching a given text disagree fundamentally on how they view reality, they will likely also disagree on how to interpret the text, or at least on whether the text, once interpreted, is to be accepted as trustworthy and authoritative.[8]

Once we recognize that various texts and various interpreters assume a variety of worldviews, the question of validity arises.

---

[7]"All historians work from some philosophical or theological base, whether consciously or not" (Miller, "Reflections," p. 65).

[8]This is not to suggest that an appeal to presuppositions, or fundamental assumptions, can be used as a short-cut by which to accept or reject specific interpretations of Scripture or specific historical reconstructions (see Silva, "Historical Reconstruction," pp. 123–25, 131); still, "one can hardly deny that a scholar's fundamental assumptions about God will radically affect one's handling of the biblical material" (ibid., p. 124).

Are all worldviews equally valid? In many modern societies there is an insistence that individuals have the right to believe what they will. But this affirmation need not, and should not, slide into the kind of relativism or subjectivism that would insist that every individual's beliefs are right. Put another way, the *right to believe* and the *rightness of belief* are separate issues, the former by no means guaranteeing the latter. Common sense would tell us that if in using the phrase *model of reality* we mean *Reality* in an ultimate sense, then by definition there can be only one completely valid worldview.[9] Only one view of the world can be in every respect true to the way things are. To be sure, no fallible human being can claim fully to have grasped this "perfect worldview." But it is still fair to say that some worldviews are better, more promising, more likely to be true than others. In his recent book entitled *Faith and Reason: Searching for a Rational Faith*, Ronald Nash explores such questions as what a worldview is, what constitutes a Christian worldview, and even how to choose a worldview.[10] Nash's treatment is generally helpful but cannot be discussed further here.

For our present purposes, it is only necessary to stress the vital importance, as a first step in the historical interpretation of the Bible, of examining worldviews—our own, that embodied in the text, that implied by the method, and those embraced by other interpreters. As already noted, where worldviews differ interpretive tensions will surely arise. A further observation can now be made. The manner in which interpreters go about arbitrating the points of tension is a sure indication of where their fundamental commitments lie. Where is the final test of truth to be found? In the Bible? In the interpretive community of faith? In the academic community? Or in the individual interpreter as a sentient and rational being? Of course, all of these are in some measure involved. But the question is who or what, in the final analysis, represents the locus of ultimate authority for the interpreter.

---

[9]For the kind of realism I have in mind here, see M. A. Noll, *Between Faith and Criticism: Evangelicals, Scholarship, and the Bible in America* (San Francisco: Harper & Row, 1986), p. 146.

[10](Grand Rapids: Zondervan, 1988), esp. chaps. 2–4. Cf. also Nash's *Worldviews in Conflict: Choosing Christianity in a World of Ideas* (Grand Rapids: Zondervan, 1992).

Some interpreters seek to accord the Bible itself this status, in keeping with the reformation principle of *sola Scriptura*. Indeed, the Bible appears to demand as much, for it teaches, as Royce Gruenler reminds us, "a definite hierarchy of authority by which God's Word takes precedence over his revelation in nature and self, requiring a rebirthing of heart and mind."[11] Thus, while not denying the light of nature or of personal experience, interpreters who take this approach will allow the biblical testimony to play the primary role in shaping their view of the world and of reality. If convinced for example that Scripture, rightly understood, claims to report instances in which God has directly intervened in the course of history, these interpreters will make room in their worldview for the occurrence of miracles, specifically those reported in the Bible, though they may well disagree over whether such miracles continue to occur today.

For other interpreters, the locus of final authority may lie elsewhere than in the biblical text—sometimes in the private sphere of their own deliberations and preferences, sometimes in the accepted standards of their community of faith, or of their academic community, sometimes simply in the cultural or intellectual *Zeitgeist* (spirit of the age). These interpreters may esteem the Bible as in some sense important, but they are hesitant to allow it *the* decisive role in determining how they view and talk about the world, religion, and reality. Consider, for example, the very fundamental question of the existence of God. Whatever ambiguities may inhere in talk about "the" worldview of the Bible,[12] it can hardly be doubted that among its most central tenets is the assertion that there is one true God, and that this God is deserving of the trust and allegiance of his human creatures. And yet many modern interpreters feel a tension in allowing this fundamental theistic truth to come to expression in their scholarly work. Robert Morgan, for example, begins with the assumption that "scholarship is bound to respect the rational norms of the day" and

---

[11]*Meaning and Understanding: The Philosophical Framework for Biblical Interpretation*, FCI 2 (Grand Rapids: Zondervan, 1991), p. xii.

[12]There is a measure of diversity exhibited within the unity that is the Bible, but I believe it is still valid to speak, in general terms, of "the worldview of the Bible."

concludes from this that "if these do not speak of God, the result is a biblical scholarship which does not speak directly of God in a believing way either." He recognizes that this approach is "bound to seem alien to those who use the Bible religiously." But he recognizes further that "the methods themselves are only a symptom of the conflict between religious assumptions and much modern thought."[13] We see, then, that where religious (or biblical) assumptions conflict with modern thought, some scholars feel compelled to side with the latter, while others feel a greater loyalty to the former. John Stott puts the matter succinctly, but profoundly, in David Edwards' recent *Evangelical Essentials: A Liberal-Evangelical Dialogue*:[14] "Perhaps the crucial question between us, then, is whether culture is to judge Scripture, or Scripture culture" (p. 168).

Having stressed the importance of reflecting on one's own fundamental understanding of the world and reality and of divulging one's background beliefs to one's audience, it is time to state explicitly what is surely implicit in the preceding pages. While this is not the place to offer a full "statement of faith," it seems appropriate to highlight at least those tenets of belief that have a bearing on the issues under consideration in this volume. The worldview and basic assumptions embraced by the present writer are founded on the belief that there is one true God who not only acts in history (through both primary and secondary causes) but also speaks (through both the Incarnate Word and the written word, the Bible; cf. Heb. 12:25). The Bible, as the word of God written—and in keeping with the very character of God—is assumed to present truth and to be authoritative. This means, to put the matter plainly, that whatever the Bible—*rightly interpreted and applied*—affirms or enjoins is to be believed and obeyed.

Stating one's position as boldly as this raises an important question. Does clarity regarding our own assumptions cut us off from all discussion with those who do not share these same assumptions? Not at all, or at least not necessarily. As the recurring phrase "rightly interpreted" suggests, there is plenty of

---

[13]*Biblical Interpretation*, p. 271.
[14]Downers Grove: InterVarsity Press, 1988.

room for debate and discussion as to a text's truth claims, whatever one's stance regarding the text's truth value. Scholars of diverse persuasions may work fruitfully together in seeking to discover what a text is saying (i.e., what its "speech acts" are), while nevertheless recognizing that there may be a parting of the ways when it comes to the question of how these speech acts are to be received.[15] Peter Craigie suggests as much in his comparison of the secular historian with the Jewish or Christian reader:

> While a secular historian will be interested in the manner in which the ancient writer has expressed history in theological terms, his own understanding will remain strictly secular. On the other hand, a Jewish or Christian reader, while sharing the interests of the secular historian, may also share the faith of the ancient writer. That is, religious readers may accept the ancient theological understanding of events as much as the historical data themselves.[16]

Having considered the importance of reality models and the significance of background beliefs, we may now turn to questions of method.

PROCEDURE: COORDINATING METHODS

While individual interpreters can commit themselves to only one model of reality, they may employ a variety of methods to get at the meaning of a text. There is, however, one qualification: each of the methods adopted must be appropriate to the model of reality embraced by the interpreter. My aim in this section is not to discuss specific methods *per se*, but rather to set forth some basic procedural steps for first discovering and then testing the historical claims of biblical texts. This procedure arranges itself around the twin issues of truth claim and truth value, of which much has

---

[15]I recognize that other, less theological (or metaphysical) assumptions may still inhibit fruitful interchange—disagreements over the sufficiency of language, the determinacy of meaning, the legitimacy of such notions as embodied intention, and the like. But, then, it is a curious inconsistency that those who hold a low view of any or all of the above nevertheless in their writings frequently exhibit an *intention* to engage in *meaningful verbal* communication.

[16]*The Old Testament: Its Background, Growth, and Content* (Nashville: Abingdon, 1986), pp. 256–57.

already been said. The proposed procedure, then, has two basic steps. The first is to *listen* to the text in an effort to discover what, if any, historical truth claims it makes. The second is to *test* the truth value of these truth claims by subjecting them to internal and external checks.

Listen: Seek to Determine the Truth Claim

Like the importance of "location, location, location" in considering a real estate purchase, the importance of *listening* in biblical interpretation can hardly be overestimated. "The task of the theologian-exegete," writes Martin Woudstra, "is a humble yet a significant one. It begins with listening; it continues and ends with listening."[17] Good listening implies, of course, asking many questions of the text—thus the need for the various exegetical disciplines such as textual criticism, linguistic analysis, literary criticism, structural analysis, and so forth. Each of these probes and explores the text in different ways and enables the interpreter to "hear" it more clearly.

Moreover, since the Bible is a "foreign book" coming to us in languages other than our own and from cultures far removed from our own both in time and place, *trained* listeners are often in a better position to "hear clearly" than are the untrained.[18] I say "often," because a measure of good faith towards one's source is also a prerequisite of good listening. This suggests a first principle of listening.

GOOD LISTENING REQUIRES AN OPEN ATTITUDE

Despite Harvey's approval of the dictum that "the beginning of wisdom in history is doubt"[19] and Ramsey's insistence that in

---

[17]*The Book of Joshua*, New International Commentary on the Old Testament (Grand Rapids: Eerdmans, 1981), p. 29.

[18]But see chap. 1 on the perspicuity of Scripture.

[19]*Historian and the Believer*, p. 111, citing Allan Nevins. To be sure, Harvey is correct in calling for a "certain toughness of mind" in those who would interpret the Bible responsibly (p. 111), but is he justified in rejecting the "old morality [that] celebrated faith and belief" and advocating a "new morality [that] celebrates methodological scepticism" and equates "integrity . . . with loyalty to the methodological procedures of the intellectual community" (p. 103)? Surely, this

assessing sources "the first requirement of a good historian is a healthy streak of skepticism,"[20] I would contend that this very much depends on the character of the sources. Gerhard Maier insists that "systematic doubt is . . . the most inappropriate procedure imaginable for dealing with the Bible."[21] Credulity (i.e., the tendency to believe on the basis of only slight evidence) is, of course, to be avoided, and carefulness and caution are to be encouraged. But overly skeptical listeners tend to make poor listeners. Assuming the worst of their sources, they sometimes fail to expend the energy necessary to discover the sense of what the sources say.

When it comes to the Bible, the energy necessary to "hear clearly" may be considerable, especially given the Bible's "remove" from the listener's own language, literary traditions, and culture. Thus, an important characteristic of the good listener or, in the case of texts, the good reader is an open, expectant attitude in approaching the text. As Jan Fokkelman has argued, "the good reader . . . has the experience that the significance of an encounter varies with the attitude he assumes during the establishment of contact. He realizes that the contact can be deepened and enriched if he goes into it with a positive attitude. Loving attention and the trust that the other partner is worth the trouble are essential conditions for a genuine dialogue." By contrast, "the attitude of treating a narrative from the very outset as a barrel full of problems creates a negative climate and runs the risk of acting as a self-fulfilling prophecy."[22]

Whether one views the Bible as deserving of initial skepticism or of trust (or of something in between) is in part a reflection

---

latter equation tends to beg the question of truth and to overlook the diversity and often shifting consensus within the "intellectual community" itself. Moreover, when Harvey condemns the "falsifying influence of the demand for belief" (p. 111), he seems to overlook the fact that unbelief can have a similarly distorting effect, constraining the historian always to come to conclusions that are compatible with this unbelief.

[20]*Quest*, p. 7.

[21]*Biblische Hermeneutik* (Wuppertal: R. Brockhaus, 1990), p. 14 (English translation here is from Robert W. Yarbrough's forthcoming translation of this work).

[22]*King David (II Sam 9–20 and 1 Kings 1–2)* (Assen: Van Gorcum, 1981), p. 4.

of one's general belief about the Bible's macro-genre[23] and in part a result of one's specific encounters with the biblical text. Certainly, no one who has seriously studied the Bible will claim that such study is without difficulties, but again Fokkelman lends a helpful perspective.

> With this I do not want to deny that Old Testament studies have their real problems. What I am pleading for, however, is that from text to text we remain aware that they are not intended to be problematical cases, and that we understand about the problems that they are *our* problems which are in part genuine inasmuch as they correspond with the great difference in time and environment between us and the Bible, but which, in part, arise from our own scholastic habits of making things difficult. I am convinced that Old Testament studies will be a Jezreel for us more often than a Negeb if we practise asking the proper questions.[24]

The ability to ask the proper questions presupposes that we come to the text with the proper expectations, and this in turn presupposes that we make an effort to bridge the spatio-temporal gap by developing, as best we can, an ancient linguistic-literary-cultural competence. Just as an understanding of the conventional workings of, say, impressionist art is very useful for rightly interpreting an impressionist painting, so too some understanding of the conventional workings of biblical narrative is a great help in "getting the picture" that individual biblical narratives wish to convey.

But even after we "get the picture" (i.e., understand the story), we may still not be sure if the *story* should be taken as *history*. We have already seen that one can no more distinguish fictional story from factual history on the basis of *formal* characteristics than one can distinguish nonreferential from referential paintings on the basis of *brush strokes*. Nor is content alone an adequate indicator; just as a work of art may be realistic and yet not specifically representational, so a narrative may be realistic and yet not historiographical. How then is one to distinguish representational/historiographical narrative from realistic but nonhistorio-

---

[23]On which, see chap. 1.

[24]*King David*, pp. 4–5.

graphical narrative? The key, as we saw already in chapter 2, is to discern the narrative's *overall sense of purpose*. But how are we to discover this sense of purpose? If not by form alone, nor even by content, then the answer has to be context. Again, as I suggested in chapters 1 and 2, the way to begin is by observing the narrative's placement within its larger narrative continuum. This brings us to a second characteristic of good listening.

GOOD LISTENING REQUIRES ATTENTION TO CONTEXT

The principle that I am suggesting runs parallel to Strauss's positive criterion for distinguishing between historical and unhistorical narratives, but in the reverse direction. As I noted in chapter 3, Strauss promoted a sort of guilt-by-association approach whereby one begins by asking whether any narrative units within a larger textual continuum "exhibit unquestionable marks of a mythical or legendary character." If such are found, then the historicity of any texts connected to these, or even proceeding from the same author, is suspect.[25] Thus Strauss extrapolates from a determination about smaller textual units to a judgment about the larger unit of which these are a part. But if the principles of discourse articulated in chapter 1 are correct (especially the principle that "upper levels of text organization, such as genre, place broad constraints on all lower levels"[26]), then the extrapolation should be reversed—viz., from the larger to the smaller. If the larger narrative complex exhibits a historiographical intent, then, barring indications to the contrary, smaller units within the complex should be assumed to share in the historical impulse.

To grasp what is at stake here, we need only consider what goes on in everyday conversation. When talking with someone, we intuitively gauge the import of individual sentences in the light of the overall tenor and direction of the conversation. A sentence like "That will be the day!" means one thing if spoken in answer to a flirtatious and insincere "Will you marry me?" and quite another if in answer to a prospective partner's serious inquiry

---

[25]*Life of Jesus*, p. 90.
[26]Bergen, "Text as a Guide," p. 330.

"How about setting December 18th as our wedding day?" Now, a form critic might easily collect numerous examples of actual verbal exchanges in which "That will be the day!" is a sarcastic rejoinder, but, as our second scenario makes clear, to ignore the larger communicative context and simply label the clause in question as a "sarcastic rejoinder formula" would be to miss the point badly.

How does this principle apply to issues of biblical historicity? Perhaps a specific example will help. Let us take a brief look at one of the more perplexing stretches of text in the books of Kings. The section comprising 1 Kings 17–2 Kings 8 recounts the prophetic activities of Elijah and Elisha. These chapters display a striking concentration of miracle stories, including even one in which Elisha throws a stick into water and causes an axhead to float to the surface (2 Kings 6:1–7). As Richard Nelson points out, this story is "something of an embarrassment for modern readers. The miracle seems both trivial and pointless."[27] Nelson has more to say on the subject, and I shall return to him later. But for the moment, the question that faces us is this: what are we to make of this fantastic story, and indeed of the whole collection of fantastic stories that comes in the midst of the books of Kings? In keeping with the significance of *context*, argued above, it would seem appropriate to begin by reflecting on the apparent purpose(s) of the books of Kings.

It is generally recognized that 1 and 2 Kings exhibit a historiographical impulse. Simon DeVries, for example, in his Word Biblical Commentary on 1 Kings,[28] observes with respect to the so-called Deuteronomistic history, of which 1 and 2 Kings are a part, that "we are blind if we cannot see that it is meaningful *historical event* that Dtr is recording and interpreting" (p. xxxiv). More specifically he writes, "1 Kgs—and the other sections of the historiographic collection—was written by men who wished to bear testimony to Yahweh's self-revelation in historical event" (p. xxxv).

And yet when DeVries comes to consider the Elijah/Elisha narratives, he describes them not as historiography but as

_____

[27] *First and Second Kings*, Interpretation (Louisville: John Knox, 1987), p. 184.
[28] Waco: Word Books, 1985.

"prophet legend," which he immediately amends to "prophet story," reasoning that " 'legend' can be popularly misconstrued as meaning fanciful or unreal" (p. xxxvii). In principle, if we follow Burke Long's definition of a prophet legend as "a story which chiefly portrays a wondrous deed or ideal virtue of an exemplary holy man,"[29] then historicity is not necessarily ruled out, at least for those who are willing to allow a place for the "wondrous" in history (see my discussion of the historical-critical method in chap. 4). In practice, however, DeVries finds little room for historicity when it comes to the Elijah/Elisha stories, preferring rather to contrast these "pious stories" with the "historiography" of the rest of Kings. Why does he come to this position? According to his own profession, it is not because of any anti-supernaturalist bias on his part. Indeed, he warns of "two errors, opposite to each other," of which we must beware in approaching the Elijah and Elisha stories: "(1) to reject them because they clash with the naturalism of the modern mind, or (2) to interpret them only literally while insisting that the biblical God always works in this way" (p. xxxvi).

Both these warnings are apt. But what is it, if not the miraculous elements in the Elijah/Elisha stories, that leads DeVries to conclude that "the aim of these stories is less to record what God *has done* (historically, at one particular time and place), than to declare what God *can do* (throughout history, in every time and place)" (p. xxxvii)? Why does he insist that "their intent is not to record what *has* happened, but what happens and can happen"? Having expressed himself so strongly on the historiographical purpose of 1 Kings, on what grounds does he exempt these prophet stories, so intertwined as they are in the careers of kings? Perhaps it is the miraculous element, after all, that gives him pause, for he later speaks of "the exaggerated supernatural element in some of them" that functions as "a metaphor for God's power and the power of God-filled men" (p. 206). But this is not the reason that he explicitly gives. Rather, beginning with the valid observation that it is not necessary that "everything narrated in the

---

[29]*1 Kings with an Introduction to Historical Literature*, The Forms of the Old Testament Literature (Grand Rapids: Eerdmans, 1984), p. 80.

Bible . . . be taken literally," DeVries moves quickly to a comparison of the Elijah and Elisha stories with the *parables* of Jesus, which are lacking in "historicity," though they are rich in "historicality"—viz., "self-awareness in historical existence" (pp. xxxvi–xxxvii).

But is this comparison apposite? By DeVries' own admission, the prophet stories' emphasis on "the wondrous and the supernatural" distinguishes them from Jesus' parables, which have no such emphasis (p. xxxvii). This being the case, surely the more appropriate comparison would be with the *miracle stories* of Jesus. Elijah's raising of the widow of Zarephath's son (1 Kings 17:17–24) might be compared with Jesus' raising of the widow of Nain's son (Luke 7:11–17); the story of Elisha's feeding of one hundred (2 Kings 4:42–44) with Jesus' feeding of the multitude (e.g., Matt. 14:16–20); Elisha's healing of Naaman's leprosy (2 Kings 5) with Jesus' healings of lepers (e.g., Luke 5:12–16); and the list could be continued. In Luke 4:25–27 Jesus himself draws a comparison between his own wonder-working ministry and the ministries of Elijah and Elisha.[30]

What, then, are we to conclude from all this? First, if the discourse principle of larger influencing smaller is correct, then the apparent historiographical impulse of the books of Kings should be taken into consideration in our reading of the Elijah/Elisha narratives.[31] We may still decide that the latter are devoid of historical value, but the burden of proof will be on us to give reasons for that judgment. For scholars who continue in the spirit of Strauss, the miraculous features of these stories may seem reason enough, but as argued in chapter 4, a naturalist presupposition should not be deemed the *sine qua non* of historical study. Second, attention should be given to the degree of integration of the smaller units into the broader context and to the presence or absence of indicators that distinctive literary forms (parables,

---

[30]Cf. Nelson, *First and Second Kings*, p. 114, which see for fuller discussion; cf. also ibid., pp. 175–76.

[31]In practice, of course, there will be something of a spiraling back and forth between close examination of the smaller units and one's understanding of the overall sense of purpose of the larger.

fables, or the like) are being introduced.[32] Where such indicators are present, the specific truth claims of the smaller units may well differ from the overall truth claims of the larger narratives. But where such indicators are absent, the discourse principle of larger influencing smaller continues in force. Third, when attempting to argue from analogous genres, or literary forms, we must take care that the most appropriate analogies are adduced. In the case before us, the accounts of Jesus' *miracles*, not his *parables*, provide the appropriate comparison. Thus, our view of the historical import of Jesus' miracle stories may play a part in our assessment of the miracle stories of Elijah/Elisha.

Returning to the specific case of the floating axhead (2 Kings 6:1–7), I would make one further observation: our first impression of an incident may reflect the limitations of our own cultural context and thus should not be implicitly trusted. As Nelson remarks, our sense that the axhead miracle is "trivial and pointless" is in part at least "caused by our inability to empathize with a poor man's consternation over an expensive borrowed tool. Iron was not cheap in those days."[33] More importantly, this incident, along with others that follow, is by no means "trivial and pointless," inasmuch as it serves to "emphasize the power of the prophet" and of the God he represents. "God's power invades the world of the ordinary to effect strange reversals. The lowly are raised to places of honor (Luke 1:51–53). The unrighteous are justified (Luke 18:9–14). The lost are found (Luke 15:3–10). The dead are raised. These are as much incredible reversals as is iron that floats."[34]

Test: Seek to Determine the Truth Value

So far in this chapter we have discussed two important elements in any responsible attempt to discover what historical information the Bible may contain. The first is to reflect on the

---

[32]See my discussion of Jotham's fable in the section "Genre Criticism and Biblical Interpretation" in chap. 1.

[33]*First and Second Kings*, p. 184.

[34]Ibid., p. 185.

importance of worldviews, or models of reality (one's own, the text's, other interpreters'). This provides the opportunity to modify, if necessary, the reality model with which one implicitly operates, or at least to become more self-consciously aware of one's own fundamental assumptions and the assumptions of others. The second is to listen as carefully and competently as possible to the biblical witness, to use every available means to discover its truth claims by approaching the text as fairly as possible on its own terms and in view of its context.

We now come to a third crucial step in the historical exploration of the Bible. Once we believe that we have some sense of what historical truth claims the biblical witness is making, our next step is to test the reliability of these claims by subjecting them to two checks. First, is the testimony internally consistent? And secondly, do its claims square with what other sources and evidences lead us to believe is true? Since our focus is on biblical testimony, some investigators will, of course, be predisposed to trust the witness while others will not. In either case, by testing our witness for internal and external consistency, we may be able to confirm or disconfirm our initial judgments.

When we find ourselves using words such as *testimony*, *witness*, and *evidence*, we are reminded of the analogy that is often drawn between the historical discipline and the law court.[35] This analogy is helpful in several respects. It reminds us that both historical study and the law court are interested in discovering what has happened in the past. It reminds us that both are *field-encompassing fields*, that is, both proceed by examining various kinds of evidence, derived from a variety of fields. It reminds us that both depend heavily on verbal testimony (e.g., written documents, depositions, the cross-examination of witnesses) and not just on the discovery and inspection of material evidence, though the latter may still play an important role. It reminds us that both are only required to establish that a particular view of the

---

[35]Simply put, "historical knowledge is based upon evidence in just the way the deliberations of a jury are" (Halpern, *First Historians*, p. 13); see also, e.g., Harvey, *Historian and the Believer*, pp. 58–59; Parker, "Methods," p. 289; Ramsey, *Quest*, pp. 22–23; Trigg, "Tales artfully spun," pp. 130–32.

past is true *beyond any reasonable doubt* and are seldom in a position to offer anything approaching *scientific proof.* It reminds us that both are required to give reasons for the judgments they reach, though these reasons may be of many different sorts. And finally, it reminds us that for testimony to be credible it must pass the two tests of internal and external consistency. We turn now to the first of these two tests.

INTERNAL CONSISTENCY OF TESTIMONY

In a court of law, an attorney can discredit a witness—even without conflicting testimony or material evidence—simply by demonstrating that the witness's testimony is internally inconsistent (i.e., self-contradictory or incoherent). It may be that the witness is lying, or perhaps simply confused, but in any case he/she is not to be trusted. The same is true of biblical testimony. If a biblical narrative is incoherent or self-contradictory, if it doesn't make sense as a *story*, then it is hardly likely to be true as *history* (though it might still contain isolated historical reminiscences).

The place to begin, then, in testing the truth value of biblical testimony that appears to make historical truth claims is with a careful literary reading of the text with an eye to internal consistency. As Ramsey remarks, when exploring the historical import of biblical texts, "the careful scrutiny of the 'internal evidence,' meaning literary study of the biblical text, should be attended to first."[36]

A word of caution is warranted here. In this first-stage scrutiny of the literary deposit with an eye to coherence or lack thereof, it is vitally important that appropriate standards of coherence and consistency be applied—viz., standards appropriate to the ancient genre under inspection.[37] In seeking to establish

---

[36]*Quest,* p. 99.

[37]See, e.g., Hemer's "guidelines to what seem to be the reasonable expectations of historicity in a writing like Acts" (*Book of Acts,* pp. 46–49). He remarks, *inter alia,* that "narratives are embodied in natural, phenomenological language, which is not to be judged by over-literal criteria. Though independent sources for the same incidents are not commonly available for Acts, it will not necessarily matter for historicity if such cases exhibit varying details and perspectives, provided the

these standards, a judicious use of comparative literature may prove useful. This point has recently been articulated and illustrated by Lawson Younger in an essay entitled "The Figurative Aspect and the Contextual Method in the Evaluation of the Solomonic Empire (1 Kings 1–11)." He writes:

> As biblical historians continue to formulate and to debate their methodology for writing histories of Israel, it is becoming more and more apparent that one of the greatest needs in establishing a method is the realization that a literary reading of the biblical text must precede any historical reconstruction. It is clear that such a reading is advantaged by anchoring the reading in the literary environment from which the text is derived.[38]

In addition to the cautious use of comparative literature, another source of guidance in assessing the coherence of biblical narrative is provided by literary approaches to the Bible such as biblical poetics, narrative criticism, discourse analysis and the like. As we have noted before, the heightened awareness of narrative conventions and literary strategies that these approaches yield sometimes calls for a reassessment of earlier judgments regarding a text's sense and coherence.

In addition to the examples presented elsewhere in this book,[39] the story of the encounter between Saul and Samuel described in 1 Samuel 9 nicely illustrates this point. The standard critical approach to this chapter has been to see in it a conflation of two originally distinct traditions, the one involving an encounter between Saul and an obscure village seer and the other involving the famous Samuel. The basis of this view is the fact that the "man of God" or "seer" remains anonymous until verse 14, where it is revealed to the reader, though not to Saul, that this "seer" is in fact

---

differences are not radically contradictory. Indeed, we should be concerned to force neither harmonization nor contradiction, if only because we stand in too distant an external position to possess a completeness of context on which such decisions are likely to depend. There may be places where we have enough information to attempt a positive fit. Otherwise we are wise to be cautious" (p. 47).

[38]In *Bible in Three Dimensions*, ed. Clines et al., p. 157.

[39]E.g., in chap. 3 (an evaluation of Strauss, pp. 111–12). The final chapter of this book will provide a more extended example on the basis of the narratives in 1 Samuel recounting Saul's ascent to the throne of Israel.

Samuel! Why is Samuel not named earlier? Diachronic scholarship has sought to answer the question by assuming two sources—an "anonymous seer" source and a "Samuel source"—which originally existed independently but at some point were conflated. Contrary to this standard approach, however, scholars such as Langlamet, Birch, McCarter, and others have argued that the masking of the identity of the seer in the early verses is not an evidence of a composite text but, rather, is a literary strategy intended to allow the reader to share in Saul's process of discovery.[40] It is "one of the dramatic highlights of the story."[41] As a slight modification of this synchronic explanation, it can be argued that the real point of the literary treatment is not so much to allow the reader to share in Saul's discovery as to highlight Saul's slowness in coming to understand what the reader has undoubtedly deduced much earlier.[42] In any case, the former consensus that 1 Samuel 9 is a conflation of two distinct sources and thus lacking in the consistency and unity to be expected of a reliable historical source has now been undercut by the literary reading that sees a unified and coherent, even sophisticated, narrative.

Does this more positive assessment of the self-consistency and coherence of 1 Samuel 9 prove its historicity? Of course not, or at least not entirely, for while internal consistency is a *necessary* condition of historicity, it is surely not a *sufficient* one. In other words, while demonstrating internal contradictions within an account would tell against its historicity, internal coherence is no guarantee of historicity. A lying witness, a clever one at least, might tell a tale that is perfectly self-consistent and yet utterly out

[40]F. Langlamet, "Les récits de l'institution de la royauté (I Sam, VII–XII). De Wellhausen aux travaux récents," *Revue biblique* 77 (1970): 173; B. C. Birch, *The Rise of the Israelite Monarchy: The Growth and Development of 1 Samuel 7–15*, SBLDS 27 (Missoula: Scholars Press, 1976), pp. 34–35; cf. 135; P. K. McCarter, *I Samuel: A New Translation with Introduction, Notes and Commentary*, AB 8 (Garden City: Doubleday, 1980), p. 185.

[41]N. Na'aman, "The Pre-Deuteronomistic Story of King Saul and Its Historical Significance," *CBQ* 54 (1992): 640.

[42]For a fuller discussion, see Long, *Reign and Rejection*, pp. 196–99; cf. also R. P. Gordon, *I and II Samuel: A Commentary*, Library of Biblical Interpretation (Grand Rapids: Zondervan, 1986), pp. 32–33.

of accord with what actually happened. Further considerations must be brought to bear: the general character and trustworthiness of the witness, the over-arching sense of purpose of the larger context within which the testimony is given, and the consistency of the testimony with external evidence. We have already had something to say on the character and context questions, so we turn now to the test of external consistency.

EXTERNAL CONSISTENCY OF TESTIMONY

This test presupposes, at least provisionally, that the interpreter has rightly understood the witness to be making historical truth claims.[43] The purpose of the external consistency test, as the name implies, is to check the truth value of these claims against whatever *external* evidences can be adduced. These evidences might include other verbal testimony—portions of the Bible or extrabiblical writings that in some way speak to the same events described by the first witness—as well as purely material remains, whether architectural, artifactual, biological, or such like.

In some instances, of course, there may be little or no external evidence that can be brought to bear on the biblical text under consideration. In these instances we are in a situation comparable to that of judge or jury who must render a verdict based on the testimony of only one witness. With neither other witnesses nor pertinent material evidence, about all judge or jury will have to go on is the character of the single witness and the coherence of the witness's story. In the same way, some purportedly historical events are recounted in only one place in the Bible and, so far as archaeology has been able to discover, are without supporting material evidence. In such instances, biblical historians have little more to consider in reaching a verdict regarding

---

[43]If, on the other hand, it has been determined that the witness's testimony is hopelessly muddled or that no historical truth claims are being made, then it might not be necessary to proceed to the external test. But even in such cases, the safest approach would be to investigate the testimony of other witnesses and to inspect whatever material evidence might be at hand, since this would allow investigators either (1) to confirm their impression that the witness is not to be trusted by amassing contradictory evidences or (2) to discover that they have misunderstood the witness and need to reevaluate their initial judgments.

historicity than their view of the character of the (biblical) witness and the coherence of the testimony.

In many instances, however, external checks on the biblical account can be made on the basis of other biblical literature, extrabiblical literature, material remains, or some combination of these three. We must make these external checks with great caution. With respect to written evidence, for example, whether biblical or extrabiblical, we must bear in mind that these sources themselves, no less than the text in question, require interpretation and testing. Moreover, we must recognize that it is almost inevitable that different sources will yield differing perspectives on historical events, and we must remind ourselves that "different" does not necessarily mean "conflicting." When due allowance is made for the genre and purpose of the literature we are reading, many assumed discrepancies turn out to be more apparent than real. As for material evidence, we must bear in mind the point made earlier that archaeological remains are neither self-interpreting nor more objective than other kinds of evidence. The minute we begin to talk about material evidence, we are interpreting it. So we dare not forget what we ourselves, or the archaeologists we read, bring to the task of assessment.

In view of such considerations as these, it should be evident that the proper application of the external consistency test, as important as it is, is no simple matter. What is more, the results that can fairly be expected from the study of external, especially material, evidence are limited. As noted in the preceding chapter, material evidence is best suited to provide information of a generalized, background nature—mode and standard of living, diet, customs, population growth and migration, and so forth. Material evidence is seldom able to confirm even that a specific event has taken place, much less to provide guidance as to the significance, or interpretation, of that event. For interpretation, we are ultimately dependant on written sources, biblical or extrabiblical, or our own theories.

About all we can hope for, then, in terms of external confirmation of an apparently historical account is that there will be a general coherence, or compatibility, between the written account and whatever can be learned from external evidences. As

is often remarked, archaeological evidence will not be in a position
to prove a biblical account true in any absolute sense, for even if it
could confirm every aspect of an event by yielding a correspond-
ing piece of material evidence, it would still fall short of
confirming the interpretative component of all history-writing.

Excursus: The occurrence of the terms *coherence* and *correspondence* in
the preceding paragraph brings to mind the two dominant *theories of
truth* that are often debated in discussions of historical method. This
is not the place to attempt a full treatment of the complex issues
involved in these discussions, but a few comments may be useful.
While a survey of the literature suggests that scholars do not always
agree on what precisely is meant by the correspondence theory and
the coherence theory, the general (if somewhat simplistic) understanding seems to be the following. The correspondence theory
defines truth in terms of correspondence to the "facts," correspondence to "the way things are."[44] The coherence theory, by contrast,
"defines truth not as the relationship of statements to facts but as the
relationship of statements to each other."[45] Statements that are
coherent with all other statements within a system of thought are
regarded as true. The former theory, with its definition of truth "in
terms of the correspondence between a proposition and a state of
affairs,"[46] is often referred to as the "common-sense theory of
truth,"[47] while the latter, with its definition of truth "in terms of the
unified nature of a system of thought," has its roots in idealism and
finds its most devoted adherents among idealists.[48]

Not surprisingly, both theories have been subjected to criticism
as regards their applicability to historical study.[49] The correspondence theory is criticized by Nash, for example, "for the simple
reason that the past to which our historical propositions are

---

[44]Cf. Brandfon, "Limits of Evidence," p. 31; Nash, *Christian Faith*, p. 108.
[45]Brandfon, "Limits of Evidence," p. 35.
[46]A. F. Holmes, "Christian Philosophy," in *The New Encyclopedia Brittanica*, ed.
J. Adler Mortimer et al., 15th ed. (1977), Macropaedia 4: 561.
[47]*Dictionary of Philosophy*, ed. Flew, p. 355.
[48]Holmes, "Christian Philosophy," p. 561.
[49]For convenient summaries, see A. R. White, "Coherence Theory of Truth," in
Encyclopedia, ed. Edwards, 2: 130–33; A. N. Prior, "Correspondence Theory of
Truth," in ibid., 2: 223–32.

supposed to correspond no longer exists."[50] The coherence theory, on the other hand, is criticized on the basis that coherence alone is no guarantee of truth. A. R. White puts it this way: "it is an objection to coherence as the meaning of 'truth' or as the only criterion of truth that it is logically possible to have two different but equally comprehensive sets of coherent statements between which there would be, in the coherence theory, no way to decide which was the set of true statements."[51] When faced with this sort of criticism, "objective idealist" proponents of the coherence theory counter by insisting that "the coherence of which they speak attaches only to a concrete system, of which human experiences form a part; it does not attach to abstract systems of mathematics or logic, where several mutually incompatible systems are possible."[52]

In the final analysis, it is probably best to make a place for both notions, correspondence and coherence, in our thinking about historical truth. Perhaps one way to attempt a synthesis is to distinguish between a *theory* of truth and a *criterion* of truth. As a *theory* of historical truth, the "common-sense" *correspondence* theory is attractive, but as a criterion, or test, of truth, it is useful only to a limited degree, since the past is unrepeatable. The *coherence* theory (in all but the most qualified formulations, perhaps) is inadequate as a theory of truth, but it offers a useful *criterion* of truth, if by it we mean, as Nash suggests, that "a proposition is true when it coheres with, fits in with, everything else that we know." Nash explains: "A police investigator who is forced to solve a crime on the basis of circumstantial evidence must use the coherence standard of truth. So must the historian in his study of history."[53]

In the light of all this, we might say that historical reconstructions that are *coherent* with all that we now know about a subject may be deemed reliable guides to the past, and may be assumed (barring discovery of conflicting evidence) to *correspond* to the past in a manner similar to the way in which a representational painting corresponds to its subject.[54] The criterion of *coherence* in the

---

[50]Nash, *Christian Faith*, p. 108.

[51]"Coherence Theory," 131, q.v. for further criticisms.

[52]*Dictionary of Philosophy*, ed. Flew, p. 66.

[53]*Christian Faith*, pp. 108–109. Unfortunately, as White ("Coherence Theory," p. 133) points out, sometimes advocates of the coherence theory confuse "the reasons, or criteria, for calling a statement true or false with the meaning of 'truth' or 'falsity.'"

[54]For an insightful discussion of coherence, correspondence, and reliability in historical study, see McCullagh, *Justifying Historical Descriptions*, pp. 1–8.

preceding statement encompasses both of my suggested tests of truth value—viz., internal consistency and external consistency. The concept of *correspondence*, on the other hand, represents an ontological affirmation of the sense in which written history represents the historical past—it "corresponds" to its subject as much as, but no more than, a representational painting does to its subject.

To sum up our discussion to this point, we may again observe that the approach to reading the Bible historically suggested in this chapter runs parallel to Strauss's tests of historicity, briefly outlined and evaluated in chapter 3. Of Strauss's several criteria for determining whether a text is to be understood as historical or unhistorical, I addressed his first negative criterion related to worldview in the section on examining models; there I differed with his opinion that "all just philosophical conceptions" mandate an anti-supernaturalist presupposition. His positive criterion that determinations regarding the historicity of smaller units may be extended to implicate the larger units of which they are a part was discussed in the section on the importance of context; there I in effect reversed Strauss's position to argue that the apparent purpose of larger discourse units places the burden of proof on those who believe that smaller units do not partake in this overarching sense of purpose. Finally, the discussion of internal and external tests of the truth value of historical truth claims parallels Strauss's second negative criterion—viz., that reliable testimony must be consistent with itself and with other reliable witnesses or evidence; there my main concern was that interpreters take care to develop a proper sense of what constitutes "consistency" in an ancient document.

As we move now to the final stage in our deliberations over how we should read the Bible historically, I shall again build on the legal analogy. A lawyer's task entails more than ascertaining what a witness is saying (truth claim) and even more than coming to a personal opinion as to the veracity (truth value) of the witness's testimony. The lawyer has not done his job until he has put the various pieces of evidence together and built a case designed to convince others, the jury or the judge, that a particular understanding of "what happened in the past" is to be accepted.

Similarly, the task of biblical historians is not only to come to informed opinions regarding the truth claims of biblical texts and to personal convictions regarding the truth value of these claims. They must also seek to put the pieces together within a plausible historical reconstruction designed to convince others that a particular understanding of "what happened in the past" is worthy of acceptance.

The manner in which lawyers and historians present their summations (their reconstructions of what actually happened) will vary, depending on their sense of how the jury is leaning, but in general they will need to do three things. First, they must briefly rehearse the testimony—recall what truth claims have been made. Second, they must evaluate the testimony—remind their hearers of which truth claims were found to be deserving of trust (e.g., by virtue of their coming from reliable witnesses whose character is well attested and whose testimony is internally consistent and also consonant with whatever external evidence is available). Finally, they must convince their hearers that their proposed reconstruction of "what actually happened," their *argument* as it were, has been arrived at logically, or at least does not rest on any logical fallacies. It is to this question of argumentation that we now turn.

PRESENTATION: CONSTRUCTING ARGUMENTS

In his book entitled *The Uses of Argument*, Stephen Toulmin develops a system for analyzing the structure of arguments (especially of the sort employed in jurisprudence) that has proved particularly attractive to historians and philosophers of history, as well as to theologians and others.[55] The essence of Toulmin's approach is to identify the various components of an argument,

---

[55]Cambridge: Cambridge University Press, 1958 (see esp. pp. 94–145). Those who have built on Toulmin's approach, to name a few, include Harvey, *Historian and the Believer*, pp. 43–64 (and through him many others; e.g., Abraham, *Divine Revelation*, esp. chap. 6); D. H. Kelsey, *The Uses of Scripture in Recent Theology* (London: SCM, 1975), pp. 122–38 (whose focus is on arguments for theological positions); N. M. de S. Cameron, *Biblical Higher Criticism and the Defense of Infallibilism in 19th Century Britain* (Lewiston: Edwin Mellen, 1987), pp. 276–89; Brown, *History and Faith*, pp. 38–40.

such as data, warrants, and backing, and to chart the argument in a candid fashion so that the function of each component in the overall argument becomes clear. The benefits of Toulmin's approach are several. It demonstrates that arguments are complex, not simple, affairs. It also affords a clear view of how an argument is put together, what data it cites, what assumptions it involves, what warrants must be true for the argument to hold, what rebuttals are conceivable that could overturn the argument, and how logically the conclusion is derived from the data. Where historians disagree in their historical reconstructions, the straightforward analysis of arguments afforded by Toulmin's scheme makes it possible to retrace the (logical) pathways by which the differing conclusions were reached and to identify specific points of strength or weakness, agreement or disagreement.

Toulmin's scheme is presented rather fully by Harvey, Kelsey, and Cameron,[56] so it will be presented only briefly here, and then exemplified. The type of argument employed in historical studies typically involves the following components in the following relation: this *datum*/these *data* (**D**) exist(s), so, with this *qualification* (**Q**; e.g., necessarily, presumably, possibly), since this *warrant* (**W**) holds, on account of this *backing* (**B**), this *conclusion* (**C**) follows, unless a *rebuttal* (**R**) of one or more aspects of the argument is forthcoming. In chart form, the structure of such an argument looks like this.[57]

---

[56]See the preceding note.

[57]This chart is essentially the same as Toulmin's, with the slight difference that I have shifted the "*so*, Qualifier" component to the left to stand over the warrant and backing, as this, it seems to me, allows the argument to be read more naturally in columns from left to right.

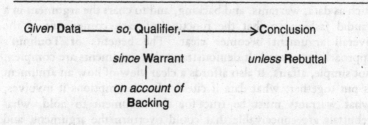

To offer a concrete example, we may chart the fairly simple argument that was tentatively suggested above with respect to how the Elijah/Elisha narratives in 1 and 2 Kings should be read. It would look something like this.

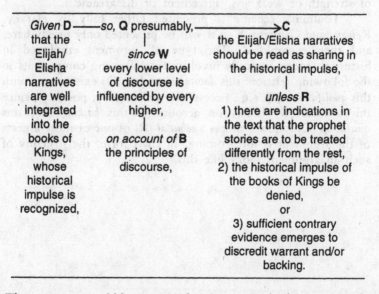

The argument could be presented, using precisely the same words, in one rather long sentence, but the advantage of Toulmin's chart is that it makes the overall structure of the argument and the function of its various components more immediately apparent.

In this particular argument, as the chart indicates, at least three rebuttals can be envisaged that would undercut the argument. The first two relate to the two-part statement of the data, while the third relates to warrant and backing. The first two rebuttals would require demonstration on exegetical grounds— namely, an identification of clues *in the text* that the prophet stories are to be treated differently than the surrounding context, or an exegetical reassessment of the overall sense of purpose and the supposed historical impulse of the books of Kings. The third rebuttal might involve a questioning of the warrant that "every lower level of discourse is influenced by every higher." In answer to such a challenge, we would need to construct a second argument, in which the former backing would become the data, the former warrant would become the conclusion, and a new warrant, with its own backing, would need to be introduced to justify the move from data to conclusion.[58] The second argument might look something like this.

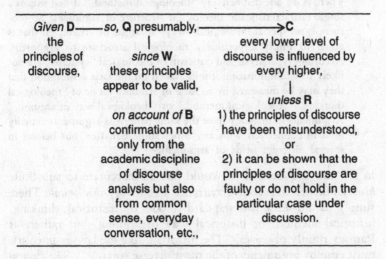

Should some aspect of this argument be challenged, then a further argument would need to be constructed, and so on. Virtually any argument (historical, theological, legal, etc.) can be analyzed in terms of Toulmin's structure, and it is very useful to

[58]Cf. Kelsey, *Uses of Scripture*, p. 127.

make a habit of subjecting one's own and others' arguments to
such analysis. Often it will be discovered that warrants or backing
are left unstated (or are lacking), possible rebuttals are not
considered, and so forth. An added benefit is that one will
constantly be reminded that history is a field-encompassing field
and that historical argumentation is complex, often involving
many steps (or sub-arguments) and making use of various kinds of
authorizations, deductions, and evidence. In his discussion of
"theological macro-arguments," Kelsey observes that "several
logically different kinds of statement may all serve to help
authorize a given conclusion, although in different senses of
'authorize.' "[59] This observation about theological arguments
applies equally well to historical ones. Similarly applicable are his
comments on theological method and reasoning.

> There is no one distinctively "theological method," if that means a
> single characteristically theological structure of argument. So too,
> there is no special theological "way" to argue or "think," if that is
> taken to imply a peculiarly theological structure to argument.
> Accordingly, analysis and criticism of theological "systems" are not
> likely to be illuminating if undertaken on the tacit assumption that
> they may be measured by an ideal or standard mode of "theological
> thinking," "theological method," or "theological way of arguing."
> Arguments in theology have the same pattern as arguments actually
> used in connection with any other subject matter, but belong in
> several different fields of argument.[60]

In the above quotation, it would not be inaccurate to substitute
history/historical for each occurrence of *theology/theological*. There
simply is no ideal or standard mode of historical thinking,
historical method, or historical way of arguing, but rather, as
Ramsey rightly observes, "The historian, like the lawyer in court,
must employ arguments of the most diverse sorts. . . . *The element
which is common to all the arguments of the lawyer or the historian (or
anyone else) is the obligation to give reasons for his conclusions.*"[61]

---

[59]Ibid., p. 135.
[60]Ibid., pp. 134–35.
[61]*Quest*, p. 22 (emphasis Ramsey's).

CONCLUSION

The present chapter began with the question, *How then should we read the Bible "historically"?* The "then" was meant to recall what had been discussed in the preceding four chapters. The specific aim of this chapter has been to move toward an answer to that question by exploring foundational issues and procedural steps, which, when further developed and refined, might yield something of a program, or hermeneutic, for approaching the Bible historically.

We considered first the importance, as preparation for any historical reading of the Bible, of gaining some awareness of the reality models, or background beliefs, that we and others bring to our reading. We are unlikely ever to understand ourselves, others, or our Bibles, unless we have some sense of where each of us, as it were, "is coming from." Having addressed the foundational issues, we then moved to a consideration of a simple, two-part procedure for exploring the historical import of the Bible. The basis of the procedure is the twofold need to *listen* carefully and competently to the biblical texts so as to detect their truth claims and to *test* the truth value of whatever historical claims are made. The procedure itself does not constitute an exegetical method but, rather, provides a framework around which the various exegetical and related disciplines might be arranged. As to the first part of the procedure, stress was laid on two requirements of good listening—viz., an open, expectant attitude and careful attention to context. As to the second part, we noted that testimony should pass two tests in order to qualify as reliable—the *internal consistency* test that requires the testimony to be coherent and self-consistent, and the *external consistency* test that requires the testimony to be compatible with whatever external evidence, rightly interpreted, might be available.

Finally, we turned to the matter of historical reconstruction and argumentation. This is where the historian seeks to assemble all the evidence that has been tested and found reliable into a convincing historical reconstruction. We likened the historian's reconstruction to a lawyer's summation at the end of a trial where witnesses have been heard and cross-examined. In this regard we explored the value of Toulmin's *anatomy of an argument* as an aid to assessing the validity and cogency of historical, and other types, of argumentation.

While there is a certain logical sequencing to the discussion in this chapter, in practice there will be more of a hermeneutical spiral, since later discoveries will often call for reassessing earlier conclusions. In the next chapter we shall consider a historically much-disputed stretch of text (the *rise of Saul* in 1 Sam. 9–11) as a testing-ground for the programmatic approach presented in this chapter.

6

AN EXTENDED EXAMPLE
The Rise of Saul

In discussions of biblical historiography, the Saul narratives in 1 Samuel have elicited much attention and interest.[1] Despite the high level of interest, however, historical study of the Saul narratives seems to have yielded rather disappointing results.[2] On the archaeological side, little has been learned to date that is of direct assistance in reconstructing the rise of Israel's first king. And this is not surprising, for as Amihai Mazar has recently pointed out, "the archaeological evidence for the period of the United Monarchy is sparse" and "often controversial."[3] In particular, "the

---

[1]See, e.g., J. Licht, "Biblical Historicism" in *History, Historiography and Interpretation: Historiography in the Ancient World and the Origins of Biblical History*, ed. H. Tadmor and M. Weinfeld (New Haven and London: Yale University Press, 1983), p. 247; H. Donner, "Basic Elements of Old Testament Historiography Illustrated By the Saul Traditions," *Die Ou-Testamentiese Werkgemeenskap in Suid-Afrika* 24 (1981): 40–54; G. von Rad, *Old Testament Theology*, trans. D. M. G. Stalker (New York: Harper & Row, 1962) 1:48–49; *idem*, "The Beginnings of Historical Writing in Ancient Israel," *The Problem of the Hexateuch and Other Essays*, trans. E. W. Trueman Dicken (Edinburgh: Oliver & Boyd, 1966), pp. 166–204; W. E. Evans, "An Historical Reconstruction of the Emergence of Israelite Kingship and the Reign of Saul," *Scripture in Context II: More Essays on the Comparative Method*, eds. W. W. Hallo, J. C. Moyer and L. G. Perdue (Winona Lake, Ind.: Eisenbrauns, 1983), p. 61; Van Seters, *In Search of History*, p. 247.

[2]A shorter version of this chapter appears in *Faith, Tradition, and History*, ed. D. W. Baker, J. K. Hoffmeier, and A. R. Millard (Winona Lake, Ind.: Eisenbrauns, 1994).

[3]*Archaeology of the Land of the Bible: 10,000–586 B.C.E.* (New York: Doubleday, 1990), p. 371.

time of Saul hardly finds any expression in the archaeological record."[4] Social-scientific and ethno-archaeological studies are in the process of providing general background information, but specific information about Israel's first kings must still be derived almost exclusively from the literary deposit in Scripture. And here we encounter a problem. A majority of scholars finds the biblical account of Saul's rise to the throne to be, as Jacob Licht puts it, "rather unconvincing as a statement of fact."[5] Indeed, most would still subscribe to the verdict rendered back in 1932 by W. W. Cannon that "the events by which he [Saul] came to the throne are and will remain a mystery."[6]

This rather unhopeful verdict may derive from one or more of several basic lines of reasoning. I noted already in chapter 3 (pp. 112ff.) the Enlightenment dictum that no narrative that includes God or the gods among the active participants in the events described can qualify as a historical account.[7] When this dictum is applied to the biblical account of Saul's rise, the resulting argument looks something like this (employing the chart described in the preceding chapter).

---

[4]Ibid. The one potential exception to this generalization — viz., the Iron I tower foundation at Tell el-Ful thought by Albright to represent the "Citadel of Saul" — is now regarded as far less certain evidence of Saulide construction than scholars had previously believed; see, most recently, P. M. Arnold, *Gibeah: The Search for a Biblical City*, JSOTS 79 (Sheffield: JSOT, 1990), pp. 51–52.

[5]"Biblical Historicism," p. 107.

[6]"The Reign of Saul," *Theology* 25 (1932): 326.

[7]For a corrective to this view, see, e.g., A. R. Millard, "Old Testament and History," pp. 39–40.

Given **D** —	*so,* **Q** presumably, —	**→C**
that the	|	the biblical account cannot
biblical	*since* **W**	be historical,
account of	divine agency can	|
Saul's rise	never play a part in	*unless* **R**
involves	historical accounts,	warrant or backing is
God as an	|	fallacious.
agent in	*on account of* **B**	
the action	"all just	
(1 Sam	philosophical	
9:15-16;	conceptions" as	
10:6, 9, 22;	defined by the	
11:6, etc.),	Enlightenment,	

Some, no doubt, dismiss the potential historicity of the Saul narratives on a basis such as this, but for those who do not share the exclusively naturalistic worldview of Strauss and his philosophical descendents, and particularly for those who regard the Bible as a distinctive book describing distinctive events, such an argument will carry no weight.

Others, such as Klaas Smelik, have argued that the Saul narratives cannot be historical because the ancient Near East provides too few "inspiring examples" ("inspirerende voorbeelden") of history writing from around the time of David or Solomon to justify any expectation that Israel might have had a historiographical tradition stemming from that time.[8] This is not the place to attempt a full critique of Smelik's contention, but a few brief comments may be in order: (1) Smelik's is an argument from silence; (2) it seems to underplay the significance of, for example, the royal apology literature attested from the chancelleries of the ancient Near East;[9] and (3) it rests, at any rate, on the

[8]*Saul: de voorstelling van Israëls eerste koning in de Masoretische tekst van het Oude Testament* (Amsterdam: drukkerij en Uitgeverij P. E. T., 1977), p. 76.

[9]In this regard it seems fairer to say, with R. K. Gnuse ("Holy History in the Hebrew Scriptures and the Ancient World: Beyond the Present Debate," *BTB* 17 [1987]: 131), that "Israelite thought was different, not unique; it moved beyond the ancient world in certain respects, but it was not diametrically opposed to the predecessor cultures."

questionable assumption that a truly new literary form can never arise spontaneously but only by means of an evolutionary development from earlier forms.[10]

Neither of the above reasons for doubting the historicity of the Saul narratives is very compelling, and indeed neither is very often cited. By far the *most frequently cited reason* for the historical agnosticism regarding Saul's kingship is the belief that the biblical narratives recounting Saul's rise simply *do not make sense as a story*. That is to say, they do not constitute a coherent, sequential narrative. Tomoo Ishida speaks for a majority of scholars when he asserts that "it is futile from the outset to attempt reconstruction of a harmonious history from all the narratives."[11] Even the (by contemporary standards) rather conservative John Bright insists that "in view of these varying accounts, we cannot undertake to reconstruct the sequence of events" by which Saul became king.[12]

In what follows, we shall focus on this last and most pervasive line of reasoning believed by the vast majority of scholars to discredit any attempt to reconstruct the historical rise of Saul from the narratives of 1 Samuel, or at least from all of them taken together. In chart form, the argument representative of the current consensus would look something like this.

---

[10]Patrick and Scult (*Rhetoric,* p. 36) seem to be closer to the mark in their observation that "the Biblical narrative was an innovative form of prose art not seen before in the ancient Near East," a form developed by the biblical writers apparently "because they found the already existing literary forms available to them, namely the chronicle and the epic, so inadequate to their purposes."

[11]*The Royal Dynasties in Ancient Israel: A Study on the Formation and Development of Royal-Dynastic Ideology* (Berlin: Walter de Gruyter, 1977), p. 42.

[12]*History of Israel,* p. 188.

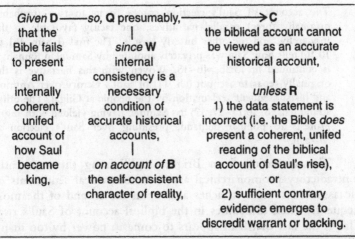

Given **D**	—so, **Q** presumably,————————→**C**	
that the		the biblical account cannot
Bible fails		be viewed as an accurate
to present	*since* **W**	historical account,
an	internal	
internally	consistency is a	
coherent,	necessary	*unless* **R**
unifed	condition of	1) the data statement is
account of	accurate historical	incorrect (i.e. the Bible *does*
how Saul	accounts,	present a coherent, unifed
became		reading of the biblical
king,	*on account of* **B**	account of Saul's rise),
	the self-consistent	or
	character of reality,	2) sufficient contrary
		evidence emerges to
		discredit warrant or backing.

Properly understood, the warrant and backing seem unassailable, so that the second rebuttal above is essentially out of the question. The first rebuttal, however, may be possible, so this is where the investigation should concentrate. The goal, then, is to *listen* once more, as carefully and competently as possible, to the biblical testimony. Despite the weight of a consensus, we must guard against presupposing in advance that the narratives will not make sense, for in so doing we are likely to foreclose any real opportunity of discovering otherwise. Rather, as we have argued in the preceding chapter, if we would be good listeners, we must approach the text with an open (though not naive or credulous) attitude.

PURPORTED OBSTACLES TO A COHERENT LITERARY READING OF SAUL'S RISE

Perhaps the place to begin is with a review of the literary, or logical, difficulties thought to stand in the way of a straightforward reading of the rise of Saul. These are basically three. First, since Wellhausen it has been customary in discussions of the rise of the monarchy as recorded in 1 Samuel 8–12 to distinguish at least two originally independent narratives detectable on the basis of discrepant attitudes to kingship. Bright explains:

The account of Saul's election comes to us in two (probably originally three) parallel narratives, one tacitly favorable to the monarchy, and the other bitterly hostile. The first (I Sam. 9:1 to 10:16) tells how Saul was privately anointed by Samuel in Ramah; it is continued in 13:3b, 4b–15. Woven with this narrative is the originally separate account (ch. 11) of Saul's victory over Ammon and his subsequent acclamation by the people at Gilgal. The other strand (chs. 8; 10:17–27; 12) has Samuel, having yielded with angry protests to popular demand, presiding over Saul's election at Mizpah.[13]

This quotation from Bright, highlighting the apparently contradictory promonarchical and antimonarchical sentiments of the assumed sources, touches also upon the second of the most frequently cited difficulties in the biblical account of Saul's rise. This is the fact that Saul appears to come to power by too many different routes. Did he come to power by distinguishing himself in battle against the Ammonites (as many historical critics believe), or as a result of his anointing followed by battle (as the combined promonarchical source would have it), or by lot-casting (as the antimonarchical source would have it)? The consensus of scholarly opinion is well summarized by Herbert Donner when he says of the various accounts, "they contradict each other: Saul could not have become king in so many ways."[14] Even restricting himself to a consideration of the so-called promonarchical source, William Irwin insists that "we are embarrassed by our very wealth! Either account [i.e., the anointing episode or the Ammonite victory] would suffice as an explanation of this revolutionary change in Hebrew history, to be given both baffles credence."[15]

To these two apparent difficulties—the differing attitudes towards the monarchy and the multiple accession accounts—must be added a third. The account of Saul's anointing in 1 Samuel 10 contains a longstanding *crux interpretum*, which comes in verse 8. In this verse Samuel instructs Saul to go down to Gilgal and wait for him, so that he may come and offer sacrifices and tell Saul what

---

[13]Ibid., pp. 187–88.

[14]"Old Testament Historiography," p. 43.

[15]"Samuel and the Rise of the Monarchy," *American Journal of Semitic Languages and Literatures* 58 (1941): 117.

he is to do. The problem is that this instruction comes on the heels of verse 7, in which Samuel tells Saul to "do what your hand finds to do." Assuming the verse 7 directive to be an unqualified authorization for Saul to act in kingly fashion whenever the need should arise, scholars have felt that verse 8 constitutes a blatant contradiction.[16] What verse 7 seems to authorize, "Do what your hand finds to do," verse 8 seems to take away, "go down to Gilgal" and "wait." To make matters worse, the fulfillment of the injunction in verse 8 does not come until chapter 13, all of which contributes to the impression that verse 8 must not be original to its present context in chapter 10, but must be a later insertion, perhaps a sort of "theological correction" inserted by a later prophetic circle unhappy with the apparently free hand being given Saul by Samuel in verse 7.[17] As a corollary to the assumption that verse 8 is secondary to chapter 10, scholars have customarily assumed that the Gilgal episode in chapter 13 (vv. 4b, 7b–15a) must also be secondary.[18]

How are we to evaluate these three arguments to the effect that the biblical account of the rise of Saul is at points contradictory and incoherent, and thus an unreliable source of historical information? I would contend that the data are now available to enable solutions to all three problems. The first two I shall

[16]See, e.g., J. Wellhausen, *Prolegomena zur Geschichte Israel*, 3rd ed. (Berlin: Georg Reimer, 1886), p. 268; K. D. Budde, *Die Bücher Samuel*, Kurzer Hand-Commentar zum Alten Testament 8 (Tübingen: J. C. B. Mohr, 1902), p. 69; R. J. Thompson, *Penitence and Sacrifice in Early Israel outside the Levitical Law* (Leiden: E. J. Brill, 1963), p. 106; H. J. Stoebe, *Das erste Buch Samuelis*, Kommentar zum Alten Testament 8/1 (Gütersloh: Gert Mohn, 1973), p. 210.

[17]Cf. J. Kegler's characterization of 10:8 as a "theologische Korrektur" in *Politisches Geschehen und theologisches Verstehen: Zum Geschichtsverständnis in der frühen israelitischen Königszeit*, Calwer Theologische Monographien 8 (Stuttgart: Calwer, 1977), p. 264.

[18]The following statement by T. Veijola (*Die Ewige Dynastie: David und die Entstehung seiner Dynastie nach der deuteronomistischen Darstellung*, Annales academiae scientiarum Fennicae, Series B, 193 [Helsinki: Suomalainen Tiedeakatemia, 1975], p. 55) is typical: "That the entire Gilgal episode in 1 Sam. 13:7b–15a (which falls outside its present context) is a secondary insertion (along with its similarly isolated anticipation in 1 Sam. 10:8), is no longer in need of demonstration" (my translation). In addition to the literature cited by Veijola, cf. also Stoebe, *Das erste Buch Samuelis*, p. 207; McCarter, *I Samuel*, p. 228.

consider only briefly, since the relevant insights necessary to their resolution have already been published by others.

In chart form, the first argument, based on the apparently differing attitudes towards monarchy, looks like this.

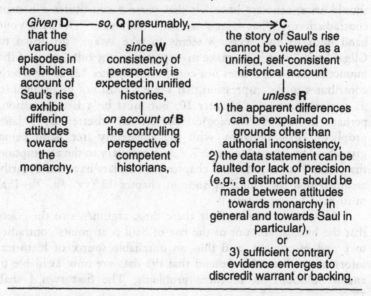

Given **D**———— *so,* **Q** presumably, ————————→**C**
that the various episodes in the biblical account of Saul's rise exhibit differing attitudes towards the monarchy,	| *since* **W** consistency of perspective is expected in unified histories, | *on account of* **B** the controlling perspective of competent historians,	the story of Saul's rise cannot be viewed as a unified, self-consistent historical account | *unless* **R** 1) the apparent differences can be explained on grounds other than authorial inconsistency, 2) the data statement can be faulted for lack of precision (e.g., a distinction should be made between attitudes towards monarchy in general and towards Saul in particular), or 3) sufficient contrary evidence emerges to discredit warrant or backing.

Those who espouse the argument from differing monarchical attitudes often fail to consider possible rebuttals such as are listed above. But, in fact, recent studies confirm the validity of at least the first two. Tsevat, McCarthy, Childs, and others have pointed out, for example, that the more antimonarchical statements are made in the episodes involving assemblies (natural contexts for expression of strong opinions) and not so much in the action reports. Eslinger has stressed that monarchical attitudes expressed are not always those of the narrator; in each instance we must ask "the simple question of who says what to whom." Others have emphasized the important distinction between attitudes that are antimonarchical *per se* and those that are merely anti-Saul.[19] When

---

[19]For bibliography and discussion pertaining to all of the above, see my *Reign and Rejection*, pp. 173–83.

we begin to look at the problem of differing attitudes to the monarchy through these corrective lenses, we discover that our sharpened vision reveals not a more clearly defined problem but the absence of any problem at all. In other words, the above argument fails, because adequate rebuttals are forthcoming.

The second challenge to the literary coherence (and thus *potential* historicity) of the biblical account of Saul's rise relates to the fact that Saul appears to have come to power via several distinct pathways. The basic argument, with potential rebuttals, may be laid out like this.

Given D —— so, Q presumably, ————→C		
that the	|	the biblical account of Saul's
various	*since* W	rise cannot be trusted as
episodes in	reliable	historiography,
the biblical	historiography	
account of	excludes	|
Saul's rise	contradictory,	*unless* R
present	mutually exclusive	1) the data statement is
multiple	renditions of how a	incorrect and it can be
(and	particular historical	shown that the episodes are
apparently	circumstance	not in fact mutually exclusive
mutually	came to be,	(e.g., that each is but a
exclusive)	|	stage in a larger process),
accounts	*on account of* B	or
of how	the self-consistent	2) sufficient contrary
Saul came	character of reality,	evidence emerges to
to power,		discredit warrant or backing.

The raw material for confirming the first rebuttal has been provided in recent work by Baruch Halpern[20] and has been further fashioned by Dianna Edelman.[21] Halpern has argued on the basis

[20]*The Constitution of the Monarchy in Israel*, Harvard Semitic Monographs 25 (Chico, CA: Scholars, 1981); "The Uneasy Compromise: Israel between League and Monarchy," *Traditions in Transformation: Turning Points in Biblical Faith,* Cross Festschrift; ed. B. Halpern and J. D. Levenson (Winona Lake: Eisenbrauns, 1981), pp. 59–96.

[21]"Saul's Rescue of Jabesh-Gilead (1 Sam. 11:1–11): Sorting Story from History," *Zeitschrift für die alttestamentliche Wissenschaft* 96 (1984): 195–209.

of both biblical and extrabiblical evidence that the process by which leaders in early Israel came to power quite likely entailed three stages, which we might describe simply as designation, demonstration, and confirmation.[22] The process would go something like this. An individual is first *designated* in some way as God's chosen instrument. The new appointee is then expected to *demonstrate* his special status and suitability for leadership by a feat of arms or military victory, whether real or merely ritual. Having thus distinguished himself publicly, he is in a position to be confirmed publicly as leader.

Both Halpern and Edelman attempt to elucidate the biblical account of Saul's rise on the basis of this tripartite pattern. Halpern isolates what he believes to be two complete exemplars of the accession pattern in the stretch of text from 1 Samuel 9 to 14.[23] The impetus for this discovery, however, appears to come more from Halpern's commitment to a theory of sources and doublets[24] than from the texts themselves.[25] Edelman improves on Halpern's analysis by discerning but one instance of the accession pattern in 1 Samuel 9–11. In her view, the divine designation is represented by Saul's anointing in the section 9:1–10:16, the demonstration by his defeat of the Ammonites in 11:1–11, and the confirmation by the "renewal" of the kingdom in 11:14–15.[26]

Edelman's scheme is plausible so far as it goes, but it leaves some unanswered questions. For example, it provides little explanation of the lot-casting episode in 10:17–27, which comes between the anointing and the Ammonite victory.[27] A further and

---

[22]While Halpern sometimes explicitly names only two stages—viz., *designation* and *confirmation* (cf. *Constitution*, pp. 125ff., 173–74)—it is clear that he presupposes a middle *demonstration* stage consisting of a real or ritual victory of some sort (cf. "Uneasy Compromise," p. 72; *Constitution*, pp. 95, 173–74). On the validity of distinguishing three stages, see also Edelman, "Saul's Rescue," p. 198 n.9.

[23]"Uneasy Compromises," p. 70.

[24]He writes, "The first step in investigating Saul's election is, as the histories recognize, a division of the sources in 1 Samuel 8ff." (ibid., p. 63).

[25]For a critical evaluation of Halpern's two-source theory, see my *Reign and Rejection*, pp. 191–93.

[26]"Saul's Rescue," pp. 197–99.

[27]Edelman (ibid., pp. 200–202) notes only that this episode "appears to augment the discussion of the first stage of the process of installing a king" and to look

more significant tension in Edelman's scheme has to do with Samuel's charge to Saul in 10:7 to "do what your hand finds to do." Edelman rightly recognizes that this charge implies some kind of military engagement, and she assumes that this must be none other than Saul's Ammonite victory. But she also recognizes—and herein lies the problem—that the real focus of 10:7 in context is not the Ammonites but the Philistines, and particularly the Philistine presence in Gibeah (which is to become the object of Jonathan's aggression in chapter 13). To come to terms with this awkward situation, some scholars postulate that the events of chapter 13 must have followed more closely on 10:7 in some hypothetical earlier stage of development.[28] In other words, they assume that episodes originally joined have now been redactionally put asunder.

This suggestion of textual dislocation brings us to the third and final challenge to the literary coherence of the rise of Saul as recounted in 1 Samuel. In what follows I shall attempt to demonstrate that this perceived difficulty actually offers the key to a rather straightforward synchronic reading of the narrative of Saul's rise.

SAUL'S FIRST CHARGE
AS A TWO-STAGE AFFAIR

As mentioned earlier, the impression of textual dislocation derives from two felt tensions in the text: first, the apparently contradictory commands given to Saul by Samuel in consecutive

---

forward to the public coronation that will eventually occur in 11:14–15; for Edelman's most recent thoughts on the issue, see her *King Saul in the Historiography of Judah*, JSOTS 121 (Sheffield: JSOT, 1991), pp. 51–58, 76–82.

[28]Ibid., p. 200. Those who seek to explain the apparent relationship between chaps. 10 and 13 in traditio-historical terms include H. J. Stoebe, "Zur Topographie und Überlieferung der Schlact von Mikmas, 1 Sam. 13 und 14," *Theologische Zeitschrift* 21 (1965): 277–80; J. M. Miller, "Saul's Rise to Power: Some Observations Concerning 1 Sam 9:1–10:16; 10:26–11:15 and 13:2–14:46," *CBQ* 36 (1974): 162; T. N. D. Mettinger, *King and Messiah: The Civil and Sacral Legitimation of the Israelite Kings*, (Coniectanea Biblica: Old Testament Series 8 (Lund: CWK Gleerup, 1976), p. 97; and most recently P. J. Arnold, *Gibeah*, pp. 89–90.

verses in chapter 10 ("do what your hand finds to do" [v.7] and "go down ahead of me to Gilgal [and] wait . . . until I come to you and tell you what you are to do" [v.8]) and, second, the fact that the trip to Gilgal is not made until chapter 13. We shall take these up in order.

As regards the commands of 10:7–8, it is my contention that they should be viewed not as contradictory but as complementary instructions, the execution of the second being contingent upon the fulfillment of the first. This view seems to be quite in keeping with the larger narrative context, which runs as follows. After a divinely orchestrated meeting between the two principals in chapter 9, Samuel anoints Saul in 10:1 as the Lord's designate to lead his people. Samuel then describes three signs that will confirm Saul in his new station (vv. 2–6). The third sign is to take place at Gibeah of God, where, as Samuel points out, there is a Philistine outpost (v. 5). This reference to a Philistine outpost is regarded by many scholars as at best superfluous, if not indeed out of place. No better justification is given for this opinion than that these scholars fail to see any reason why the biblical narrator should mention a Philistine installation at this particular juncture in the narrative.[29] When we recall, however, that Saul was appointed especially to deal with the Philistine menace (cf. the Lord's instructions to Samuel in 9:16), and when we notice that it is as soon as the three signs have come to pass that Saul is to do what his hand finds to do (10:7), then the mention of a Philistine presence at the site of the third and final sign takes on special significance. There is much to commend the view that Samuel's mention of the Philistines in 10:5 represents a fairly obvious hint to Saul of what, in fact, his hand should find to do.[30]

---

[29]P. K. McCarter (*I Samuel*, 182), for example, remarks simply that "this notice is immaterial at this point and probably secondary, having been added along with the instructions in v 8 as preparation for c 13."

[30]This understanding of the significance of 10:5 is attested already in the writings of grammarian and biblical commentator David Kimchi (1160–1235), who sees in Samuel's reference to the "officers of the Philistines" (Kimchi's apparent understanding of the Philistine presence) a hint that Saul "should remove them from there and save Israel out of their hands" (my translation of Kimchi's commentary to 1 Sam. 10:5 found in standard editions of the rabbinic Hebrew Bible). Other commentators who have sensed something of the significance of 10:5 include R.

Against this background, and recalling the tripartite accession process worked out by Halpern and Edelman, we are
prompted to ask what could possibly serve as a more appropriate
demonstration, after Saul's divine *designation*, than that he should
"throw down the gauntlet" to the Philistines by attacking one of
their installations? Samuel, of course, realizes that such an act of
provocation will signal only the beginning and not the end of
trouble, and so he issues a *second* instruction to Saul in verse 8: "Go
down ahead of me to Gilgal. I will surely come down to you to
sacrifice burnt offerings and fellowship offerings, but you must
wait seven days until I come to you and tell you what you are to
do." In other words, as soon as Saul has done what his hand finds
to do, thereby provoking the Philistines, he is to repair to Gilgal,
where Samuel will join him in order to consecrate the ensuing
battle with sacrifices and to give him further instructions.[31]

In this way, then, the two injunctions of 10:7–8 appear to be
not contradictory but complementary and sequentially contingent.
We still have a problem, however, since the prescribed trip to
Gilgal does not take place until chapter 13. The wording of 13:8,
which speaks of Saul waiting "seven days, the time set by
Samuel," leaves no room for doubt that the allusion is to 10:8—on
this point there is universal agreement. What is often overlooked,
however, is that a similar relationship exists between the notice in
13:3 that Jonathan has attacked the Philistine outpost at Geba and
Saul's first charge in 10:7. In other words, in 13:3 we see Jonathan
doing what Saul was instructed to do back in 10:7. As Stoebe
succinctly puts it, "the deed that is here [13:3] ascribed to Jonathan
is what one awaits as the continuation of Saul's Spirit-endowment
in Gibeah and of the charge 'Do what your hand finds to do'

Kittel, *Geschichte des Volkes Israel*, 7th ed. (Gotha: Leopold Klotz, 1925), 2: 82; A.
Lods, *Israel from its Beginnings to the Middle of the Eighth Century*, trans. S. H. Hooke
(London: Kegan Paul, Trench, Trubner, 1932), p. 353: C. J. Goslinga, *Het eerste
boek Samuël*, Commentaar op het Oude Testament (Kampen: J. H. Kok, 1968),
p. 223; Smelik, *Saul: de voorstelling van Israëls eerste koning*, p. 107.
    [31]For a discussion of the prophet's role in pre-battle consecration and instruction,
see my *Reign and Rejection*, pp. 61–63.

(10:7)" (my translation).[32] It is noteworthy that Jonathan's provocative act in 13:3 is immediately followed by Saul's going down to Gilgal to wait for Samuel (13:4). Thus, we see the procedure *envisaged* in chapter 10 (i.e., provocation of the Philistines followed by convocation in Gilgal) actually *followed* in chapter 13. While this double attestation of the provocation-followed-by-convocation pattern does not constitute a proof of the genuineness and originality of the pattern in either context, it would at least seem to shift the burden of proof to those who would wish to assert the contrary.

In view of the obvious relationship between chapters 10 and 13, are faced then with a final, very crucial question. How are we to explain the rather large gap, in both narrative time and real time, between Samuel's two-part instruction to Saul in 10:7–8 and its evident fulfillment three chapters and several episodes later? Must we assume traditio-historical or redactional dislocation of originally sequential episodes, or *might we not consider the possibility that Saul simply falters in his first assignment*, that he simply doesn't do what his hand finds to do, thus delaying indefinitely the execution of his second instruction—viz., the trip to Gilgal? The latter alternative seems to offer a rather promising possibility for explaining the gap between the issuance of Saul's first charge and its eventual fulfillment through the agency of Jonathan. The objection might be raised, however, that if Saul falters at the start, why does the text not explicitly say so or condemn Saul for his inaction? In addressing this objection, it will be helpful to contemplate a different kind of gap or gapping.

"GAPPING" AS LITERARY DEVICE AND THE GAP BETWEEN 1 SAMUEL 10 AND 13

In his *Poetics of Biblical Narrative* (pp. 186–88), Meir Sternberg points out that all literary works establish "a system of gaps that must be filled in" by the reader in the process of reading.

---

[32]*Das erste Buch Samuelis*, p. 247; cf. p. 207. More recently, Halpern (*Constitution*, pp. 155–56) has also drawn attention to the command/fulfillment relationship between 10:7 and 13:3.

Every literary work raises a number of questions in the mind of the reader, but it only provides explicit answers to a few of these. The remaining questions, the "gaps" as Sternberg calls them, are to be answered or filled in by the reader on the basis of clues in the text itself. Sternberg illustrates what he means by citing the following Hebrew nursery rhyme.

> Every day, that's the way
> Jonathan goes out to play.
> Climbed a tree. What did he see?
> Birdies: one, two, three!
>
> Naughty boy! What have we seen?
> There's a hole in your new jeans!

How did Jonathan tear his jeans? In the tree, of course. Even a child can draw this conclusion quite readily from the information given in the rhyme, though the point is never explicitly made. Of course, gap-filling may not always be as simple as this, especially in narratives as artful and sophisticated as the Samuel narratives. Sternberg writes: "gap-filling ranges from simple linkages of elements, which the reader performs automatically, to intricate networks that are figured out consciously, laboriously, hesitantly, and with constant modifications in the light of additional information disclosed in later stages of reading."

It seems fair to say that the *literary* gap created by the *literal* gap between Saul's first charge and its eventual fulfillment is of the more difficult sort described above. That it should take conscious effort to fill it should not surprise us, for as Sternberg remarks, "in works of greater complexity, the filling-in of gaps becomes much more difficult and therefore more conscious and anything but automatic." The test of any attempt at gap-filling is, of course, whether the hypothesis is "legitimated by the text."

One way to formulate an argument against the coherence of the Saul story on the basis of the datum that there is a gap between the charge of 1 Samuel 10:7-8 and its apparent fulfillment in chapter 13 would be the following.

Given **D**——so, **Q** presumably, ————————➤**C**		
that the fullfillment of the charge given in 1 Sam 10:7-8 does not come until 1 Sam 13, after several intervening episodes,	| *since* **W** proper sequencing is a usual aspect of storytelling (unless there are specific indications of flashback, prolepsis, etc.), | *on account of* **B** the importance of establishing cause-effect relationships in coherent narratives,	either there is no intent to convey a coherent, sequential account, or the texts must have suffered some dislocation, | *unless* **R** 1) it can be shown that, despite appearances, proper sequencing has in fact been preserved, or 2) sufficient contrary evidence emerges to undermine warrant or backing.

Even leaving aside the possible rebuttals for the moment, we can see that the above argument is not a very tight one, for it tacitly assumes that "proper sequence" inevitably means that fulfillment follows *immediately* after charge. But everyday experience belies such an assumption; as every parent knows, the charge, "Clean your room!" is often followed by many intervening episodes before the fulfillment finally comes. Thus, even were we to grant absolute status to the warrant, the conclusion would not necessarily follow from the data.

Moreover, and perhaps more importantly, we have seen that greater sensitivity to the literary device of *gapping* establishes the first rebuttal listed above as a distinct possibility. In what follows we shall take a necessarily cursory look at how my theory that Saul "faltered in the starting gate" might help to explain the entire narrative sequence of his rise to power.

MAKING SENSE OF SAUL'S RISE

Immediately following the anointing episode, the text recounts a rather enigmatic conversation between Saul and his uncle (10:14–16), the significance of which has largely eluded scholars. In this conversation, Saul is reasonably loquacious on the topic of his search for his father's lost donkeys and even as regards his "chance" meeting with Samuel, but he is absolutely silent, as our narrator informs us, on the matter of the kingship. Saul's silence regarding the "big news" of the day has baffled most commentators. But might this not simply be the behavior of a man who is shrinking back from a fearful first duty as the "Lord's anointed" and who would just as soon not talk about it, at least not with one of such militant leanings as Uncle Abner (if that is who is in view)?

Moving on to the next episode (10:17–27), I would argue that Saul's failure to carry out his first charge also helps to explain why it is necessary for Samuel to convene an assembly in Mizpah and why there is a certain negative tone to the proceedings there. Saul's inaction after his designation means that he has done nothing to gain public attention or to demonstrate his fitness as a leader. This means, of course, that the normal accession process, whereby designation was to be followed by demonstration that would then lead to confirmation, has stalled. The Mizpah assembly may be viewed as Samuel's attempt to bring Saul to public attention by a different route than that originally envisaged and to show by the lot-casting that Saul is the leader given by God in response to the people's request for a king (chap. 8). If this reading of the episode is basically correct, it becomes increasingly difficult to interpret Saul's hiding behind the baggage at the time of his selection as evidence of laudable humility. One senses, rather, a timidity and even fearfulness in Saul, the crouching "giant" (cf. 9:2), that will express itself again in Saul, the cringing "giant" of chapter 17, who shrinks back in fear and dismay before the Philistines' own giant (17:11). Moreover, if my theory is correct that there has yet been no demonstration of Saul's valor or fitness in battle, then it is not too surprising that some troublemakers protest, when Saul is dragged from behind the baggage, "How can this one save us?" (10:27).

In chapter 11 Saul's rescue of Jabesh-gilead from the Ammonite threat provides the long-awaited *demonstration,* and the kingship is "renewed" (v. 14), that is, the accession process, derailed by Saul's initial faltering, is set back on track. The defeat of the Ammonites serves, then, as a sort of substitute for the demonstration originally envisaged by Samuel in 10:7, which was to have been a provocation of the Philistines. After Saul's Ammonite victory, all the people are delighted with their new king (11:12–15). Only Samuel seems to remain cautious, issuing in the next chapter rebuke and warning that kingship can yet fail. Samuel's tone in chapter 12 suggests that the experiment of kingship, and in particular Israel's new king, must yet stand a test. It is my contention that this test relates directly to Saul's first charge. It is no mere coincidence, then, that the very next chapter recounts Jonathan's attack upon the Philistine outpost in Geba (13:3), phase one of Saul's first charge (cf. 10:7), followed by Saul's immediate retreat to Gilgal to await Samuel's arrival (13:4), in accordance with phase two of his first charge (10:8). Lamentably, Saul fails in the execution of phase two, and receives a stinging rebuke from the belated Samuel (13:8–14). Although Samuel's reaction to Saul's failure has often been interpreted as excessively harsh, this assessment no longer seems justified once we recognize the link between Saul's failure in chapter 13 and his all-important first charge in 10:7–8.

Space limitations do not allow a full exploration of the significance of Saul's first charge, but one may at least observe that it seems designed to create an authority structure whereby human kingship can be accommodated within what remains essentially theocratic rule. In the new order established by Samuel in his first charge to Saul, the king is to become the military agent, but the prophet is to remain the recipient and mediator of the divine initiative.[33] If the king will but obey the word of the Lord as mediated by the prophet, then the experiment of kingship can succeed (see 12:13–15, 24–25). Saul does not obey, however, either in chapter 13 or subsequently in chapter 15, and so proves himself unfit to remain on the throne of Israel.

---

[33]On the mediatorial role of prophets in the monarchical period, see my *Reign and Rejection of King Saul*, pp. 60–65.

GOOD STORY, BUT IS IT HISTORY?

If the foregoing study of the Saul traditions is moving in the right direction, it seems more likely than has generally been assumed that the Bible does present an internally coherent account of Saul's rise to power. The *story* makes sense. But does this mean that we should understand the story as *history?* Not necessarily, for as noted in the preceding chapter, the consistency of a story is no guarantee of its truth, including historical truth. Moreover, so far we have focused exclusively on the chapters recounting Saul's rise and have yet to look to the broader context and overall sense of purpose of the books of Samuel. To this point, we are only able to suggest that the account of Saul's rise is "possibly" to be read as a historical account. This is how my argument would look.

Given **D**—— that the Bible presents an internally coherent, unified account of how Saul became king,	*so,* **Q** possibly, | *since* **W** internal conistency is a necessary (but not a sufficient) condition of accurate historical accounts, | *on account of* **B** the self-consistent character of reality,	——————>**C** the biblical account could be viewed as a historical account, | *unless* **R** 1) the data statement is shown to be incorrect after all, or 2) sufficient contrary evidence emerges to discredit warrant or backing.

All we know to this point is that the account of Saul's rise could possibly be a historical account. In order to discover whether it probably should be understood in this way, we must broaden our investigation to consider the larger context of which the Saul narratives are a part. If these display a historiographical character, and if the Saul narratives are lacking in textual indications that they should be treated differently from their context, then the presumption will be in favor of reading the Saul narratives historically. The important question of the overall sense of purpose of the books of Samuel is deserving of at least a chapter, if not an entire book, so it cannot be treated adequately in the short compass of the present volume. Perhaps the best we can do in the space available is to recall what was said at the beginning of this chapter about the central place the books of Samuel have enjoyed in discussions on ancient Israelite historiography and to note that, despite a minority opinion to the contrary, most scholars are agreed that a historical impulse is evident in these books. As sophisticated as is the literary art of 1 and 2 Samuel, and as prominent as is the ideological/theological impulse, the historiographical character of the stories is still felt. A majority of scholars would concur that the same can be said of the larger literary context of which the books of Samuel are a part (i.e., the so-called Deuteronomistic History, or the Former Prophets). Taking the larger context into consideration, then, we may construct the following argument. We are still focusing on truth claim, not truth value, and the effect of the argument is to shift the *qualifier* from *possibly* to *probably*.

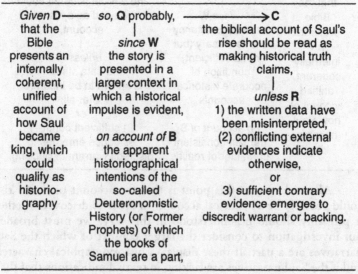

Given **D** —— *so,* **Q** probably, ————➤**C**		
that the	|	the biblical account of Saul's
Bible	*since* **W**	rise should be read as
presents an	the story is	making historical truth
internally	presented in a	claims,
coherent,	larger context in	|
unified	which a historical	*unless* **R**
account of	impulse is evident,	1) the written data have
how Saul	|	been misinterpreted,
became	*on account of* **B**	(2) conflicting external
king, which	the apparent	evidences indicate
could	historiographical	otherwise,
qualify as	intentions of the	or
historio-	so-called	3) sufficient contrary
graphy	Deuteronomistic	evidence emerges to
	History (or Former	discredit warrant or backing.
	Prophets) of which	
	the books of	
	Samuel are a part,	

To assert that the biblical account of Saul's rise probably should be *read* as historiography (i.e., to recognize that the text makes historical truth claims) is not the same as saying that the account must be *accepted* as history. What one decides on the latter issue may depend in part on how the text's truth claims square with external evidences (which in the present instance are minimal, as noted earlier). How one weighs up the various evidences, however, will be affected by one's fundamental assumptions about the Bible's *macro-genre*. On the one hand, for those who regard the Bible as an ancient document of *merely* human origin, there may be little reason to assume the truth value of the Bible's truth claims, and it may take very little conflicting evidence to cast these claims into doubt. Moreover, no quantity of positive correlations will by themselves be likely to bring about a rethinking of the Bible's origins. On the other hand, for those who accept the Bible's self-testimony to its divine as well as human origin, there will be warrant for accepting the testimony as reliable, and there will be a profound reluctance to overturn this confidence on the basis of apparently negative correlations.

In the argument below, the backing is admittedly a dogmatic one, but it is presented without apology, for I am convinced that, as Soggin has said, "no historian starts from an ideological void."[34] And what is ideology if not, at its most basic level, dogma? It is inevitable, it seems to me, that as arguments are pushed deeper and deeper to the level of basic warrants and backing, they all will be found to rest ultimately on some fundamental set of beliefs about God, self, the world, the Bible, and so forth—in other words, on dogmatically held positions.

My final argument looks like this.

---

[34] J. Alberto Soggin, *Introduction to the Old Testament*, 3d ed., trans. John Bowden, Old Testament Library (Louisville: John Knox, 1989), p. 182.

Given D ——	so, Q probably,	——→C
that the		the historical Saul became
Bible	*since* **W**	king basically as described,
presents an	the Bible speaks		
internally	truth,	*unless* **R**
coherent,			1)the data statement is
unified	*on account of* **B**	incorrect—i.e. written data
account of	its status as the	have been misinterpreted,
how Saul	word of God,	or
became		2) sufficient contrary
king that		evidence emerges to
(probably)		discredit warrant or backing.
should be		
viewed as a		
historical		
account,		

What is interesting about this argument is that even with its dogmatic backing the conclusion is only "probably" true. This is so because the degree of certainty of the conclusion is limited by the degree of certainty of the data (truth claim) as established in the earlier arguments. This means that one may affirm the total trustworthiness of the Bible and still hold only a qualified assurance that Saul became king in a certain way.

CONCLUSION

The aim of this chapter has been to offer a more extended example than was possible in the earlier chapters of how one might approach a biblical narrative with historical questions in mind. Our consideration of the narratives in 1 Samuel having to do with Saul's rise to power has illustrated how intertwined literary reading and historical reconstruction often are. It has also illustrated some of the ways in which interpreters' background beliefs and fundamental assumptions influence (to a limited degree) assessments of a text's truth claims and (to a large degree) assessments of a text's truth value.

Proceeding along lines suggested in the preceding chapter, we sought to listen afresh to the story of Saul's rise to power. And with the aid of some of the newer insights of modern literary study, we discovered a more coherent storyline than has previously been recognized by most scholars. The coherence of a story is not, of course, a guarantee of its historicity. As already noted, coherence is a necessary but not a sufficient condition of historicity. But discovering a sensible, sequential story in 1 Samuel 9–13 does at least remove the most common reason for assuming that the events surrounding Saul's rise to power must forever remain a mystery.

Anything approaching "scientific proof" is, of course, impossible in matters of history, since the object of study—the past—no longer exists and is certainly not susceptible to repeated experimentation and observation. But this does not mean that a cumulative case cannot be built for the *probability* that a given narrative fairly represents its historical subject . . . in the same way that a portrait fairly represents its subject. But even if the biblical narratives prove to be sensible, how are we to choose between the "pictures" of the past they present and the sometimes widely divergent "pictures" presented by some modern scholars? Abraham Malamat puts it very simply: "We could all do well to give heed to Wellhausen's dictum, astounding for him: 'If it [the Israelite tradition] is at all feasible, it would be utter folly (*Torheit*) to give preference to any other feasibility.' "[35]

---

[35]"The Proto-History of Israel: A Study in Method," in *The Word of the Lord Shall Go Forth: Essays in Honor of David Noel Freedman in Celebration of His Sixtieth Birthday*, ed. Carol L. Meyers and M. O'Connor (Winona Lake: Eisenbrauns, 1983), p. 309. The quotation is from Wellhausen's *Die Composition des Hexateuchs und der historischen Bücher des Alten Testaments*, 3d ed. (Berlin: Reimer, 1899), p. 347, and is, as Malamat notes, "limited in context."

EPILOGUE

Following a precedent set by several other volumes in this series, I have decided to bring this book to a close with an epilogue rather than a conclusion. This seems fitting, as the journey of exploration that we began at the start of this volume has not yet reached its conclusion—at least not its final conclusion. At this juncture in the writing process I feel much the same as I did several years ago when making my first climb in England's Lake District. From the base of the small mountain, called Barrow, the climb to the top looked achievable within the allotted amount of time, even if not particularly easy. As it turned out, Barrow has several "false peaks." I can well remember the mixture of satisfaction and deflation I felt, as a first-time climber unaware of this feature, upon reaching what I thought was the top of the mountain, only to discover that it was a false peak and that the trail, after running level for a short stretch, continued sharply upward to another peak, and even another after that!

Still, there is value in attaining a peak, even if not the final one. Even from lesser heights, one can get a view of the surrounding terrain. One can see more clearly where one has been. And one can see other paths that might have been taken and can at least imagine the kinds of things that would have been seen along the other routes. Perhaps most importantly, it is only upon reaching the false peak that the climb still ahead can be seen.

This is where we are—at a point where we can look back

over the ground we have covered and recall what we have seen. At an early stage in our journey we discovered that the Bible, though not a history book *per se*, is a book deeply concerned with history. Amidst the library of literary genres that constitutes the Bible, there are those—particularly (but not exclusively) its narratives— that evidence a historiographical impulse, albeit not of the modern, secular variety. The Bible's narratives concern themselves not merely with the human actors on the stage of history but with the Lord of history himself and with his perspective on and participation in the unfolding drama. The story is, as the well- worn phrase puts it, *His* story. And it is masterfully told. Thus, with the historical impulse are combined two others: the theologi- cal and the literary.

Respecting the latter, we discovered in the second stage of our journey that literary artistry plays as important a role in (narrative) historiography as does visual artistry in portraiture. We even explored the idea that a good way to view ancient historiography is as a kind of *verbal representational art*, with all that this implies about the interplay of creativity and constraint in the depiction.

At the third stage of our journey, we looked at the fundamental question of the importance of history for faith. We discovered that how one answers this question is often a reflection of one's understanding of the essence of Christianity. We noted that for classic Christianity the gospel of redemption from sin and of new life in Christ has depended for its validity on redemptive history, not redemptive fiction.

At the fourth stage of our journey we halted to have a look round at our fellow travelers and to ask why it is that there is so often radical disagreement on historical questions. We observed that several of the more prominent approaches to biblical interpre- tation have, in addition to their strengths, also some weaknesses that prevent them from doing full justice to the biblical testimony.

We then resumed our journey and in its fifth stage began to develop a basic hermeneutical strategy for approaching biblical texts with historical questions in mind. After considering the importance of contemplating fundamental assumptions—ours, others' and the texts'—we stressed the need for first seeking to

discover the truth claims of biblical texts by *listening* to them as
carefully and competently as possible, and then thoughtfully *testing*
these claims on the basis of both internal and external considerations. We also explored a method of analyzing, constructing, and
presenting historical arguments. Finally, having sketched out a
basic approach, we tried it out on a specific example.

This, in brief, is the ground we have covered. We can now
turn and look at the climb still ahead. Several areas come into view
that invite further exploration. The concept of historiography as
representational art and the implications of this view invite further
discussion, as does the question of how literary theory may
impinge on some of the specific historical-critical conclusions
reached by earlier scholars. The related disciplines of narrative
theory and biblical poetics are still relatively new, and it can be
hoped that the future will see further developments and
refinements in these approaches. The exploration of comparative
literatures from the ancient Near Eastern and Hellenistic worlds
represents an ongoing task. And perhaps most importantly, one
would like to see in the future further reflection on the Bible's own
theology of history.

So it appears that the journey must continue (though not
within the confines of this small volume). In the preface, I
commented with respect to journeys that "getting there is half the
fun." At this stage, looking back but also looking forward,
perhaps all I can hope for is that some of my fellow travelers will
agree and will be encouraged to continue to explore the historical
dimension of the Bible.

FOR FURTHER READING

A complete list of works cited in this volume may be found in the index of authors and titles. In this section I have selected contributions in English that should prove helpful for those wishing to research further some of the topics discussed in the preceding pages.

Since I am convinced that a proper historical assessment of biblical texts is dependent, in the first instance, on a proper literary reading of them, I shall begin by mentioning works that offer guidance in reading biblical literature more competently. Beginning students might well want to start with Robert Alter's stimulating book *The Art of Biblical Narrative* (New York: Basic Books, 1981). For the study of poetry, James Kugel's *The Idea of Biblical Poetry: Parallelism and Its History* (New Haven: Yale University Press, 1981) offers seminal insights, which are further developed by Alter in *The Art of Biblical Poetry* (New York: Basic Books, 1985). Tremper Longman III's *Literary Approaches to Biblical Interpretation*, FCI 3 (Grand Rapids: Zondervan, 1987) is a useful, brief introduction to both prose and poetry in the Bible, and it includes example readings. Alter's *World of Biblical Literature* (New York: Basic Books, 1992) also treats both prose and poetry as well as a number of general issues arising from the study of the Bible as literature. Literary critic Leland Ryken has contributed a number of studies on the Bible as literature, including *How to Read the Bible as Literature* (Grand Rapids: Zondervan, 1984) and *Words of Delight: A Literary Introduction to the Bible* (Grand Rapids; Baker, 1987).

Influential treatments of the narrative poetics of the Hebrew Bible include Shimon Bar-Efrat's *Narrative Art in the Bible*, JSOTS 70 (Sheffield: Almond Press, 1989 [Hebrew orig. 1979, 2d ed. 1984]), Adele Berlin's *Poetics and Biblical Interpretation* (Sheffield: Almond Press, 1983), Jacob Licht's *Storytelling in the Bible* (Jerusalem: Magnes Press, 1978), and, of course, Meir Sternberg's magisterial *Poetics of Biblical Narrative: Ideological Literature and the Drama of Reading* (Bloomington: Indiana University Press, 1985). A strength of Sternberg's tome is its stress on the complementarity of literary,

227

historical, and theological study; a weakness, with respect to beginning students, is its length and high literary style, which beginners will find challenging. A perspective on biblical narrative that differs philosophically from Sternberg's is offered by David M. Gunn and Danna Nolan Fewell in *Narrative in the Hebrew Bible*, Oxford Bible Series, ed. P. R. Ackroyd and G. N. Stanton (Oxford: Oxford University Press, 1993). Mark Allan Powell's *What Is Narrative Criticism?* (Minneapolis: Fortress, 1990) is a well-written introduction to the study of New Testament narrative. The best "literary commentary" on the entire Bible is entitled *A Complete Literary Guide to the Bible*, ed. Leland Ryken and Tremper Longman III (Grand Rapids: Zondervan, 1993). Also useful is *The Literary Guide to the Bible*, ed. Robert Alter and Frank Kermode (Cambridge, Mass.: Belknap Press of Harvard University Press, 1987). The list of works in the burgeoning field of modern literary criticism of the Bible could easily be continued, but perhaps this is enough to give students a start. For more, see Mark Allan Powell, *The Bible and Modern Literary Criticism: A Critical Assessment and Annotated Bibliography* (New York: Greenwood Press, 1991).

The historical study of the Bible is deeply enmeshed in issues of general hermeneutics. This is made particularly evident by Robert Morgan (with John Barton) in *Biblical Interpretation*, Oxford Bible Series, ed. P. R. Ackroyd and G. N. Stanton (Oxford: Oxford University Press, 1988). Morgan helpfully traces the development of modern, liberal critical study of the Bible and exposes many of the philosophical/hermeneutical influences that have led to the current crisis among biblical scholars wishing to embrace the rational methods of secularism without jeopardizing religious convictions. For an evangelical perspective on the history of biblical interpretation, Moisés Silva's *Has the Church Misread the Bible? The History of Interpretation in the Light of Current Issues*, FCI 1 (Grand Rapids: Zondervan, 1987) is recommended. Recent full-length, evangelical introductions to biblical hermeneutics include Grand R. Osborne's *Hermeneutical Spiral: A Comprehensive Introduction to Biblical Interpretation* (Downers Grove: InterVarsity Press, 1991) and Anthony C. Thiselton's monumental *New Horizons in Hermeneutics: The Theory and Practice of Transforming Biblical Reading* (Grand Rapids: Zondervan, 1992). Also worthy of note is Gerhard Maier's *Biblische Hermeneutik* (Wuppertal: R. Brockhaus, 1990), now available in English translation by Robert W. Yarbrough under the title *Biblical Hermeneutics* (Wheaton: Crossway, 1994). Summaries of current mainline thinking on a broad range of topics is conveniently accessible in *A Dictionary of Biblical Interpretation*, ed. R. J. Coggins, and J. L. Houlden (Philadelphia: Trinity Press International, 1990). Among general discussions of historical knowledge and historical method, I have found to be most useful Michael Stanford's *Nature of Historical Knowledge* (Oxford: Basil Blackwell, 1986), C. Behan McCullagh's *Justifying Historical Descriptions* (Cambridge: Cambridge University Press, 1984), and David Carr's *Time, Narrative, and History* (Bloomington: Indiana University Press, 1986). For a brief description of traditional historical-critical interpretation of the Bible, see J. Maxwell Miller's *Old Testament and the Historian* (Philadelphia: Fortress, 1976). And for an insightful analysis of the historical-critical method as applied to the Bible, I know of nothing better than William J. Abraham's *Divine Revelation and the Limits of Historical Criticism* (Oxford: Oxford University Press, 1982).

A number of works treat special topics that fall under the general heading of biblical historiography. As regards the historiography of the Old Testament, for example, some scholars argue that it should be dated very late (e.g., John Van Seters, *In Search of History: Historiography in the Ancient World and the Origins of Biblical History* [New Haven: Yale University Press, 1983]; *idem, Prologue to History: The Yahwist as Historian in Genesis* [New Haven: Yale University Press, 1992]), while others argue that the Old Testament texts for the most part do not intent to be taken as historiography in the first place (e.g., Thomas L. Thompson, *Early History of Israel: From the Written and Archaeological Sources*, Studies in the History of the Ancient Near East 4, ed. M. H. E. Weippert [Leiden: E. J. Brill, 1992]). While often rich in individual insights, such works, it seems to me, are unable to sustain their major theses. I find more of value in Baruch Halpern's *First Historians: The Hebrew Bible and History* (San Francisco: Harper & Row, 1988). As regards historical study of the New Testament, Craig L. Blomberg's *Historical Reliability of the Gospels* (Leicester: Inter-Varsity, 1987) and Colin J. Hemer's *Book of Acts in the Setting of Hellenistic History*, Wissenschaftliche Untersuchungen zum Neuen Testament 49 (Tübingen: J. C. B. Mohr, 1989), merit special mention.

On the relationship between historical study and Christian faith, students may benefit from reading David Bebbington, *Patterns in History: A Christian Perspective on Historical Thought* (Grand Rapids: Baker, 1990); Colin Brown, *History and Faith: A Personal Exploration* (Grand Rapids: Zondervan, 1987); *idem, ed., History, Criticism and*

Faith (Leicester: Inter-Varsity Press, 1976); Ronald H. Nash, *Christian Faith and Historical Understanding* (Grand Rapids: Zondervan, 1984).

Those wishing to explore the homiletical potential of Scripture's diverse literary genres, including its historiographical portions, might wish to consult Sidney Greidanus, *The Modern Preacher and the Ancient Text: Interpreting and Preaching Biblical Literature* (Grand Rapids: Eerdmans, 1988), and the relevant essays in Michael Duduit, ed., *Handbook of Contemporary Preaching* (Nashville: Broadman, 1992).

INDEX OF AUTHORS/TITLES

INDEX OF BIBLICAL PASSAGES

239

INDEX OF SUBJECTS

Page numbers in bold type indicate major discussions of the respective topics.

Supernaturalism. *See also* Divine intervention
  anti-, 103, 125, 182, 202
Synchronic vs. diachronic reading,
  47n, 52, 111–12, 149, 187–88
Synoptic histories of the Old Testament, 77–86
Testimony/witness, 74, 107, 116.
  See also Evidence
  external consistency of, 185–86,
    189–94, 199, 226
  internal consistency of, **185–89,**
    194, 199, 256
  listening to, 177–85
Theology
  history-centered, 102
  philosophical, 102
Troeltsch, E., 121, 128–32
Truth, 24, **91–93, 191–93**
  coherence theory of, 191–93

establishment of, 26
illustration of, 26, 102
truth claim, 24–25, **29–30,** 48,
    61n, 90, **90–93,** 95–96,
    166, 168, 170–71, **176–85,**
    189, 193–94, 199, 220–22,
    226
truth value, 24–25, **29–30,** 92,
    116, 170–71, 176–77, **184–
    94,** 199, 20–21
Tübingen school, 104
Universal History, 75
Vatke, W., 104
von Rad, G., 105
Wellhausen, J., 104, 205, 223
Witness. *See* Testimony
Worldview/background beliefs, 43,
    93, 108, 110, 115, **120–22,**
    131–34, 147, 167, **171–76,**
    184–85, 199, 121–22, 225

Printed in the USA
CPSIA information can be obtained
at www.ICGtesting.com
LVHW051532210724
785408LV00008B/76

9 780310 431800